JUSTINIAN'S DIGEST 9.2.51 IN THE WESTERN LEGAL CANON

JUSTINIAN'S DIGEST 9.2.51 IN THE WESTERN LEGAL CANON

Roman Legal Thought and Modern Causality Concepts

Wolfgang Ernst

intersentia
Cambridge – Antwerp – Chicago

Intersentia Ltd
Sheraton House | Castle Park
Cambridge | CB3 0AX | United Kingdom
Tel.: +44 1223 370 170 | Fax: +44 1223 370 169
Email: mail@intersentia.co.uk
www.intersentia.com | www.intersentia.co.uk

Distribution for the UK and Ireland:
NBN International
Airport Business Centre, 10 Thornbury Road
Plymouth, PL6 7PP
United Kingdom
Tel.: +44 1752 202 301 | Fax: +44 1752 202 331
Email: orders@nbninternational.com

Distribution for Europe and all other countries:
Intersentia Publishing nv
Groenstraat 31
2640 Mortsel
Belgium
Tel.: +32 3 680 15 50 | Fax: +32 3 658 71 21
Email: mail@intersentia.be

Distribution for the USA and Canada:
Independent Publishers Group
Order Department
814 North Franklin Street
Chicago, IL 60610
USA
Tel.: +1 800 888 4741 (toll free) | Fax: +1 312 337 5985
Email: orders@ipgbook.com

Justinian's Digest 9.2.51 in the Western Legal Canon. Roman Legal Thought and Modern Causality Concepts

ISBN 978-1-78068-832-9
D/2019/7849/75
NUR 820

British Library Cataloguing in Publication Data. A catalogue record for this book is available from the British Library.

Ille se profecisse sciat,
cui Iulianus valde placebit.

To be able to delight in Julian,
mind, this is progress indeed!

cf Quint 10.1.112

TABULA GRATIARUM

John Adams
John Cairns
Andrew Dickinson
Shane Finn
Tomasz Giaro
Benjamin Goodyear
Richard Hyland
David Ibbetson
Horst Heinrich Jakobs
Jonathan Katz
Francesca Lamberti
Ian Maclean
Francesco Milazzo
Thomas Rüfner
Martin Schermaier
Daniel Schwennicke
Jakob Fortunat Stagl
Andreas Thier
Thamar Xandry

CONTENTS

LIST OF ABBREVIATIONS

Abt	Abt(h)eilung
AC	Appeal Cases
Anm	Anmerkung
AnnPal	Annali del Seminario Giuridico della Università di Palermo
ANRW	Aufstieg und Niedergang der Römischen Welt
ArchGiur	Archivio Giuridico
Art	article
Bas	Basilika
BIDR	Bulletino dell'Istituto di Diritto Romano
C	Codex Iustiniani
ca	circa
CCC	Constitutio Criminalis Carolina
CE	Christian era
cf	confer/conferatur
cap	caput
caut	cautela/ae
c Iul Imp	contra Iulianum opus imperfectum
col	columna, -ae
comp	compilatio
const	constitutio
CRRS	Corpus der römischen Rechtsquellen zur antiken Sklaverei
D	Digesta Iustiniani
d	died
dig	digesta
disp	disputatio
diss	dissertatio
DNB	Dictionary of National Biography

ed(s)	editor(s); edictum
edn	edition
e.g.	exempli gratia
et al	et alii
ER	English Reports
f/ff	(and) following (pages/columns)
ff.	Digesta
fin	finis
frag	fragment
h.t.	hoc titulo
I	Institutiones Iustiniani
ibid	ibidem
IECL	International Encyclopedia of Comparative Law
i.f.	in fine
HLL	Handbuch der lateinischen Literatur der Antike
Iul	Iulianus
KanAbt	Kanonistische Abteilung
l	lex
lib	liber, -ri
LQR	Law Quarterly Review
MS(S)	manuscript(s)
n	nota, notae, footnote
n p	no place
Po	Potthast
OCD5	(New) Oxford Classical Dictionary
OIR	Orbis Iuris Romani – Journal of Ancient Law Studies
qu, quaest	quaestio(nes)
RomAbt	Romanistische Abteilung
sec	sectio
tit	titulus, -i
tom	tomus, -i
tr	translated, translator
TR	Tijdschrift voor Rechtsgeschiedenis
p	pagina, page

pr	principium
Quint	Quintilian
RIDA	Revue internationale des droits de l'Antiquité
Sab	Sabinus
schol	scholion
SDHI	Studia et documenta historiae iuris
s v	sub voce/verbo
UKHL	House of Lords, United Kingdom
Ulp	Ulpianus
v	versus
vol	volume(n)
X	Liber Extra
ZRG	Zeitschrift für Rechtsgeschichte

CHAPTER 1
THE QUAESTIO

This investigation follows the main contributions to the doctrinal history of the antinomy between D.9.2.11.3 and D.9.2.51. Both texts concern the liabilities, under the *lex Aquilia*,[1] of two offenders: the first mortally wounds a victim and the second finishes him off. According to the former text, the second attacker is liable for killing, whereas the first attacker is liable for wounding; the author of the text, Domitius Ulpianus (*ca* 170–223), attributes this view, of which he approves, to Juventius Celsus (67–130). The latter text by Julian (*ca* 110–*ca* 175) advocates holding both attackers liable as killers and is thus taken as marking a contrarian view.

In the evolution of Roman legal scholarship, the following solutions to this problem have been suggested. (1) The Digest allows us to spot a disagreement between Celsus (followed by Ulpian) and Julian. From this starting point, secondary questions emerge, most importantly concerning the precise legal point about which Celsus and Julian disagree. Or (2), the cases can be distinguished. The distinguishing element has been found in (a) the different quality of the first blow (the degree of certainty with which the first act could be expected to result in the victim's death), as assumed by the Ordinary Gloss and many others, or (b) the different quality of the second blow (deadly as such or deadly only because directed against an already mortally wounded man). In a variant of the last distinction, the second blows are distinguished as to the immediacy of their effect: they are either instantly deadly (D.9.2.11.3) or a mere accelerating contribution to a dying process still continuing (D.9.2.51). (3) Last but not least, the licence to strike out and/or replace words and passages, as claimed by the

1 For a quick overview of our knowledge of the *lex* and the Roman jurisprudence which developed on its basis, cf J Sampson, 'lex Aquilia on wrongful damage to property' (25 June 2018), *OCD5*, http://oxfordre.com/classics/abstract/10.1093/acrefore/9780199381135.001.0001/acrefore-9780199381135-e-8261?rskey=2JrK2S&result=1, retrieved 23 Feb 2019; B Winiger, *Responsibility, Restoration and Fault* (2018) 55 ff.

20th-century authors of the interpolationist persuasion, allowed our texts to be liberally morphed into variants which are free of contradictions.

The development of the various interpretations that have been provoked by the tension between two passages of the Digest shall, in a nutshell, make for a case study on the history of Roman law research, from its medieval beginnings to our day. The contributions will be reported in chronological order. Along the way, we shall find the classical lawyers' texts mirrored in a colourful spectrum of intellectual responses. We are revisiting a classic, and 'the classic is intricate and crowded, it is a place filled with people, and voices, and things and memories – vibrating with echoes' (Simon Leys).[2] This book is a resonance analysis for the echo-chamber around D.9.2.51 and its tension with D.9.2.11.3. Tracing back our steps, a return to the Roman origins is sought – and but another note added to the echo-chamber's polyphony.

Inevitably, the changing understanding of the Roman jurists' texts has been coloured by the respective contemporary frameworks that provided the analytical grasp of 'wrongdoing' in general, the elements of the injuring act and how they are interrelated, as well as the specific consequences of the act and how they are linked to it. Roman law scholars have shifted the legal issue here at stake around, opting somewhat arbitrarily for different systematic localisations, according to the author's preferred concept of the structure of the delict: is it a matter of *culpa*, or of causation? And if it is a causation issue, is it about the causal link between the inflicted wound and its deadly effect, or is it about the damages that result, in a proper causal link, from the liability-triggering wound? Do the jurists' decisions rely on divergent interpretations of the republican statute[3] (or, rather, the edictal *formulae*), or do the difficulties emerge only at the level of evidence, with no dispute about the 'substantive' law as such? Or was it for the Roman lawyers primarily a problem of how joint liability worked among several perpetrators, thus touching the issue of concurrence of actions?

It is a widespread notion that modern Roman law scholarship properly began sometime in the late 19th century, and that it then developed specific features that now set it apart from all pre-modern handling of the Roman law sources. A part of this narrative is the changing role of Roman law, from being the law of the land, used (and sometimes abused) by contemporary methods of statutory interpretation, to the object of

2 S Leys, *The Hall of Uselessness* (2011) 274.

3 There have been various attempts to reconstruct the lost text of the *lex Aquilia*, none of which can claim to avoid a speculative element, cf e.g. M Crawford, *Roman Statutes* vol 2 (1996) 607 ff.

historical research, which is controlled by standards of critical scholarship alone. A causal link is implied: losing its role as the law of the land was the presumed starting shot that let 'true' Roman law scholarship for the first time run its course. Looking at the test case here examined, we shall find an impressive continuum of exegetical attempts, a seemingly timeless dialogue of interpreters, each trying to outdo everyone else, overcoming past misconceptions, in perpetual search of the ultimate, true understanding. From this point of view, no particular stretch in the evolution of Roman law scholarship should be declared intellectually off-limits and unfit for consideration. While the philological and interpretative achievements of pre-1880 scholars are not to be dismissed out of hand, more recent Roman law research has added an impressive variety of highly specific approaches, most notably studies of single jurists' methodologies and ideologies. Today, we are also equipped with refined tools that our predecessors did not have at their disposal. These include improved editions or/and photographic reproductions of the Digest and the Basilika, as well as palingenetical studies. Celsus's and Julian's texts shall here be revisited, using the broad range of insights that have accrued over centuries of scholarship, and inspired by the hope of progressing to a more historically acute understanding of the Roman lawyers' thinking.

This study is a case of diachronic microhistoriography. Along the way, a number of adjacent issues come into view that would also merit closer inspection. The matter of joint tortfeasorship and accessorial liability for Roman delicts is but one example. However, if loss of focus was to be avoided, these issues could not be subjected to in-depth studies in their own right. Likewise, much secondary literature which is only a hair's breadth away from our texts had to be side-lined.

For this book, covering eight centuries, ideally every major contribution should have been included. All evidence matters. For a number of reasons, however, not the least limits to the author's linguistic abilities, this survey must fall short.[4] The 15th to 18th centuries are underreported, due to the impression, maybe false, that there was less variance in opinions found then, compared to the more diverse and individualistic theorists of the 19th to 21st centuries. There was no reason to include authors who have just restated the texts or referred to them in passing only. The viewless do not count. While no substantial contribution spotted has been omitted, the author's personal point of view, as well as his unconscious biases, may have prevented the discovery of yet more contributions. Eurocentricity could

4 Translations from foreign languages are mine, unless otherwise indicated.

not be avoided, insofar as the story here told was a European affair for half a millennium. Since the 18th century, however, Roman law studies have been pursued in non-European universities as well, and it is a matter of regret that in all likelihood a considerable number of non-European contributions will have been overlooked. For most of the authors dealt with, providing biographical information seemed superfluous; only for the occasional 'minor poet' is a reference given.

Acts covered by the *lex Aquilia* triggered what was in essence a private law liability for damage done to personal property, a penal element notwithstanding. The mortal attacks discussed in this context are all directed against a slave, the loss falling on the slave's owner. These Aquilian cases could (and later would) also be viewed from the angle of criminal law. If one substituted the slain slave for a free person, the problem became a matter of the law of homicide. Carrying the texts over into the field of criminal law, the sequence of mortally wounding (first offender) and killing (second offender) a person could thus entail two death sentences, if one followed Julian. Some criminal law writers will have to come into the field of vision too.

For a considerable time now, conceptually similar problems to the ones dealt with by the Roman jurists have also been identified in many modern tort law systems, regardless of the fundamentally changed conceptual frameworks of contemporary tort theories. Today, the problem is commonly identified as one of an 'interrupted' or 'broken' causal nexus; another catchphrase frequently used is that of an 'overtaking causality'. References to the pertinent Roman texts have found their way into one decision or another,[5] which is a good example of what David Johnston has called 'the sheer intellectual vitality of Roman law'.[6] Nonetheless, modern case law is not reported here. The occasional exception notwithstanding, the contemporary judge will have no professional ambition to advance our understanding of the Celsus–Julian debate.

Many contributions are dense, multi-layered pieces, and the compressed summaries through which they are represented here will often fail to do them full justice. Insofar as this report also covers authors of the interpolationist school, the then-customary diacritical marks will be

---

5 From *Scott v Shepherd* (1773) 96 ER 525, to *Fairchild v Glenhaven Funeral Services Ltd* [2002] UKHL 22; [2003] 1 AC 32, on which see H Scott, 'Killing and Causing Death in Roman Law', (2013) 129 *LQR* 101. Presumably, comparable examples could be pulled together from most jurisdictions.

6 *The Cambridge Companion to Roman Law* (2015) 8.

retained, namely '[…]' for words/passages assumed not to be part of the original text, and '<…>' for original text presumed to be cut out.

The core texts will be referred to as *l.*11.3 and *l.*51, with pr/§1/§2 as references to the three subsections into which the latter text has usually been broken down since the late Middle Ages. Comments upon other Digest texts will be taken into account as well, most notably pertaining to D.9.2.15.1, referred to as *l.*15.1.

D.9.2.51 Iulianus libro LXXXVI digestorum[7]

Ita vulneratus est servus, ut eo ictu certum esset moriturum,
medio deinde tempore heres institutus est et postea ab alio ictus decessit:

quaero, an cum utroque de occiso lege Aquilia agi possit.

respondit: occidisse dicitur vulgo quidem, qui mortis causam quolibet modo praebuit:
sed lege Aquilia is demum teneri visus est, qui adhibita vi et quasi manu causam
mortis praebuisset, tracta videlicet interpretatione vocis a caedendo et a caede.

rursus Aquilia lege teneri existimati sunt non solum qui ita vulnerassent,
ut confestim vita privarent, sed etiam hi,
quorum ex vulnere certum esset aliquem vita excessurum.
igitur si quis servo mortiferum vulnus inflixerit
eundemque alius ex intervallo ita percusserit,
ut maturius interficeretur, quam ex priore vulnere moriturus fuerat,
statuendum est utrumque eorum lege Aquilia teneri.

(1) Idque est consequens auctoritati veterum, qui, cum a pluribus idem
servus ita vulneratus esset,
ut non appareret cuius ictu perisset, omnes lege Aquilia teneri iudicaverunt.

(2) Aestimatio autem perempti non eadem in utriusque persona fiet:
nam qui prior vulneravit, tantum praestabit,
quanto in anno proximo homo plurimi fuerit
repetitis ex die vulneris trecentum sexaginta quinque diebus,
posterior in id tenebitur, quanti homo plurimi venire
poterit in anno proximo, quo vita excessit,
in quo pretium quoque hereditatis erit.

eiusdem ergo servi occisi nomine alius maiorem,
alius minorem aestimationem praestabit, nec mirum, cum uterque eorum
ex diversa causa et diversis temporibus occidisse hominem intellegatur.

quod si quis absurde a nobis haec constitui putaverit,
cogitet longe absurdius constitui neutrum lege
Aquilia teneri aut alterum potius,
cum neque impunita maleficia esse oporteat
nec facile constitui possit, uter potius lege teneatur.

multa autem iure civili contra rationem disputandi pro
utilitate communi recepta esse
innumerabilibus rebus probari potest: unum interim posuisse contentus ero:
cum plures trabem alienam furandi causa sustulerint,
quam singuli ferre non possent,
furti actione omnes teneri existimantur,
quamvis subtili ratione dici possit neminem eorum teneri,
quia neminem verum sit eam sustulisse.

---

7 The texts follow the (small) Mommsen edition (*editio stereotypa*); the translations are based on Lawson's.

D.9.2.51 Julianus, Digest, Book 86

A slave was wounded so seriously that it was certain that he would die of the blow; then after a while he was appointed an heir and afterwards, hit by another assailant, died:

I ask whether an action for killing under the Lex Aquilia can be brought against both.

He answered: a person is popularly said to have killed if he furnishes a cause of death by applying force in whatever way: but he is being held liable under the Lex Aquilia only if he furnishes a cause of death by applying force and, so to speak, with his own hand; the interpretation of the word 'occidere' being derived from 'cædere' and 'cædes'.

Again, liability under the Lex Aquilia is understood to attach not only to those who wound in such a way as to deprive at once of life, but also those inflict a wound of which it is certain that someone will die. If therefore a person inflicts a mortal wound on a slave and another person strikes the same slave after a while, so that he is put an end to earlier than he would have died of the former wound, we must decide that both of them are liable under the Lex Aquilia.

(1) And this is in keeping with the authority of the older jurists, who, where the same slave was wounded by several persons in such a way that it was not clear of whose blow he died, decided that all are liable under the Lex Aquilia.

(2) Now the valuation of the dead slave will not be the same for both persons; for the one who first wounded him will pay whatever was the highest value of the slave in the past year, counting back three hundred and sixty-five days from the wound, the later assailant will be liable for the highest price the slave could have been sold for in the year next before he departed his life, and in this the value of the inheritance will be included.

Accordingly, for the killing of the same slave one will pay a higher and the other a lower valuation, which is not surprising since each of them is taken to have killed the slave under different circumstances and at a different time.

But if anyone should think that we have given an absurd ruling, let him reflect that it would be a far more absurd ruling if neither should be liable under the Lex Aquilia, or one rather than the other; for on the one hand misdeeds should not go unpunished and on the other it is not easy to decide which of the two is more clearly liable under the Lex.

It can be proved by countless examples that many solutions have been accepted by the Civil Law, overcoming dialectic for the common good; I shall content myself for the moment with one: Where several persons with intent to steal remove another's beam which any one of them could not have carried, all are held liable to an action of theft, although the fine point might be taken that no one of them is liable because no one of them really removed it.

D.9.2.11.1–3 Ulpianus libro XVIII ad edictum

(1) Si alius tenuit, alius interemit,
is qui tenuit, quasi causam mortis praebuit, in factum actione tenetur.

(2) Sed si plures servum percusserint, utrum omnes
quasi occiderint teneantur, videamus.
et si quidem apparet cuius ictu perierit, ille quasi occiderit tenetur:
quod si non apparet, omnes quasi occiderint teneri Iulianus ait,
et si cum uno agatur, ceteri non liberantur:
nam ex lege Aquilia quod alius praestitit,
alium non relevat, cum sit poena.

(3) Celsus scribit, si alius mortifero vulnere percusserit,
alius postea exanimaverit,
priorem quidem non teneri quasi occiderit, sed quasi vulneraverit, quia ex alio
vulnere periit, posteriorem teneri, quia occidit.
Quod et Marcello videtur et est probabilius.

D.9.2.15.1 Ulpianus libro XVIII ad edictum

Si servus vulneratus mortifere postea ruina vel naufragio
vel alio ictu maturius perierit,
de occiso agi non posse, sed quasi de vulnerato;
sed si manumissus vel alienatus ex vulnere periit,
quasi de occiso agi posse Iulianus ait.
Haec ita tam varie, quia verum est eum a te
occisum tunc cum vulnerabas,
quod mortuo eo demum apparuit:
at in superiore non est passa ruina apparere an sit occisus [...].

D.9.2.11.1–3 Ulpian, On the edict, Book 18

(1) If one man held a slave and another killed him,
the one who held him is liable to an action *in factum*, on the ground that he furnished a cause of death.

(2) But if several persons strike a slave, let us see whether all are liable as having killed him.
And if it is clear by whose blow he perished, that person is liable as having killed him;
but if it does not, Julian says that all are liable as having killed him;
and if one is sued, the others are not released;
for under the Lex Aquilia what one man pays does not relieve, since what is paid is a penalty.

(3) Celsus writes that if one man strikes a slave a mortal wound, and another afterwards deprives him of life,
the former is not liable as having killed, but as having wounded, because he dies of a different wound, but the latter is liable as having killed.
Marcellus also agrees with this and it is the better view.

D.9.2.15.1 Ulpian, On the edict, Book 18

Where a mortally wounded slave afterwards, by the fall of a house or a shipwreck or some other kind of blow, dies sooner than he would have done,
an action cannot be brought for killing, but for wounding;
but if he dies from the wound after being manumitted or alienated, Julian says an action can be brought for killing.
And the reason for the difference is that the truth is that he was killed by you at the time when you wounded him,
though this came to light only when he died;
whereas in the former case the fall of the house did not allow it to come to light whether he was killed [...].

CHAPTER 2
THE EVIDENCE

I. SETTING THE STAGE

1. ACCURSIUS'S ORDINARY GLOSS

In Accursius's Ordinary Gloss (*Glossa Ordinaria*), the gloss '*teneri*' on D.9.2.51 tries to explain the tension between this fragment on the one hand and D.9.2.15.1/D.9.2.11.3 on the other:[8]

> *Being liable* – as for killing. Because each of the two is liable for the closest year's maximum value, calculated from the moment he was wounded, as here submitted, *lex aestimatio autem* [= D.9.2.51.2], below *de dam. infect. lex fluminum § idem Servius* [=D.39.2.24.5] at the end, above *lex ait* [= D.9.2.21]. With regard to a [slave] wounded [only], the damages are assessed within 30 days according to the third chapter. No argument against this can be taken from above *lex huic § si servus* [=D.9.2.15.1] or *lex item Mela § Celsus* [= D.9.2.11.3], where he says that the first is liable because of the wounding, although the wound was deadly, because it was not certain that he would die from this wound.[9]

This has a counterpart in the gloss '*mortifere*' to D.9.2.15:

> *Mortal* – as it was believed to be, and yet it was not certain & hence this is not in conflict with D.9.2.51.[10]

---

8 Accursius has lifted this gloss from the apparatus of Azo (*ca* 1150–1230), as it can be found in the following MSS of the *Digestum vetus* which preserve Azo's glosses: Vatican lat 1408, Bamberg jur 11, and Munich 14028. I am grateful to H H Jakobs, who provided me with images.

9 *Teneri* – ut de occiso. nam uterque tenetur quanti plurimi in anno proximo a tempore sui vulneris: ut hic subiicit *aestimatio autem etc.* [= D.9.2.51.2], infra *de damn. inf. l. fluminium § idem Servius* i.f. [= D.39.2.24.5], supra *l. ait* [= D.9.2.21]. de vulnerato autem fieret aestimatio intra xxx dies ex tertio cap. Nec est contr. supra *eo. l. huic § si servus* [= D.9.2.15.1] & *l. idem Mela § Celsus* [= D.9.2.11.3], ubi dicit primum ut de vulnerato teneri licet esset vulnus mortiferum: quia non erat certum ex vulnere moriturum.

10 *Mortifere* – ut putabatur, non tamen erat certum & sic non est contra *infra eodem ita vulneratus* [= D.9.2.51].

Another gloss to *l.*51.2 (gloss '*disputandi*') comments upon the *ratio stricta*-passage:

> *Of that which is to be discussed* – This is against the strictness of the law, since by strictness of the law neither is liable. The first not, since he did not slay, the second not, since he [the slave] was to die regardless of the wound [inflicted] by him.[11]

This was the 'solution' adopted by Accursius (*ca* 1182–1263): in the case of an absolutely mortal first wounding, both wrongdoers incur liability for killing, whereas a first wounding that could lead to the slave's death, but does not necessarily have to, allows a Chapter III liability only, leaving the second wrongdoer as the only one liable for killing.[12] The strategy of the Gloss was once aptly described thus: 'One does not try to resolve the contradictions found through a higher-level principle, but each statement and each opinion gets its own limited range of application which lets it co-exist with the other text.'[13]

The interpretation accepted by the Gloss became the *communis opinio*. From early on, both decisions were brought into a rule/exception relationship. The general rule was the one for the *vulnus letale plurimum*, triggering one liability for wounding and one for killing, with *l.*51 being an exception to the rule, giving rise to two liabilities for killing. To quote a much later jurist, the law is stated by paraphrasing *l.*11.3 and *l.*15.1, to which then is added *nisi vulnus simpliciter & per se letale sit, ut certum sit ex eo vulnere moriturum fuisse.*[14] The gloss '*disputandi*' reinforces the impression that the 'correct' solution to which the strict law points would not be the one proposed by Julian. Subsequent generations of authors supplied smart terms for these two kinds of mortal wounds, for example *vulnus letale per se*, also called *letale simpliciter*, on the one hand, and *vulnus letale plurimum* – commonly lethal – on the other. Later canon law terminology juxtaposed 'individually mortal' and 'absolutely mortal'.[15]

---

11 *Disputandi* – id est contra rigorem iuris, nam de rigore iuris neuter tenetur. prior non, quia non occidit; secundus non, quia et sine eius vulnere esset mortuus.

12 The *ut putabatur* in the gloss '*mortifere*' seems to put it slightly more strongly, in that here the deadliness is only presumed, although perhaps with good cause.

13 R Stintzing, *Geschichte der Deutschen Rechtswissenschaft* vol 1 Abt 1 (1880) 106 [my translation].

14 O Westenberg (1667–1737), *Opera Omnia Juridica* vol 2 (1747) 203.

15 N München (1794–1881), *Das kanonische Gerichtsverfahren und Strafrecht* vol 2 (1866) 378.

2. THE BYZANTINE PERSPECTIVE

For the Basilika,[16] D.9.2.51 has been considerably compressed, resulting in Bas.60.3.50.[17] The text does not include the argumentation directed against the solution that finds neither attacker liable for killing. The Greek text may perhaps be attributable to Dorotheus/Pseudo-Dorotheus.[18] D.9.2.15 has become Bas.60.3.15; the citation of Julian, which could trigger doubts as to the consistency of his position, has been omitted.[19] A fuller reproduction of Julian's essay is preserved in a scholion, obviously drawing from the Digest original. Two other scholia are concerned with the distinction between Bas.60.3.50 [≈ D.9.2.51] and Bas.60.3.15 [≈ D.9.2.15].[20] This is the longer one:

> 'deals a slave a lethal blow': from this moment the slave was definitely bound to die, and another could not bring death upon him; for if he were expected to survive and died through the blow of the other, the one who dealt the first

16 On the palingenesia of Bas.60.3 see M Miglietta, 'Towards a palingenetic study of Bas. 60,3: the contribution of the Byzantine ἴνδικες: part I', (2014) IX *Subseciva Groningana* 59, and M Miglietta, 'Towards a Palingenetic Study of Bas. 60.3: The Contribution of the Byzantine "ΙΝΔΙΚΕΣ. Part II', *Il diritto romano e le culture straniere. Influenze e dipendenze interculturali nell'antichità* (2015) 283.

17 Ἐάν τις δοῦλον θανατηφόρως πλήξῃ καὶ τὸν αὐτὸν δοῦλον γραφέντα κληρονόμον ἄλλος ἀνέλῃ, οἱ δύο τῇ περὶ φόνου ἀγωγῇ ἐνάγονται καὶ ἐπὶ μὲν τοῦ πρῶτον πλήξαντος ἀπὸ τοῦ τραύματος καὶ εἰς τὰ ὀπίσω ὁ ἐνιαυτὸς ψηφίζεται, ἐπὶ δὲ τοῦ δευτέρου ἀπὸ τῆς ἀναιρέσεως, καὶ αὐτὸς δίδωσι τὴν ἀποτίμησιν τῆς κληρονομίας. Εἰ γὰρ καὶ πολλοὶ πλήξουσι καὶ μὴ ἔστι δῆλον, ἐκ ποίας πληγῆς ἀπέθανε, πάντες τῇ ἀγωγῇ τῇ περὶ φόνου ὑπόκεινται· πολλὰ γὰρ ὁ νόμος διὰ τὴν κοινὴν ἀσφάλειαν παρὰ τὸ ἀκριβὲς εἰσάγει, ὡς ἔνθα πολλοὶ δοκὸν κλέψουσιν, ἣν ὁ καθ' ἕνα οὐ δύναται βαστάσαι, πάντες ἐνέχονται τῇ περὶ κλοπῆς ἀγωγῇ, καίτοι τῆς ἀκριβείας βουλομένης μηδένα ἐνέχεσθαι. (If someone deals a slave a lethal blow, and another kills the same slave, who has been nominated heir, both are prosecuted for homicide; for the one who dealt the first blow, a year is counted backwards from the wounding, but for the second, from the killing, and he himself (the owner) gives an estimate for the inheritance; for, even if many deal blows and it is not evident from which blow he died, all will be prosecuted for homicide. For the law admits much contrary to strict sense on account of public security, just as where many steal a beam which one alone could not lift, all are liable for theft, even though strict sense demands that none be liable.) Heimbach had numbered this text as Bas.60.3.51; cf Miglietta (2015) (n 15) 313 ff. Thamar Xandry and Daniel Schwennicke have assisted me with the Graeca throughout.

18 On Dorotheus see F Brandsma, *Dorotheus and his Digest translation* (1996).

19 On this text Miglietta (2014) (n 16) 84 ff.

20 H J Scheltema et al, *Basilicorum Libri LX* Series B vol VIII (1983) 3162 (schol 18) = Heimbach V 319 (schol 2), and H J Scheltema et al, *Basilicorum Libri LX* Series B vol VIII (1983) 3161 (schol 10) = Heimbach V 319 (schol 7).

> blow would be prosecuted not for having killed but for having wounded him, according to theme 2 chapter 15 [=Bas.60.3.15 ≈ D.9.2.15]. Which is then the difference between that chapter and the present one? That the blow is greater than the wound, and therefore this is the difference between chapter 15 [=Bas.60.3.15 ≈ D.9.2.15] and the present one.[21]

This comment stresses the absolute deadliness of the first blow, contrasting this with some expectation of survival, which then leads to the decision as set out in Bas.60.3.15 [≈D.9.2.15].[22] A lengthy scholion attached to this text stresses the evidentiary aspect.[23]

> If a slave who has received a lethal blow shortly after dies from an earthquake or a shipwreck or from being struck in another way, he who dealt him the blow is not prosecuted for his killing but for having wounded him. But if a slave who has been manumitted, or one who has been alienated to another, dies after having received the lethal blow, one will sue under the Aquilian law for his death. But the reason why one sues in one case for his killing and in another case for his wounding under the Aquilian law is evident. For where he has died without having suffered another blow, it is evident that he died as a result of the first blow, and hence he who struck him is prosecuted for his killing. But where an earthquake or a shipwreck killed the slave after the blow, he is prosecuted only for his wounding, since it was impossible for us to learn whether he was killed by the blow. […][24]

---

21 δοῦλον θανατηφόρως πλήξῃ· 'Αφ' οὗ πάντως ἔμελλεν ἀποθνήσκειν, κἂν ἄλλος μὴ ἐπήγαγεν αὐτῷ τὸν θάνατον· εἰ γὰρ προσδοκήσιμος ἦν εἰς τὸ ζῆσαι καὶ διὰ τῆς ἑτέρου πληγῆς ἀπέθανεν, ὁ πρώτως πλήξας οὐχ ὡς φονεύσας, ἀλλ' ὡς τραυματίσας ἐνήγετο ἂν κατὰ τὸ β'. θεμ. τοῦ ιε'. κεφ. Τίς δὲ ἡ διαφορὰ αὐτοῦ καὶ τοῦ παρόντος; Ὅτι ἡ πληγὴ μείζων ἐστὶ τοῦ τραύματος· καὶ ἐντεῦθέν ἐστιν ἡ διαφορὰ τοῦ ιε'. κεφ. καὶ τοῦ παρόντος.

22 Cf Miglietta (2015) (n 15) 331.

23 H J Scheltema et al, *Basilicorum Libri LX* Series B vol VIII (1983) 3109 f (schol 8) = Heimbach V 278 f (schol 6).

24 Ἐὰν οἰκέτης θανατηφόρον πληγὴν δεξάμενος μετὰ ταῦτα ἀπὸ σεισμοῦ ἢ ναυαγίου ἢ ἄλλως πληγεὶς συντομώτερον τελευτήσῃ, οὐκ ἐνάγεται ὡς περὶ ἀναιρεθέντος αὐτοῦ ὁ πλήξας αὐτόν, ἀλλ' ὡς τραυματίσας αὐτόν. Ἐὰν δὲ ἐλευθερωθεὶς ἢ ἐκποιηθεὶς ἑτέρῳ ὁ τὴν θανατηφόρον πληγὴν δεξάμενος τότε τελευτήσῃ, ὡς περὶ ἀναιρεθέντος αὐτοῦ κινεῖται ὁ Ἀκουΐλιος. Διὰ τί δέ ποτε μὲν ὡς ὑπὲρ ἀναιρεθέντος, ἄλλοτε δὲ ὡς ὑπὲρ τραυματισθέντος κινεῖται ὁ Ἀκουΐλιος, πρόδηλός ἐστιν ὁ λογισμός. Ἔνθα μὲν γὰρ μηδεμιᾶς ἑτέρας ἐπενεχθείσης αὐτῷ πληγῆς τελευτᾷ, πρόδηλόν ἐστιν, ὡς ἐκ τῆς πρώτης πληγῆς ἐτελεύτησε, καὶ διὰ τοῦτο ὡς περὶ ἀναιρεθέντος ἐνάγεται ὁ πλήξας αὐτόν. Ἔνθα δὲ μετὰ τὴν πληγὴν ὁ σεισμὸς ἢ τὸ ναυάγιον ἀνεῖλε τὸν οἰκέτην, ἐπειδὴ οὐ συνεχώρησεν ἡμῖν αὐτὰ μαθεῖν, εἰ ἐκ τῆς πληγῆς ἀνῃρέθη, διὰ τοῦτο ὡς περὶ τραυματισθέντος μόνον ἐνάγεται. […].

Finding an antinomy in the text of the Basilika would require that one read the *alius ictus* in Bas.60.3.15 as the blow of a second attacker, thus equating this case with the one in Bas.60.3.50. The first attacker's liability would then be one for wounding in the former text, one for killing in the latter. Stephanos, however, averted this antinomy by arguing that *alius ictus* must be understood to refer to another accident (ἄλλως πληγεὶς = *aliter perculsus*).[25]

3. CANONISTS TAKE NOTE

In the Latin west, canonists gave attention to the text and problem of *l.*51. In the time of Pope Innocent III, we see the first re-use of the part of *l.*51.2 where Julian invokes the *utilitas communis*, arguing that misdeeds should not go unpunished: from Julian's text the maxim *ne crimina remaneant impunita* was derived.[26] In the decretal *Inauditum* of 1199, the Pope demanded that King Henry of Hungary punish a thief of church property, stating that *rei publicae interest ne maleficia maneant impunita.*[27] The decretal was preserved in the collection of Alanus Anglicus,[28] who noted that the origins of the maxim were Roman law: *ff. ad leg. Aquil. Item uult [Ita uuln?] penult.*, an obviously flubbed reference to *l.*51.2.[29] As has been rightly remarked, the idea was considerably transformed: while Julian dealt with a matter of substantive private law liabilities, advocating that the owner should be compensated by both attackers, the papal chancery used his maxim to support the idea of mandatory public prosecution.[30] A few years later, another decretal, which dealt with the suppression of

25 C Ferrini, 'Postille esegetiche ai frammenti del commentario di Ulpiano alle formule edittali ad legem Aquiliam', *Opere di Contardo Ferrini* vol 2 (1929) 95, at 102.

26 D Liebs, *Lateinische Rechtsregeln und Rechtssprichwörter* 7th edn (2007) 110 (no 117).

27 *Inauditum*, Po 591 (1199 CE).

28 On him, see J Canning, s v 'Alanus Anglicus', *Oxford DNB*, https://doi.org/10.1093/ref:odnb/53478.

29 K Pennington, 'Innocent III and the Ius Commune', *Grundlagen des Rechts: Festschrift für Peter Landau zum 65. Geburtstag* (2000) 349, at 352 f.

30 There is a debate whether the idea had been formulated by learned clerics before it surfaced in *Inauditum*; Richard M Fraher assumed that an Anglo-Norman canonist had done the pioneer work: R M Fraher, 'The Theoretical Justification for the New Criminal Law of the High Middle Ages: "Rei Publicae Interest, Ne Crimina Remaneant Impunita"', (1984) 3 *University of Illinois Law Review* 577, at 590; other canonists have been suggested by G Jerouschek, '"Ne crimina remaneant impunita." Auf dass Verbrechen nicht ungestraft bleiben: Überlegungen zur Begründung öffentlicher Strafverfolgungen im Mittellalter', (2007) 89 *ZRG KanAbt* 323, at 379; Lotte Kéry pointed to Fulbert of Chartre, to whom the phrase is attributed *sed cum*

violence among Swedish clergy, relied on the maxim again; the necessary steps, however, could be left to the secular authorities, who had to act, because *publice utilitatis intersit, ne crimina remaneant impunita.*[31] It has been noted that *maleficium* was replaced here by *crimen*, completing the shift into criminal procedure territory: the *utilitas publica* requires consistent prosecution of crimes. This decretal was picked up for learned collections and later included in the *Liber Extra* (X 5.12.18). Quoting Tancred's opening words of his *Summula de criminibus* (1210),[32] *quoniam rei publice interest ut crimina non remaneant impunita*, Kenneth Pennington observed that by now 'the maxim's career was established':[33]

> '*Ne crimina remaneant impunita*' became a standard maxim of the Ius commune in the later Middle Ages. It was used by canonists and civilians alike. Although not included under the title 'De regulis iuris' in the Decretales of Gregory IX or the Sext of Boniface VIII, its exclusion did not impede its illustrious career. Like many of the *regulae iuris* that became part of medieval jurisprudence, *Ne crimina remaneant impunita* had its ultimate origins in Roman law. In the jurisprudence of the Ius commune, Roman law, particularly the Digest, became a rich quarry for building juridical concepts.

Following Richard Fraher, Pennington finds that the 'maxim spoke to the age; one might observe that it speaks to every age.'[34] The paroimia *publice utilitatis intersit ne crimina remaneant impunita* made its entry into the field of criminal procedure, but it did not take long for it to also refer to ideas which we today would classify as criminal law theories of deterrence and general prevention.[35] However, the later uses of the idea here identified were no longer concerned with the antinomical text of *l.*11.3, so we do not have to follow this strand of intellectual history in this book.

Not much later, in 1209, Innocent III had to deal with a real-life case bearing some resemblance to the cases set out in *l.*11.3 and *l.*51.[36] A priest

---

iuris sit ad utilitatem rei publicae cunctos punire maleficios: L Kéry, 'Ein neues Kapitel in der Geschichte des kirchlichen Strafrechts: Die Systematisierungsbemühungen des Bernhard von Pavia (†1213)', *Medieval Church Law and the Origins of the Western Legal Tradition* (2012) 229, at 247.

31 *Ut famae tuae* – X 5.39.35 = Comp III 5.21.8 = Po 2038 (1203 CE).

32 R M Fraher, 'Tancred's Summula de criminibus: A New Text and a Key to the Ordo iudiciarius', (1979) 9 *Bulletin of Medieval Canon Law* 23–36.

33 Pennington (n 29) 352.

34 *Ibid*, 353.

35 R M Fraher, 'Preventing Crime in the High Middle Ages: The Medieval Lawyers' Search for Deterrence', *Pope, Teachers, and Canon Law in the Middle Ages* (1989) 212.

36 X 5.12.18 = Comp IV.5.6 [= *de homocidio*] c 2, Po 3757.

had hit a fleeing thief of church instruments when parishioners rushed in and finished him off. The legal issue was whether the priest's behaviour had triggered the so-called *irregularitas*, with the result that the priest would be deposed. *Irregularitas*, an impediment regarding one's consecration, was an automatic consequence of homicide. The parishioners' liabilities did not come into view. Innocent III found that the priest should not be deposed unless he had administered a deadly blow (which would have led to the thief's death anyway) and had done so with intent to kill. For the priest to go free it was also necessary that the parishioners' actions had not been carried out on his behalf (*studio, consilio vel mandato*). In order to establish the effect of the first blow, it was necessary to consult medical experts. The decretal thus introduced an element that was not an express topic in the deliberations of the Roman jurists, namely the evidentiary issue.[37] If it was not possible, by way of expert examination, to establish whose blow had killed the thief, the priest was taken to be the killer and would suffer the required punishment: *in hoc dubio tanquam homicida debet haberi sacerdos, etsi forte homicida non sit* ('If the matter is doubtful, the priest is to be dealt with on the basis of murder, even if by chance it was not murder'). One may note that an evidentiary protection along the lines of '*in dubio pro reo*' is not in play at all. While the cases are not a perfect match, the papal decision seems somewhat more in the line of Julian in D.9.2.51pr, insofar as the prior offender, the priest, is held liable for killing. If one were to make this comparison, the decretal even goes beyond Julian, who had made the first offender's liability for killing dependant on the finding that the wound first inflicted would have ended in the victim's death 'with certainty', whereas for Innocent III it was sufficient that there was doubt as to who ultimately effected the victim's death. A gloss to X 5.12.18 indeed notes that the canon law and the civil law differ.[38]

X 5.12.18 and, as companion texts, Ulpian's and Julian's decisions were to remain part and parcel of the doctrine of *irregularitas*.[39] There is no need to follow in detail the pursuant interpretations of X 5.12.18 by learned canonists. It suffices to say that some controversy emerged concerning the understanding of X 5.12.18, with a strong trend of pulling the decretal law closer to the civilian sources. The developed canon law

---

37 This can be seen as a precursor towards compulsory post-mortem procedures, as later prescribed, for example, by Art 149 Constitutio Criminalis Carolina (1532).

38 Gregorius Papa IX, *Decretales cum glossis restitutae* (1615) 1210.

39 Cf, for example, G de Villadiego, *Tractatus de irregularitate, suspensione et interdicto ecclesiastico* (1589) ex cap sexto, n 18, p 101 ff.

was later summarised by Justus Hennig Boehmer (1674–1749), whose line coincided with that of Accursius:[40] everything depended on the quality of the wound first inflicted – did it necessarily lead to death or not? It was a matter for the medical expert. The civil law, Boehmer explained, had adopted this distinction in view of the *lex Aquilia*, *l.*15.1 and *l.*51pr.

4. THE LETHAL WOUND: CRIMINAL LAW AND THE MEDICO-LEGAL ASPECT

The matter of the lethality of a wound was to become a cornerstone of medieval and early modern criminal law. The lethality of the wound came to be seen as the criterion to delineate crimes of homicide from crimes of assault. What constituted the lethality of a wound? Must a small wound that leads to a lethal infection then be considered lethal? For many centuries, such questions constituted the core of homicide doctrines. A rich set of presumptions and rules developed over time, from the canon law side as well, often focussed on the evidentiary aspect of how lethality was proven in court.[41] Presumptions of lethality were typically limited by a maximum time-span between wounding and death. A rich casuistry ensued, addressing, for example, the significance of an intervening medical treatment or the lack thereof, or of fever caused by the wound versus by another infection. To this evolving, complex field of criminal law, the distinction between the absolutely lethal and the mostly lethal, used by the Accursian Gloss to harmonise *l.*11.3 and *l.*51, came as a convenient add-on. Conversely, treatises elucidating the lethality requirement usually also tended to include references to one of these texts or to both of them. However, they rarely took a fresh view of the tension between the two texts. It is not necessary to report the history of the lethality element in the development of the criminal law of homicide in full. Some select remarks will be made, however, to provide a background, in order to better understand the success of the Azonian/Accursian contribution to our antinomy.

The earliest pertinent treatise from the 13th century circulated under the title 'De percussionibus'. Throughout the middle ages it was seen – and cited – as a work of Odofredus (*d* 1265). Its authorship is now considered

40 J H Boehmer, *Ius Ecclesiasticum Protestantium* vol 5 (1736) 75 f.

41 A handy summary of the *Ius Commune* view of the lethality issue can be found in the consilium 415 of Decius; Ph Decius, *Consilia sive responsa* (1588) 453 f.

to be a matter of doubt.[42] *L.*15.1 is cited as the authority for a slightly rephrased statement of law, namely that an attacker can only be held liable *de vulnerato*, if the lethally wounded victim is 'slain by another, or the collapse of a house, or in a shipwreck'. The original *'vel alio ictu'* has become *'ab alio occisus'*, thus neatly absorbing the cases of *l.*11.3 and *l.*51pr into *l.*15.1. The author supports the following general presumption of fact: if a person dies after being wounded, it is supposed to be due to the wound, and hence the wound is taken to have been lethal. This is based on the end of *l.*15.1 (*'quod eo mortuo apparuit'*). The word *'mortifere'* at the beginning of *l.*15.1 does not mean lethal, but rather 'presumably lethal' (or 'at first sight lethal'). *L.*51, on the contrary, shows that an upgrade to 'true' lethality was possible.

The treatise 'De percussionibus' was used by Albertus Gandinus (1245–*ca* 1310), who integrated much of its discussion into his 'Tractatus de Maleficiis'.[43] Gandinus discusses the liability for the infliction of a minor wound that leads to fever and death (infection?). The liability for wounding is not a problem. But what about killing? Amidst a range of arguments, *l.*15.1 and *l.*51.2 come into view. Albertus Gandinus's solution starts with the issue of *dolus* to kill. If such *dolus* is missing, the attacker should be liable for wounding only. Alternatively, one could contemplate always opting for a liability for killing, which then would have to be mitigated taking into account the type of delict, the state of the wrongdoer and the degree of fault. Gandinus claims to have been present when someone was convicted, along these lines, of manslaughter in Modena, the conviction carrying a heavy monetary fine, or alternatively the loss of a foot.

In all cases where death ensued *ex intervallo*, the initial lethality of the wound distinguished wounding from killing. If the lethality could not be established, the attacker could only be culpable of wounding: *vulnerans non de occiso, sed de vulnere tenetur* became an important adage of criminal law. It made sure that a wounding did not automatically turn into killing, if the victim had died *ex intervallo* for reasons insufficiently related to the wound.[44] To establish the mortality of a wound, medieval scholars

42 The text has been edited, on the basis of the extant manuscripts, with an attempt to clarify the palingenetical background, by O Cavallar, 'Agli albori della medicina legale: I tattati "De percussionibus" e "De vulneribus"', (1999) 26 *IUS COMMUNE* 27, at 76–89.

43 H Kantorowicz, *Albertus Gandinus und das Strafrecht der Scholastik, Zweiter (Letzter) Band: Die Theorie. Kritische Ausgabe des Tractatus de Maleficiis nebst textkritischer Einleitung* (1926) 300 ff.

44 A Aretinus (ca. 1400–1461), *Tractatus super maleficiis* (1555), tit *'et ex intervallo'* n 13 f.

developed complex evidentiary rules and presumptions, factoring in the time-lag between the affliction of the wound and the moment of death, as well as other factual elements.[45]

To start criminal proceedings *per inquisitionem*, a specific requirement needed to be met, dubbed *corpus delicti*.[46] The term denoted the deed as such, without regard to its doer.[47] For the crime of homicide the lethality of the wound was considered to be part of the *corpus delicti*. In order to start proceedings for homicide, it was therefore necessary to show that the victim had suffered a wound that qualified as lethal.[48]

The reliance on a host of mechanical presumptions, which have not been reported here, was later overcome by the Constitutio Criminalis Carolina (CCC).[49] Its Article 147 was entitled 'If someone has been wounded and it is doubtful whether the wound was that cause of death' and stated:

> Item, if someone has been hit and dies some time afterwards, so that it is doubtful whether he died of the blow (of which he is accused) or not, in such cases both parties (as of old) need to give evidence; also one has to call expert surgeons and other persons who have knowledge as to the deceased's development after the blow and event, to give evidence regarding the time for which the deceased survived after the blows; a deliberation among the aldermen ('*urteiler*') and in between the jurors and the legal experts has to take place, at place and time as regulated in this order.[50]

---

45 Recent research has tried to identify aspects of victimology in the Ius Commune, and has from this angle looked anew into such attempts to classify wounds; M-C Lault, 'La prise en compte médiévale de la victime dans quelques traités criminels et statuts urbains', (2015) 25 *Histoire de la justice* 107 ff.

46 E Dezza, *Lezioni di storia del processo penale* (2013) 59, 84 f., 96.

47 The Roman law basis for this approach – establishing first that a crime has happened, before asking for the person of the criminal – was Ulp 50 ed D.29.5.1.24, pertaining to the SC Silanianum: an interrogation (under torture) of slave members of the household could only begin once the *paterfamilias* has been found dead.

48 For details, cf Benedict Carpzow (1595–1666), *Practica Nova Imperialis Saxonica Rerum Criminalium* (1677) Pars I qu 26 n 22.

49 On the CCC, see J H Langbein, *Prosecuting Crime in the Renaissance: England, Germany, France* (1974) 167 ff.; Dezza (n 46) 42 ff.

50 Item so eyner geschlagen wirt, vnnd über etlich zeit darnach stürb, also das zweiffelich wer, ob er der geklagten streych halb gestorben wer oder nit, in solchen fellen mögen beyde theyl (wie von weisung gesatzt ist), kundtschafft zur sach dienstlich stellen, vnd sollen doch sonderlich die wundtärtzt der sach verstendig vnnd andere personen, die da wissen, wie sich der gestorben nach dem schlagen vnd rumor gehalten hab, zu zeugen gebraucht werden, mit anzeygung wie lang der gestorben nach den streychen gelebt hab, vnd inn solchen vrtheylen, die vrtheyler bei den rechtverstendigen, vnd an enden vnd orten wie zu end diser vnser ordnung angezeygt, radts pflegen.

A later commentator of the CCC explained that the lethality of the wound – as an element of the *corpus delicti* – was to be established so as to satisfy the *moralis certitudo* of the judge. There was no legal basis to insist on a regular post-mortem (*sectio cadaveris*).[51]

The identification of the lethality of the wound as a core requirement for homicide introduced a crucial causality element in to all legal analyses of that crime. As a 17th-century jurist was later to complain: 'many can contend to avoid [being convicted for] homicide, namely on the ground that the wound had not been the adequate cause of death'.[52] An accused could simply plead that the wound had not been *re vera letale*, but only *per accidens causa mortis*. Focussing for homicide on the infliction of a lethal wound gave the delict a structure similar to the Roman *causam mortis praebere*: the killer must have inflicted a wound that could be shown to have been the true cause of the ensuing death. From early on, the criminal lawyers had found that there was no difference between someone who has slain the victim (*occidit*) and someone who has caused his/her death.[53] For this, one relied on a statement by Ulpian to be found in the Digest title pertaining to the *Lex Cornelia de sicariis*, Ulp 8 ad Leg Iul et Pap D.48.8.15: *nihil interest, occidat quis an causam mortis praebeat*. The technical niceties of the role of *occidere* within the *lex Aquilia* could thus be left to one side. Although homicide was conceptualised as causing death by a lethal wound, a notion closer to the Roman concept of *occidere quasi manu* popped up occasionally. In his great commentary to the CCC, Johann Samuel Friedrich von Böhmer (1704–1772), one of the lawyer sons of Justus Henning Böhmer, relied, for the law of complicity, on the distinction between providing a *causa physica* and a *causa moralis*. In the case of homicide, von Böhmer found that only one single perpetrator could become the *causa physica*, by delivering the deadly wound, whereas eventual accomplices could only contribute *causae morales*.[54] The idea did not catch on.

The continued discussion of issues pertaining to the presumed or proven lethality of wounds, mostly from a criminal law perspective, has

---

51 H C Meckbach, *Anmerkungen über Kayser Carl des V Peinliche Halsgerichts-Ordnung* (1756) 287.

52 C Haubold (1766–1824), *De jure et justitia commutativa* tom I (1671) tract II no 680: *multi se ab homicidio liberare contendunt, nempe vulnus non fuisse adaequatam causam mortis*.

53 'De Percussionibus', (1999) 26 *IUS COMMUNE* 27, at 76.

54 J S F von Boehmer, *Meditationes in Constitutionem Criminalen Carolinam* (1770) Art 177 §2 III.

created a persistent contact point between legal and medical experts. 'De percussionibus' is often seen as a pioneering publication for the field of medico-legal analyses.[55] The antinomy of *l*.11.3 and *l*.51, especially if harmonised by the concept of graded degrees of lethality, came with an invitation to clarify the role of the medical expert in the field of evidence.

II. THE LATE MIDDLE AGES

In a remarkable doctrinal turn, Baldus de Ubaldis (1327–1400) understood Julian as promoting a legal fiction, namely that a person had been killed twice, which in the natural world was impossible.[56] Baldus then considers an advocate who advises the first offender to hire a third party to finish off his mortally wounded victim, thus making sure that his liability remains limited to one for wounding. Of course, Baldus found, such an advocate deserves to be hanged. However, justice should be administered speedily. I take this to imply that a speedy judgment against the first offender for wounding also protects him from seeing his liability upgraded to murder. There is no express reference to the defence of *res iudicata*, to which Baldus here seems to allude. Another controversial matter, also taken up by Baldus and later authors, will not be pursued here: when prosecution proceedings have been initiated while the victim is still alive, how does one procedurally accommodate his/her supervening death?

A 'minor poet' among the so-called post-glossators, Florianus de Sancto Petro (Sampieri) (*d* 1441),[57] stood out by virtue of his quite extensive commentary on the *Digestum vetus*, thus also giving close attention to title 9.2.[58] He deals with the *mirabilis modus evadendi* mentioned by Baldus, strongly cautioning against it. It is dangerous. It does not help if

---

55 Cavallar (n 42) sets out pre-Renaissance authors and their works at the intersection of law and medicine. For the authors of the Renaissance, see I Maclean, 'Evidence, Logic, the Rule and the Exception in Renaissance Law and Medicine', (2000) 5 *Early Science and Medicine* 227; for the 17th-century history, see A Pastore, 'Médecine et droit, compétition ou collaboration?', (2017) 11 *Histoire, médecine et santé – Revue d'histoire sociale et culturelle de médecine, de la santé et du corps* 19, available: http://journals.openedition.org/hms/1077, accessed 18 December 2018; DOI: 10.4000/hms.1077, all with further references.

56 B de Ubaldis, *In primam Digesti veteris partem commentaria* (1599) ad *l*.51 *si ita vulneratus*.

57 On Florianus see J F von Schulte, *Quellen und Literatur* vol 2 (1877) 252 n 26, 280, 303 n 1.

58 F de Sancto Petro, *In primam & secundam Digesti veteris partem commentaria* (1576) ad l *Celsus ait* (*l*.11.3) 169.

the first wound is found to be certainly lethal, in which case according to *l.*51 the offender is held liable, retrospectively, for killing. Apart from this, the canon law will consider him a murderer anyway, citing X 5.12.18. Furthermore, while the victim is still alive, the offender cannot be prosecuted for murder, and in the meantime the victim can be killed by accident. Florianus also hints at liability for attempted murder. Aside from these pragmatic considerations, in his commentary on *l.*51 he follows Baldus in attributing a legal fiction to Julian.[59]

Related reflections are found in the medieval commentary on D.24.3.10.1, the *l. si ab hostibus §1 D. solut. matr.*, another text which addresses a problem of consecutive wounding resulting in the victim's death. As Pomponius sets out, if a husband kills his wife, the dowry is to be returned to her heirs. The question was whether the husband who had set his wife on a sure path to death would lose the dowry, regardless of, for example, ensuing medical malpractice, where sound treatment could have saved her life. If *l.*11.3 were relied on to downgrade the husband's liability to wounding, would this also mean that he did not lose the dowry? And was the *mirabilis modus defendendi*, as set out by Baldus and others, available to the husband? The matter was addressed *inter alia* by Jason di Mayno (1435–1519),[60] who takes a negative stand, referring to *l.*51pr. The problem is nicely unpacked into a broad range of variants by Alexander de Tartagnis (de Imola) (*ca* 1424–1477):[61] the husband omits to call in a doctor for his wounded wife, he calls in an inexperienced doctor, etc. Most importantly, it needs to be determined, in retrospect, whether the wound inflicted by the husband was truly lethal. Can a medical expert's statement that turns out to come from an inexperienced doctor be overturned by another, more qualified doctor?

Bartholomaeus Caepolla (1420–1475)[62] looked at the matter from the angle already addressed by Baldus and Florianus: how can the more severe penalty be avoided?[63] The hypothetical counsel is addressed to someone who has mortally wounded a victim. If this client finds a judge willing to prosecute him speedily for the lesser offence, he will be protected on the

59 *Ibid*, 206 n 2.

60 J di Mayno, *In primam Infortiati partem Commentaria* (1573) n 9 ad hunc locem.

61 A de Imola, *Super prima infortiati parte Commentaria* (1549) fol 23r.

62 On him, see G Rossi (a cura di), *Bartolomeo Cipolla: un giurista veronese del Quattrocento tra cattedra, foro e luoghi del potere* (2009); O Ruffino, s v 'Cipolla, Bartolomeo', *Dizionario biografico degli italiani* vol 25 (1981).

63 *Cautaellae iuris* (1535) caut V.

strength of the *ne bis in idem* principle, citing *l. Si quis crimine C. de acc.* [=C.9.2.9]. The possibilities for the client to self-initiate such proceedings are discussed. Caepolla then turns to the *cautela mirabilis*, that the client should induce a third party to also lethally wound the victim. The dangers of such an action are explained, following Florianus.

III. RENAISSANCE MEN

When the handling of the Digest shifted from a text-focussed reading, with all jurists' excerpts taken to be on the same plane, to a historical view of the world of antiquity, with discernible actors who worked at different times and sometimes held divergent legal views, it became possible, for the first time, to consider the two texts as expressions of irreconcilable legal opinions pertaining to the same set of material facts. At the same time, it was possible to let go of forced harmonisations. Most writers of the legal humanism reacted strongly to the harmonisation established by the *Glossa Ordinaria*.

Among the subtle vignettes published by Udalricus Zasius (1461–1535), there is one entitled 'De intellectu l. item Mela § Celsus ff. ad l. Aquiliam'.[64] Zasius forcefully disagrees with the *Glossa Ordinaria*. He chastises the Gloss for corrupting the text by suggesting that the 'mortal' in *l.*15.1 is only imagined. *Vides nebulas, adduc lucem si poteris*: Zasius develops a theory all of his own. If the second wound effects the death without a delay (*in continenti*), this blow has to be held to be deadly, and the first blow must be classified as a wounding only. If, however, there is a delay between the second blow and the ensuing death, no distinction can be made between the first and the second wrongdoer, and rather than letting both off the hook, both have to be held liable as killers. The death coming about by *casus fortuitus*, which is what Zasius sees in *l.*15.1, cannot count as *occidere*. The *alio ictu* in this text therefore has to be read as *ictu casu fortuito*, excluding human action. Of course, should the *ruina* etc. have been caused by someone's action (*culpa hominis*), that person would be liable, too. Zasius also criticises Caepolla and his insistence that a *vulnus* is deemed *mortalis* only if there is a 100 per cent certitude that it will result in death: *phantasia est*! For the law, a certitude that cannot fail – we would today speak of 100 per cent certainty – can never be necessary.

---

64 U Zasius, 'Singulares intellectus etc', *Opera Omnia* vol 5 (1550) col 169 ff.

Zasius is also reluctant to see the matter as solvable by reference to a medical expert.[65] One has to deal with an uncertainty caused by the confluence of two accidents, not merely by the occult state of natural affairs.

In an erudite manner, Andreas Tiraquellus (1488–1558) dealt with the topic from the viewpoint of moderating penalties.[66] He comes back to Baldus's *mirabilis modus defendendi* and its shortcomings, highlighting the difference between civil and canon law, and refers the reader to Florianus and Caepolla.

Diego de Covarrubias y Leyva (1512–1577)[67] wrote 'De vulneribus a pluribus inflictis', systematically addressing various scenarios.[68] Our cases are dealt with under the sub-heading 'Vulnus ab uno illatum, quando ei imputetur ad homicidium, si vulneratus ab alio exanimatus fuerit?'. Covarrubias sets out the antinomical texts, lining up X 5.12.18 with D.9.2.51. He notes a controversy among canon lawyers as to the interpretation of X 5.12.18. Covarrubias extensively discusses Zasius's dissenting view, which, however, is ultimately discarded again in favour of the *opinio communis*.

The Nuremberg scholar Jakob Ayrer (the younger) (1543–1605), famous for writing the 'Historische Processus juris',[69] published a handbook-style treatise on the law of murder and manslaughter.[70] Going through a variety of cases, he arrives at *l.*11.3, which he identifies as a case of a brawl. Julian's text seems to offer a divergent result. Ayrer subscribes to the distinction of the Accursian Gloss, according to which *l.*51 provides the solution only in cases of certain lethality. If the matter remains doubtful, one cannot hold the earlier attacker liable *de occiso*. For this result a considerable a number of authorities are cited.

Nicolaus Vigelius (1529–1600) reshuffled the law of Justinian's Digest to represent it in a more systematic, understandable order. In the sixth part

---

65 For his scepticism concerning the medical expert Zasius cites Alexander de Imola: A de Tartagnus Imola, *In primam partem infortiati commentaria* (1562) ad D.24.3.10 n 10, p 23.

66 A Tiraquellus, 'De poenis legume temperandis aut remittendis, causa 61', *Tractatus Varii* (1587) 363; on Tiraquellus, see G Rossi, *Incunaboli della modernitá. Scienza guiridica e cultura umanistica in André Tiraqueau (1488–1558)* (2007).

67 On Covarrubias, cf J G Sánchez/B G Fueyo, *Diego de Covarrubias y Leyva. Summa de delictis et eorum poenis. Año 1540* (2018) 17 ff.

68 D de Covarrubias y Leyva, *Opera Omnia* (1734) 688–93.

69 Cf E Schumann, 'Von "Teuflischen Anwälten" und "Taschenrichtern"', *Ulrich Tenglers Laienspiegel, Ein Rechtsbuch zwischen Humanismus und Hexenwahn* (2011) 431, at 456 ff.

70 J Ayreri, *Tractatus Methodicus & accuratissimus De Triplici Genere Homicidiorum* (1647) 397 ff.

of this seven-volume work,[71] Vigelius deals with the question *utrum de occiso, an de vulnerato quis teneatur*, reproducing *l.*15.1 and *l.*11.3. But, *contradicit l. si ita 51 D. ad l. Aquiliam* [= D.9.2.51]. No attempt is made to harmonise the texts. Rather, the contradiction is accepted as such. Vigilius notes, however, that *l.*51 is concordant with *l.*11.2.

Jacques Cujas (1522–1590)[72] gave the interpretation a completely new turn. In one of his 'observations', he asserted that one was looking at a controversy, Celsus and Julian being the adversaries:[73]

> As in many other cases, so in particular in D.9.2.21, Julian disagrees with Celsus, if one [attacker] mortally wounds a slave and another later finishes him off: Celsus thinks that the latter force makes liable for killing under the first chapter of the lex Aquilia, the former for wounding under Chapter III, D.9.2.11.3; Julian thinks both for killing. In the case of a mortally wounded slave who dies later, Celsus computes the backwards year from the day of the death, Julian from the day of the wounding; D.9.2.21.1. But of course, for no other reason does Julian set out his own opinion in a long essay (*l.*51) than that Celsus disagrees with him, whom he also notes and tacitly refers to in that bit of *l.51 Quod si quis absurde a nobis haec constitui putaverit, etc.*[74]

Cujas points to a multitude of disagreements between Julian and Celsus. He does not fail to point to the controversy between Celsus and Julian concerning the date from which the one-year period is to be reckoned if there is a hiatus between the mortal wound and the death. Cujas also thinks he identifies the sceptical '*quis*' in *l.*51.2 as Celsus, a conjecture from then

---

71 N Vigelius, *Digestorum juris civilis libri quinquaginta* vol 6 *(de obligationibus & actionibus ex delicto descendentibus)* lib XLVI cap XII (1584) col 5652–4.

72 On Cujas see X Prévost, *Jacques Cujas (1522–1590), Jurisconsulte humaniste* (2015); X Prévost, 'Reassessing the Influence of Medieval Jurisprudence on Jacques Cujas' (1522–1590) Method', *Reassessing Legal Humanism and its Claims. Petere Fontes?* (2016) 88.

73 I Cuiacius, 'Lib XXVII Observ, cap 13', *Opera, quae de iure fecit, et edi voluit* vol 4 (1595) col 640.

74 Ut in plerisque aliis causis, sic in specie *l. ait ad legem Aquiliam* [= D.9.2.21], Iulianus a Celso dissentit si alius servum mortifere vulneravit alius postea exanimaverit: Celsus vim posteriorem de occiso ex primo capite legis Aquiliae teneri putat, priorem de vulnerato ex tertio *l. 11 § Celsus eodem tit.* [= D.9.2.11.3]. Iulianus utrumque de occiso. Celsus homine mortifere vulnerato & postea mortuo annum retrorsum computari ex die mortis, Iulianum ex die vulneris *l. 21 §1 eod.* [= D.9.2.21.1]. Nec sane aliam ob rem in *l. 51* magnum studium ponit in adferenda sententia sua quam quod Celsus ab eo dissentiret, quem etiam notat & refellit tacite illo loco dicta *l. 51 Quod si quis absurde a nobis haec constitui putaverit, &c.*

on followed by most, disputed by some. More extensively, but also more conventionally, Cujas dealt with the matter in his extensive commentary on Julian's Digest, published after his death.[75] Here, Cujas follows and paraphrases Julian's essay in close detail. He sees a tension between the *leges Dialecticorum*, which seem to lead to Celsus's decision, and the *utilitas omnium, ne maleficia sint impunita*, advanced by Julian: *subtilitatem vincit utilitas*. The relationship between *utilitas* and *aequitas* is discussed at length and with examples, with the somewhat utilitarian result that *utilitas nihil aliud est, quam aequitas mera, sive aequitatis mater, ut Socrates ait*. In this perspective, which can perhaps be traced back to the gloss '*disputandi*', Julian forsook sober legal logic and went soft in order to accommodate a public policy interest. This view was hardly apt to increase Julian's future fanbase. The position of the Ordinary Gloss was thus superseded in two steps: Zasius destroyed the glossators' cheap harmonisation, and Cujas put the discussion on a new footing with his hypothesis that two opposing views had been recorded in the Digest. The solution in the Ordinary Gloss, however, did continue to find supporters.

Hugo Donellus (1527–1591) advanced a high-grade analysis.[76] First, Donellus dismisses the solution of the Gloss as 'ridiculous': one cannot say that something is deadly if the deadliness is not really established. Then Donellus distinguishes both cases, in a way similar to the one proposed by Zasius: in the case of *l*.11.3 the later offender kills the victim immediately, and only he can be held liable since the effectiveness of the first wound can no longer be tested; the *ratio* of *l*.15.1 is thus carried over to the case addressed by Celsus. By contrast, in the case dealt with by Julian (*l*.51), the slave, twice wounded, does not die immediately, but with a delay. This can be deduced from §1, where Julian states that it is uncertain by whom the victim has been slain: '*hic optima ratio est, cur omnes teneantur de occiso: quia non potuit intellegi utrum magis ex priore vulnere an posteriore interfectus fuerit, quia utrumque mortiferum vulnus fuit.*' There is no hint of a controversy, and no criticism of Julian is voiced by Donellus. Given the speed with which Cujas's theory of conflicting opinions would take hold, Donellus's position was soon to become non-conformist.

One and the same victim cannot be killed by two different persons at two different times – that is the *ratio dubitandi* set out by Anton Faber

---

75 I Cuiacius, 'Recitationes solemnes ad libros XC Digestorum Salvii Iuliani, Lib LXXXVI ad l. 51 Ita vulneratus', *Opera Postuma* vol 2 (1637) col 484 ff.

76 H Donellus, 'Ad Tit D ad Legem Aquiliam', *Opera Omnia* vol 10 (1761) cap IV no 8.

(1557–1624) for *l.*51.[77] The first wrongdoer should be liable for wounding, and only the second one for killing. Faber finds Julian in conflict with the rest of the Roman lawyers. The argumentative apparatus mustered by Julian is a reaction, according to Faber, to the doubtful position he meant to support. Faber wonders why Ulpian can in *l.*15 refer to Julian as supporting the wounder's liability in the case of a later *ruina*, unless Julian should have contradicted himself, something that would be *nec novum, nec mirum*. Faber rejects the Accursian harmonisation, since 'lethal' already means that the ensuing death is certain. As to Julian's following argument, Faber thinks that in the case where it is unclear whether the first blow was lethal, it is preferable not to convict at all, since convicting both implies the conviction of an innocent. This can be seen as an allusion to what we would refer to as the *in dubio pro reo* principle.

IV. EARLY MODERN JURISTS

By this time, two basic approaches had been brought into play, namely the Ordinary Gloss's distinction, turning on the definitiveness of the first wound's lethality, and the notion that a classical controversy had slipped into the Digest. During the centuries to come, neither of these understandings prevailed over the other. The Ordinary Gloss once more proved its resilience. Important writers, like Voet[78] and Suarez, still followed the *Glossa Ordinaria*; others, like Bachovius,[79] followed Cujas.

The mainstream of the time is well represented by Henricus Zoesius (1571–1627).[80] Zoesius reports that Cujas had thought he identified, in *l.*51, a reference to Celsus. Rather than acknowledging a controversy, a *pugna*, it seems preferable to him to distinguish the cases along the lines of the *Glossa Ordinaria*. If in a case like that of X 5.12.18 the lethality of the first wound should be doubtful, the corresponding liability should be limited to that for wounding: '*Cujus ratio est, quod in poenalibus leges sint proniores ad absolvendum, quam ad condemnandum.*' Another author reaffirming the solution of the Accursian Gloss was Petrus de Greve

77 A Faber, *Rationalia in secundam partem pandectarum* (1616) 903.

78 J Voet, *Commentarius ad pandectas* vol 1 (1778) ad lib IX tit II n 9, p 428 f.

79 R Bachovius von Echt (1575–*ca* 1640), *Notae et animadversiones ad disputationes Treutleri* vol 1 (1688) disp 18, thesis 9, p 341, where Bachovius reports both Cujas's diagnosis of a controversy as well as the distinction proposed by the Accursian gloss.

80 H Zoesius, *Commentarius ad Digestorum libros L* (1718) ad lib IX tit II n 22, p 216.

(1621–1677),[81] who inserted a temporal element in the definition for the *simpliciter letale* criterion: the wound must effect the death with necessity within a few hours or days.[82]

Grotius's (1583–1645)[83] microscopic contribution is worth mentioning. To the passage '*Quod si – lege Aquilia teneri*' in *l.*51 he laconically remarks: '*Id quod minus absurdum est, valet pro ratione*'. This sentiment is echoed later by Jean Domat (1625–1696), who reproduces Julian's own words:[84] '*multa jure civili, contra rationem disputandi, pro utilitate communi recepta esse, innumerabilis rebus probari potest.*' It is a position which, not unlike that of Cujas, somewhat reluctantly accepts Julian's text, deliberately setting aside reservations as to the soundness of his logic.

For centuries, in fact until the publication of Pernice's work in 1867, the book of authority for the law of the *lex Aquilia* were Ioannis Suarez de Mendoza's (*d* 1681) *Commentarii ad Legem Aquiliam*, first published in 1640, here used in the edition included in Meerman's *Thesaurus*.[85] His is very much a mainstream approach. Lethal wounds do not necessarily lead to a death – this is Suarez's starting point. From here, he easily proceeds to the reason for the Chapter III liability in the *ruina* case of *l.*15.1: the effective lethality can no longer be established. Furthermore, *l.*51 is not a problem, since here the lethality is an absolute certainty: we are back at the solution of the Gloss. Suarez slightly shifts the criterion, in that he looks into the curability of the first wound, which to him is the core of the distinction. Suarez draws from medical literature in delineating which wounds qualify as curable and which do not. The reason why Julian is so verbose, Suarez opines, is the difficulty of the distinction and not, as Cujas maintained, that Julian disagreed with the accepted approach. Suarez does, however, see a problem that holding the first offender liable for killing makes it difficult to also hold the second offender liable for killing. Or would not holding the

---

81 On him, see J A H Bots, 'Harderwijkse professoren (1648–1812) en net benoemingsbeleid van de Gelderse curatoren', *Het Gelders Athene: bijdragen tot de geschiedenis van de Gelderse universiteit in Harderwijk (1648–1811)* (2000) 51 ff.

82 P de Greve, *Exercitationes ad pandectarum loca difficiliora* (1660) 248.

83 H Grotius, *Florum sparsio ad ius Iustinianeum* (1642) 131; on Grotius's use of the Roman law of delict in general, see J Sampson, *The Historical Foundations of Grotius' Analysis of Delict* (2017).

84 J Domat, 'Legum Delectus ex libri Digestorum et Codicis, ad 9, 2 n. XVIII', *Les Loix Civiles* (1767).

85 G Meerman, *Novus thesaurus juris civilis et canonici* vol 2 (1751) 42 ff. Our problem is dealt with in lib I cap III sec III. A critical edition of Suarez's work is being prepared by Paulina Święcicka, Krakow.

second offender liable for killing require downgrading the first offender's liability to wounding? As between different evils the lesser evil is to be preferred, so among absurd solutions is the least absurd. This is the line taken by Grotius. To supplement eruditely the parallel case of the beam stolen by co-thieves, where no one can be considered a freeloader, Suarez quotes Antiphanes:[86]

> For we, ten men, contribute now for supper,
> But no one of them all bears what he brings,
> So here's a case where he who bears bears not,
> And this is just the meaning of a griphus.

Matthaeus (II) (1601–1654) looked into the matter from a criminal law perspective.[87] He sides with the *Glossa Ordinaria.* Only if the first blow is *simpliciter letale* will both be liable as killers; if not, the first wrongdoer will be liable for wounding, the second for killing. Julian addresses the former case; for the latter case Matthaeus finds support in *l.*15.1: since the shipwreck or the *ruina* make it impossible to assert that the first blow qualified as *simpliciter letale,* the first wrongdoer cannot be convicted as a killer. Matthaeus concludes that if the case were altered so that the first blow was *simpliciter letale,* and the *runia* could not make its (potential) deadly effect uncertain, the wrongdoer should be held liable as a killer. What if, Matthaeus asks, neither the first nor the second blow qualifies as *simpliciter letale,* with both blows together making for the deadly outcome? Both must be held liable as killers, because it would be absurd to let them go free in this case.

Turning to some intellectually ambitious authors, Ulricus Huber (1636–1694) summarises D.9.2.15.1, which he finds contradicted by Julian in *l.*51.[88] If the slave is slain *continuis ictibus,* both wrongdoers will be held liable, as set out in *l.*11.1–2. However, both conflicting jurists take it that there has been an *intervallum.* He takes Julian's words *si primo ictu certum esset, hominem moriturum* as a clue for the mediation: *mortifere* implies that there is no chance that death will not follow; this is in line with the Ordinary Gloss. In 1685, Christian Thomasius (1655–1728) had commented upon Huber's positions in his *Scholiae ad Ulrici Huberi Positiones ad Instituta et Pandectas.* Huber incorporates these comments,

---

86 Athenaeus of Naucratis, *The Deipnosophists* vol 2 (1854) 708, transl. by Yonge.
87 A Matthaeus, *De Criminibus* 5th edn (1761) lib XLVIII tit 5 n 19, p 382 f.
88 U Huber, *Praelectiones iuris civilis* vol 3 (1735) 824 f.

together with replies of his own, in later editions of his *Praelectiones*; in turn, Thomasius's rebuttals in support of his positions (*Scholia ad Ulrici Huberi Positiones ad Instituta et Pandectas*) were also included. Regarding Huber's interpretation, Thomasius doubts that the Roman lawyers had thought of a distinction between *vulnus letale per se* and *vulnus letale plurimum*; he also questions whether all medical doctors approved of this distinction. He rather sees a controversy, in which, to him, Julian seems to muster the stronger arguments. To this, Huber replies by giving an example of an actual post-mortem in 1668. The prefect of the security of the Rijks Athenaeum Franeker, in Groningen, had died some days after being hit by a stone. A post-mortem by the professor of anatomy, D Frenzelius,[89] found that the wound had neither been lethal nor as such led to the death. The public prosecutor, informed by his own medical experts, held otherwise. A compromise was facilitated by the distinction of *vulnus absolute letale* and such wounds that only provide a cause for death: here the wound had caused a fever, which in turn had led to the prefect's death. This proved, in Huber's view, that the distinction works well in practice. Huber also rejects a reference to *l*.21.1, which text describes a disagreement between Julian and Celsus, as this dispute has a different subject matter. To this, Thomasius had the following to reply: the dispute among the Groningen doctors rather supported his own, Thomasius's, scepticism. Thomasius defends his diagnosis of a jurists' controversy, since the synonymous wording of both texts, and the use of the term *mortifere* especially, does not allow the assumption that Julian and Ulpian were writing about different cases. He never maintained, Thomasius concludes, that he had identified the dispute to be found between *l*.11.3 and *l*.51, with the different dispute regarding the issue of the proper reckoning of the one-year period (as set out in D.9.2.21.1). Ulricus Huber's son, Zacharias Huber (1601–1678), also took up the issue, in the context of an erudite dissertation 'De lege Julia, cuius meminit Suetonius vita Neronis, cap. xxxiii'.[90] He thinks that the reasoning of Julian in *l*.51 can be carried over to the handling of the action arising under the *lex Cornelia de sicariis et veneficis*. An aspect already touched on in Huber's writing, but well covered by many authors, was the precise meaning of *mortifere*: can something be called lethal if it was in fact cured somehow? To quote just one jurist on this matter, we learn from Samuel de Cocceji (1679–1755) how he thinks the *vulnus letale* is to be

89 On him, see J W Napjus/G A Lindeboom, *De hoogleraren in de geneeskunde aan de Hogeschool en het Athenaeum te Franeker* (1985) 70 f.

90 Z Huber, *Dissertationes Juridicae et Philologicae* vol 2 (1702) 28 ff.

understood: '[t]he potential to cause death is decisive, and in one person a wound cannot be helped, which in a more robust person could be cured. The judgement of the medical doctor counts.'[91]

In his much-used commentary on the Digest, Johann Brunnemann (1608–1672) followed Cujas in the diagnosis of a *dissensio jurisconsultorum*.[92] He reports Julian's reasoning, but thinks it is inapplicable in criminal proceedings, insofar as murder with necessity triggered a fixed (non-discretionary) penalty (*poena ordinaria*), since the wound first inflicted, albeit lethal, did not cause the victim's death.

Johannes Voet (1647–1713) devoted a full section to our issue.[93] Rejecting the theory that Julian contradicted himself, which he finds lacking textual support, he forcefully returns to the view first set out by the glossators. For Julian's deliberations, the absolute certainty of death, following from the first wound, is crucial. Voet also musters support from *l*.15.1: the argument that the *ruina* etc. made it impossible to establish the certainty with which the wound would have killed the slave does not make sense, he held, if that certainty would have been beyond doubt. For the case as set out and decided by Julian, Voet adds a public policy consideration: if a perpetrator has inflicted a (certainly) mortal wound, and thus has already become guilty of manslaughter, why should his guilt/liability be expunged (or rather reduced) as a result of another wrongdoer's top-up action? He sees a potential conflict with the decision concerning the slave killed in a brawl (*l*.51.1): in spite of the uncertainty, all participants are held to be killers, and why should, between two persons who without doubt both contributed to the victim's death, only one be held liable?[94] While Voet returns to the *communis opinio* of learned lawyers, he also somewhat strengthens Julian's much maligned solution for the case of *l*.51pr, as understood by the glossators and their followers.

Gerard Noodt (1647–1725)[95] writes with a strong tendency to neutralise *l*.51, most likely because Julian's solution for cases of the structure 'two perpetrators: wounding/killing', if carried over in the field of criminal law, came with the danger of a proliferation of death penalties. Noodt discredits Julian as best he can. In Noodt's view, the first wrongdoer could face a liability only on the basis of his *causam mortis praebere*, since the wound he

91 S de Cocceji, *Ius Controversum Civile* vol 1 (1713) qu VI ad lib IX tit II, p 514.
92 J Brunnemann, *Commentarius in Pandectas* vol 1 (1752) ad D.9.2.51, p 340.
93 J Voet, *Commentarius ad pandectas* vol 1 (1778) ad lib IX tit II n 9, p 428 f.
94 Voet adds an argument from D.48.6.15.4 which is not set out here.
95 G Noodt, 'Ad legem Aquiliam Liber singularis, cap. 10', *Opera Omnia* vol 1 (1724) 137, at 154 f.

inflicted only leads to the slave's actual death on the strength of the second wounding. Only the second wrongdoer commits homicide: why should one interpret the first wrong as homicide, if it clearly is not? This leads Noodt to side with Ulpian. The assumption that we face a jurists' controversy ran into an additional problem, since Julian, in *l*.15.1, is reported by Ulpian as approving a decision which came from the presumably opposing camp and which can be distinguished from the case dealt with in *l*.51pr only with great difficulty (if at all). Does the *alius ictus* mentioned in *l*.15.1 not easily include a blow like the (second) one which is the crux of *l*.51? Noodt, in this regard following Faber, supplements the controversy theory with the novel idea that Julian had indeed changed his mind. He assumes that Julian reverted to the line later confirmed by Ulpian.[96] Noodt then heaps praise on a wise man's ability to see through and correct his own past mistakes. Julian's view, Noodt maintains, has never become the law of the land, and thus also has to be disregarded today. Noodt's proposition that Julian gave up his view did not go unchallenged: in dealing with real and apparent controversies in the Digest, Karl Friedrich Walch (1734–1799), in his re-edition of Christian Heinrich Eckhard's *Heremeneutica Iuris*, reviewed alleged retractions by Roman jurists and from this angle criticised Noodt, siding with Suarez:[97] both Marcellus and Ulpian surely would have expressly noted that the view they advanced had also found Julian's support, especially if that had come by way of a retraction, had that only been the case.

Bavius Voorda (1729–1799)[98] discusses the whole complex in an inspired manner.[99] He does not blame the oldest interpreters, the glossators, for coming up with the distinction between the fully lethal and the 'only accidentally' lethal, since at their time the research into this field was still underdeveloped. But it is incredible, he thinks, that Ulricus Huber walked the same line, in spite of authors like Cujas or Noodt who had by then shown the right way. Voorda thoroughly investigates the problem of whether Julian contradicts himself. Against Noodt, he dismisses as incredible the idea that Julian had gone over to the position of Celsus.

---

96 Ulpian then would have here used a different book by Julian, written later than the *libri digestorum*.

97 C H Eckhard, *Hermeneutica Juris* (1779) 355 ff.

98 On Voorda, see M Hewett, 'Voorda resurgens: An introduction to Jacobus Voorda and his unique lectures on the Ius Hodiernum at the University of Utrecht', (2003) 9 *Fundamina* 103.

99 B Voorda, *De crimineele ordonnantien van Koning Philips van Spanje* (1792) cap 2, 250–4.

To avoid the problem of Julian contradicting himself, he suggests that Julian's reported approval in *l.*15.1 relates only to the immediately preceding variations *sed si manumissus – agi posse.* This is a way out which would return, supported by future authors, most notably Hans Ankum.

Robert Jean Pothier (1699–1772) reports Julian's decision (*l.*51) at length, adding *l.*11.3 as a view at odds with Julian's. As it seems that the reference to Julian here pertains to both cases, thus including *ruina/ naufragium/alius ictus*, one is compelled to deduce that Julian changed his mind:[100] Pothier follows Noodt.

*L.*51 also popped up in an 18th-century commentary to the 'Sachsenspiegel', the 13th-century mirror of justice for Saxony.[101] The author stresses that under the terms of the 'Sachsenspiegel' the judge does not need to consult a *medicus* in order to find the wound *pro causa efficiente* of the death. He was not bound to distinguish between *vulnus letale per se* and *per accidens. L.*51 is taken to support the presumption that someone who had attacked the victim has thereby already become *causa mortis*.

V. 19TH-CENTURY PANDECTISTS FROM GLÜCK TO WINDSCHEID

Christian Friedrich von Glück's (1755–1831)[102] interpretation turns on the matter of uncertainty: is it permissible to take a slave as slain in the moment of the act only if the ensuing death is already a matter of fact? As long as there is uncertainty, the act cannot be counted as slaying. Glück does not follow Voet and Suarez (and the Gloss) in their argument that Julian addresses the case of the absolutely lethal first stroke, but Ulpian that of a merely contingently, but not absolutely, lethal first stroke. The elaborate argument set out by Julian (*l.*51) shows, Glück writes, that Julian tried to overcome an opposing view (of Celsus). For Julian, one could advance the argument that an illegal act (the second stroke) could hardly have the effect of excusing another (the first stroke). However, he finds the argument of Julian's adversaries weightier, namely that a mortal wound

[100] J R Pothier, *Pandectae Justinianeae in novum ordinem digestae* tom 1 (1782) ad D.9.2, sec I art I n IV, p 280 n (a).

[101] H C Meckback, *Commentar über den Sachsen-Spiegel* 2nd edn (1789) 944 f.

[102] C F Glück, *Ausführliche Erläuterung der Pandecten nach Hellfeld*, Theil 10, Abt 1 (1808) 346 ff.

could not be seen as deadly if a later stroke was the immediate and direct cause of the death. Glück follows Noodt in his diagnosis that Julian later changed his view (*l.*15.1).

Another, quite crude, method to dissolve the presumed conflict between Celsus and Julian was employed by a number of authors who invoked the *lex posterior* rule to give precedence to *l.*11.3 and *l.*15.1, which are Ulpian's, and hence derogate from the earlier text by Julian. This solution was advanced by, *inter alia*, Albrecht Schweppe (1783–1829)[103] and Freiherr Rudolph Christoph Karl Sigmund von Holzschuher zu Harrlach und Thalheim-Aschbach (1777–1861),[104] both authors of widely used practitioners' handbooks. It was quite a popular idea, but did its proponents not overlook the fact that both texts had become statutory law at the same moment when the Digest was promulgated?

Throughout the 19th century, we gradually see the idea of *culpa* taking centre stage in the analyses of liability problems. Scholars tried to find a common *culpa* requirement, which was seen as the hallmark of individual responsibility, underlying all sorts of liability.[105] Taken with a grain of salt, this movement can be seen as also advocating a more restrictive handling of liabilities; expansive interpretations of the Roman law could be rejected on the ground that no *culpa* could be found in the defendant's behaviour. An early author who focussed on the concept of *culpa* was Egidius von Löhr (1784–1851).[106] He proposes a common-sense understanding of *l.*11.3. Since the death cannot have resulted from the first wound, the liability must take its measure from Chapter III; we just lack the necessary consequence to qualify the act as a killing. *L.*51, on the other hand, only slipped into the Digest due to negligent compilers.[107] In due course, Alfred Pernice was to take up the viewpoint established by von Löhr and Hasse in his analysis of our texts.[108]

Criminal lawyers also took note. Heinrich Luden (1810–1880), an influential jurisprudential writer,[109] contributed a high-calibre discussion

---

103 A Schweppe, *Das Römische Privatrecht in seiner heutigen Anwendung* 4th edn (1831) §548, at p 434.

104 F R C K S von Holzschuher zu Harrlach und Thalheim-Aschbach, *Theorie und Casuistik des gemeinen Civilrechts* vol 3: *Obligationenrecht* 3rd edn (1864) 1119.

105 A seminal contribution was Johann Christian Hasse's (1779–1830), *Die culpa des römischen Rechts. Eine civilistische Abhandlung* (1838).

106 E von Löhr, *Die Theorie der Culpa* (1806).

107 *Ibid*, 126 ff.

108 Below p 39 f.

109 For Luden, see S Mattasch, *Der Tatbestand des Verbrechens bei Heinrich Luden* (2005).

from a criminal law perspective.[110] *L.*11.3 and *l.*51 are best understood as referring to different cases. Roman jurists only accepted such wounds as deadly which in fact led to the victim's death. Julian in *l.*51 deals with a constellation where the actual causation is doubtful. It is the interplay of both wounds which brings about the death. By contrast, in the case dealt with by Ulpian, the second wounding is the undisputable cause of an immediate death. This is, in a nutshell, the same idea as advanced by Zasius. Interestingly, Luden accepts Julian's solution for private law liability, while rejecting it with regard to criminal liability, a juxtaposition which had already been advanced by Brunnemann. Another thoughtful criminal lawyer looked to *l.*51 as a model for Article 148 of the CCC: Franz Victor Ziegler (1816–1888) used our texts to elucidate the topic of concurrent tortfeasors, who act with no plan agreed between them.[111] Ziegler pays close attention to the details of the case set out by Julian. While killing requires the infliction of death, here a reliable proof that the second wound has immediately killed the victim may be difficult. In view of this uncertainty, both are held liable, since both inflicted lethal wounds. If, however, the second blow can be determined as the cause of the actual death, the first attacker can only be held liable for wounding.

Aloys Brinz (1820–1887), one of the most original pandectists, developed a theory of his own. His core idea would become highly popular in the 20th and 21st centuries, although it would be linked to other authors, his pioneership all but forgotten:[112] Julian wished to hold attackers liable for killing, even if the act had not gone beyond the stage of attempt, provided the wound inflicted was truly mortal.

Adolph von Vangerow (1808–1870) undertook a thorough examination of our texts.[113] A first distinction had to be drawn between contemporaneous and sequential wounding. Contemporaneous wounding resulted in individual liability under Chapter I, according to Ulpian in *l.*11.2, referencing Julian. This reference, Vangerow holds, points to the text in *l.*51.1, where, in turn, it is backed up by the *auctoritas veterum*. As to cases dealing with subsequent wounding, *l.*11.3, *l.*15.1 and *l.*51 are looked at: the first appeared to represent the general rule, the last at first sight 'an entirely deviant dogma'. The Gloss's lethal/certainly lethal distinction,

---

110 H Luden, *Über den Thatbestand des Verbrechens nach gemeinem teutschen Recht* (1840) 263 ff.

111 *Die Theilnahme an einem Verbrechen nach P.G.O. Art. 148. Eine criminalistische Abhandlung* (1845) 79–83.

112 *Pandecten* vol 2, 2nd edn (1879) §281b n 6, 15.

113 K A von Vangerow, *Lehrbuch der Pandekten* vol 3, §681 Anm 1, 7th edn (1876) 585 ff.

while more convincing than the idea of Julian's unsteady change of views, seems to Vangerow an unlikely explanation, too. Another distinction needs to be found. Vangerow looks to the second act. In his view, *l*.11.3 deals with a killing of the slave, which is lethal as such, with no contributing effect of the prior wound, just as in the case of supervening death in a shipwreck or by a *ruina*. The second blow, in other words, must have been of a kind that would also have finished off a sound, unwounded person. The first striker cannot be held liable as a killer of the slave, *quia ex alio vulnere periit*. Vangerow also relies on the verb *exanimare*. By contrast, Vangerow finds *l*.51 to be dealing with a second stroke that only accelerates the dying process (*ut maturius interficeretur*). The second wound as such would not have been deadly, had it not been inflicted on an already dying man. Thus, both wounds together bring about the death in its concrete occurrence, and this is reflected in both wrongdoers' liability as killers. An additional argument for this view is taken from the following §1: his decision, Julian claims, is in line with the position of the *veteres* according to which, if several persons wound a slave *ut non appareat, cuius ictu perisset*, they all become liable as killers. This argument, in Vangerow's opinion, only works if in *l*.51pr there is a similar uncertainty in the overlay of the two contributions; it would not work if the death were a clear-cut consequence of the second act alone. Last but not least, Vangerow also points to §2, where the alternatives, namely letting both wrongdoers off the hook, or holding one liable as a killer, but not the other, also presuppose that none of the wrongdoers can be seen as having inflicted a wound which would by itself qualify as a sufficient cause of death. The distinction, according to Vangerow, thus has to be based on a quality of the second act: if the second act in itself is an outright and immediate killing, for which the wounded state of the slave is of no import, the first wounding remains under Chapter III. If the second act is not of this quality, but capable of accelerating the dying process, which would have run its course in any case (with certainty), both perpetrators come under Chapter I.

Incidentally, around 1886 Frederick Pollock (1845–1937) evinced a very similar understanding, albeit not publicly. In his personal copy of Erwin Grueber's *The Roman Law of Damage to Property*,[114] he noted at *l*.51pr: 'semble, it is to be taken that the 2d wound was not in itself mortal'.[115]

---

114 On this book see p 40.

115 This has been brought to light by J Cairns, 'English Torts and Roman Delicts: The Correspondence of James Muirhead and Frederick Pollock', (2013) 87 *Tulane Law Review* 867, at 879.

The translator of the Digest, Charles Henry Monro (1835–1908),[116] took the same line: 'It seems to be assumed that the death of the victim would not have happened at the time when it did without both wounds, but not that the second alone would necessarily have been fatal.' Monro disagrees with commentators who rely on *l*.11.3 to diagnose a controversy over the very same case: 'but this I think is impossible.' *L*.51.1 brings in the element that one does not know who was the killer and 'this would establish a strong difference between this case as the one in *l*.11.3, for there is it is perfectly plain who killed, namely the second assailant, who "exanimated" the wounded man.' Monro finds Julian's text unnecessarily wordy, and wonders why the fuss.

Turning to Bernhard Windscheid (1817–1892), we find our texts dealt with in yet another context.[117] Windscheid addresses the problem from the angle of the measure of damages, which, of course, had been in play all along as one aspect among others, given the different provisions for Chapter I and Chapter III. For a then-fashionable doctrine of *id quod interest*, Windscheid compares the actual economic development (losses and gains) of the victim and a hypothetical development in a scenario where the injury, which is the basis of liability (the 'critical fact'), has not occurred. For this reckoning, some exceptions come into play, one for the case that 'the loss, for which compensation would fall due, would have resulted from the critical fact, but in reality, the same loss has resulted from another fact'. He exemplifies this with the wounding of an animal, which is then struck dead by a lightning. As to the Roman law sources, *l*.11.3 and *l*.15.1 are cited. Windscheid registers Julian's view, which 'did not prevail'. He rejects Vangerow's interpretation, which he sees as being in conflict with the temporal basis for the assessment of compensation for the second blow set out in *l*.51.2. It is difficult to see Windscheid's original view as a progressive contribution to furthering our historical understanding, since his measure of damages test is obviously at odds with the relevant particular provisions of the *lex Aquilia*. As a general observation, modern tendencies to unify the bases of liability, merging Chapter I and Chapter III into a unified category of damage done to property, tend to shift our problem into the measure of damages field, since a liability of the same category is triggered for both attackers.

---

116 *Digest IX.2, Lex Aquilia* (1898) 71–2. On Monro see s v 'Monro, Charles Henry', *Dictionary of National Biography* supplement 2 (1912).

117 B Windscheid, *Lehrbuch der Pandekten* vol 2, 8th edn (1900/01) §258 n 15.

VI. MODERN ROMAN LAW SCHOLARSHIP SINCE THE LATE 19TH CENTURY

1. PIONEERS OF CRITICAL HISTORICISM

In the jurisdictions where Justinian's Digest had been part of the law of the land, there had been an urge to resolve the antinomy in a way that avoided contradictions in favour of certainty and consistency. This time drew to a close. The contemporary applicability of Justinian's codification petered out in one country after the other. More scientifically-minded inquiries, supported by a broad neo-humanist turn of scholarship, gained momentum throughout the 19th century. New critical editions, following systematically thought-through editing principles, supplanted older and cruder editions. Roman law scholars re-focussed their activities, aiming at a historically correct understanding of the law in action in Roman antiquity. For the *lex Aquilia*, Pernice, Grueber and Willems published the first monographs of the new era in 1867, 1886 and 1896, one German, one English and one French. All three books, as a matter of course, addressed our texts. One might have expected these authors to come to a reading unhampered by the scholarly controversies of the past, with a common view emerging from a fresh start. This was not to be. We shall see these authors at odds, as they also link back to and refresh positions established in the preceding centuries.

A book by Alfred Pernice (1841–1901), *Zur Lehre von den Sachbeschädigungen nach römischem Rechte*, initially his *Habilitationsschrift*, published in Weimar in 1867,[118] was to become the standard monograph for almost a century. He starts with *l*.15.1,[119] which in his eyes has as a predominantly evidentiary *ratio*, attributed to Julian. For Pernice, the element which must be proven is the offender's *culpa*. If the intervening act is 'quite extraordinary', unforeseeable from the first wrongdoer's perspective, there is no *culpa* with regard to the effects of the intervening act. To prove the wrongdoer's *culpa*, one would have had to show that the wound culpably inflicted must have led to the death in a predictable manner; such proof

118 The monograph needed to qualify as a German professor. The university regulations required Pernice to provide a printed work, which he did using the first 25 pages of the well-known book then already in print. It is the same text, although the title for the thesis was *Bemerkungen zur lex Aquilia* (= *Remarks to the lex Aquilia*); this work is available online at https://books.google.de/books?id=tGQMAAAAYAAJ&printsec=frontcover&hl=de&source=gbs_ge_summary_r&cad=0#v=onepage&q&f=false.

119 *Zur Lehre von den Sachbeschädigungen nach römischem Rechte* (1867) 176 ff.

is not possible. This lack of *culpa* for the deadly effect that can be sufficiently proven requires a restriction of the liability to Chapter III. The cases in which the deadly effect comes to light after *manumissio* or *alienatio* do not have this problem; hence a liability under Chapter I is possible (*l.*15.1). Of course, *l.*51 does not fit into this line of thought. Pernice rejects Vangerow's attempt to distinguish the cases of *l.*11.3 and *l.*51pr. In his view, the texts deal with lethal wounds, but he assumes that the concept of lethality was fluid, and that Julian wanted to turn the exception into the rule. Pernice further states that Julian did not prevail and, moreover, that he changed his view, as *l.*15.1 showed. So, the diagnosis is a controversy, and Julian again the man of volatile views, as first portrayed by Noodt. While Pernice was an early advocate of the 'interruption of the causal nexus' concept, for him the 'interruption of the causal nexus' negates *culpa*. To be more precise, 'interruption of the causal nexus' excludes the foreseeability of events, which Pernice thinks is a prerequisite of *culpa*. Later authors have seen 'interruption of the causal nexus' as negating another, quite separate requirement, namely that of causation. The major prominence that Pernice attributed to the requirement of *culpa* is surprising, since none of our texts really talks about *culpa*. None of the later authors, as far as I can see, has tried to link the problem of our texts to a requirement of *culpa*.

The most elaborate of the three works was Erwin Grueber's (1846–1933)[120] *The Roman Law of Damage to Property*, published in 1886.[121] Unlike Pernice's work, it has not become a focal point of reference, though it is difficult to say why not.[122] According to Grueber, *l.*51 is 'not at all in contradiction' with *l.*11.3 and *l.*15.1. He took it that according to Julian, the first attacker was liable for killing, 'for he has inflicted a wound from which death must have necessarily followed, and from which death has apparently resulted in the given case, although under the concurrent influence of another wound, and therefore earlier than was to be expected.'[123]

Joseph Willems (1871–1944)[124] discarded the views of Glück and Pernice, who had found not only a disagreement between Celsus and

---

120 On Grueber, see J Cairns, 'The Early Historiography of the *Lex Aquilia* in Britain: Introducing Students to the Digest', *Wrongful Damage to Property in Roman Law. British Perspectives* (2018) 3, at 13–8.

121 E Grueber, *The Roman Law of Damage to Property* (1886) 35 ff, 52 ff, 164 ff.

122 Grueber's work was reviewed by Muirhead: J Muirhead, 'Grueber on the Lex Aquilia', (1886) 2 *LQR* 379.

123 Grueber (n 121) 164.

124 Willems was one of the Belgians who fled Belgium in 1914, to settle in the 'Belgian colony' of Royal Tunbridge Wells and Southborough; cf *The Shock of War – Tunbridge Wells in the First World War* (2014).

Julian, but also Julian contradicting himself.[125] He reports, side by side, the solution of the Gloss and that of Vangerow. He finds both approaches reconcilable; the lethality of the first and of the second wound are both material in distinguishing the cases. In the case set out by Julian, it is a certainly lethal first wound, to which is added another wound of unclear lethality. The case addressed by Celsus deals with a first wound of a degree of lethality not firmly established, followed by a second wound of unquestionable lethality. There is no antinomy. Willems's text does not bring in any considerations of causation.

While Pernice had already made considerable use of Byzantine sources, it was Contardo Ferrini (1859–1902) who systematically brought his expertise of Byzantine scholars to our texts. In an article first published in 1886,[126] Ferrini reports the solution of the Gloss, but opines that the eminently practical Roman lawyers would hardly have had a distinction in mind that could be so difficult to establish and would be fraught with uncertainty. Ferrini closely considers Vangerow's proposal, but sides with Windscheid's criticism of Vangerow, adding that the words *quo vita excessit*, if combined with Julian's opinion that the one-year-period is to be reckoned from the moment of wounding, require the second blow in *l.*51 to be instantly deadly. This eliminates a distinguishing element relied upon by Vangerow and leaves the mainstream view that Julian had put forward a minority position, which could not successfully be established. It is not unusual for Celsus and Julian to clash. Ferrini points to a parallelism between *l.*51 and *l.*11, with Julian cited in each paragraph of *l.*11, except on our point, where the words *quod et Marcello videtur et est probabilius* rather suggest a controversy. Julian's view, he thinks, is best understood as a recourse to the law of accessorial liability in order to tackle the otherwise unsurmountable problems of proving the lethality of the second (!) blow. As to *l.*15.1, Ferrini argues that *alius ictus* here must be understood to refer to another accident, relying on Stephanos (ἄλλως πληγεὶς = *aliter perculsus*).[127] In this case there is no difficulty as to a second offender's liability and as to how the lethality of his blow could possibly be proven if the slave was already facing certain death.

---

125 J Willems, *La Loi aquilienne: théorie du dommage aux choses en droit romain* (1896) 65–8.

126 C Ferrini, 'Postille esegetiche ai frammenti del commentario di Ulpiano alle formule edittali ad legem Aquiliam', *Opere di Contardo Ferrini* vol 2 (1929) 95, at 97–108. Ferrini has dealt with our problem repeatedly, namely in Contardo Ferrini, 'Ottaveno e le sue dottrine', *Opere di Contardo Ferrini* vol 2 (1929) 113, at 127 n 1.

127 *Ibid*, 102 ff.

Giovanni Pacchioni (1867–1946) wrote the first English-language article exclusively devoted to our antinomy.[128] He rejects Grueber's and Vangerow's approaches. While he is somewhat more sympathetic towards the recent interpretation by Ferrini, in the end this does not convince him either. He would have liked to see a more precise statement as to the exact understanding of complicity: does it require a conspiracy among the wounders (subjective test), or is it sufficient that there be an objective complicity? Furthermore, does not the objective test fail in a case where the first blow is considered to be deadly? Harmonisation like the one used by the Gloss is 'not allowed nowadays'.[129] It is best, Pacchioni finds, to recognise the heterogenous nature of the Corpus Iuris, which brings together texts from different authors from different times. Therefore 'little theoretical discordances' could not be avoided altogether. We are confronted with one of them. This leaves the problem of *l.*15.1: did Julian change his mind?[130] Pacchioni rejects this idea, now stressing that the cases here dealt with are quite different from the one set out in *l.*51pr: *l.*15.1 deals with unavoidable events ('the Roman ideas of fate and fortune'), breaking the causal connection (*alio ictu* is not specifically addressed). Julian's modernist approach, he assumes, allowed considering a slave, after a blow *quo certum esset periturum*, as already dead; the owner could bring an action 'whilst the slave was still alive'. Pacchioni takes *l.*15.1 as a veiled rejection of this view. Pacchinio asks which solution one should follow today, and while he acknowledges that most writers are inclined to accept Ulpian's view, today Julian's theory is to be preferred, 'considering the progress of medicine in our age'. These are musings which go back to the Middle Ages and early modern times. Awkwardly, the editor Frederick Pollock (1845–1937) added a word of caution:[131]

> I am not sufficiently versed in the Digest to have a decided opinion as to what Julianus was capable of. But I cannot help thinking that a Roman lawyer who held that an action would lie for killing a man before the man was dead would have seemed to colleagues *capable de tout*; and with all deference to specialists in Roman law, I submit that we ought to have stronger and less ambiguous evidence before we attribute such a view to any lawyer of the classical period.

128 G Pacchioni, 'A Disputed Point in the Lex Aquilia', (1888) 4 *LQR* 178.
129 *Ibid*, 181.
130 *Ibid*, 182.
131 *Ibid*, 184.

William Warwick Buckland (1859–1946), in his *opus magnum* on the Roman law of slavery, considers our cases, since slaves are the victims.[132] He reports the relevant cases, systematically lined up, ending with *l*.51. Here he thinks it is 'immaterial, whether death does or does not immediately follow the second injury. The fact that it follows at once does not prove that the second injury was of itself mortal', which Buckland assumes is the case in *l*.51, since Julian counted the year backwards from the moment of wounding and here takes the death as the starting point. Hence the second wounding and the actual death must here have happened contemporaneously. Buckland with wonderment registers the controversy. To him, it is plain that *l*.11.3 and *l*.51pr are not about one and the same case. *L*.51 leaves it uncertain whether the second wound was itself mortal, which is express information given in *l*.11.3: 'Thus the contradiction, improbable in itself, appears to be non-existent.' Buckland clarifies that the immediacy with which death here followed the second wound (as he supposes) does not imply that the second injury was in itself mortal: 'It does not shew that it was mortal apart from the first'.

Buckland gave advanced lectures on the *lex Aquilia* in Cambridge in the 1920s. These lectures were delivered on the basis of a typescript, which has recently been discovered and edited by David Ibbetson.[133] This is the analysis which Buckland set out for his students:

> Difficult questions arise where there are two or more woundings by different people. […] A number of people attack a man and he dies of their assault. In h.t. 51.1 Julian discussing primarily successive attacks lays down rules applicable to this case. All are liable for killing. He says you must either say all are or none is and that whatever may be said logically for this last solution, the contrary rule is established, in the public interest, on the authority of the '*veteres*', the republican jurists, lest wrongful acts go unpunished. He says that it is like the case of several men carrying off a thing none of them individually could have moved. Ulpian in h.t. 11.2 quotes and approves this opinion, adding that if it is clear which wound killed the man, that one is liable for the killing, the others only for wounding. He adds also, what we know from other sources, that what one pays does not release the others as it is a *poena*. Passing to the actual case of successive assaults it must be said that there is much controversy. It is commonly held that there is conflict in the texts, but not all think this and

132 W W Buckland, *The Roman Law of Slavery* (1908) 29 f.

133 D Ibbetson, 'William Warwick Buckland on the Lex Aquilia', *Wrongful Damage to Property in Roman Law. British Perspectives* (2018) 46.

I think the view that there is not is right. The rule of the texts as I understand them is as follows.

If it is clear which killed him that one is liable for killing, the others (we assume only two assaults) are liable only for wounding. But if it is uncertain all are liable for killing. H.t. 11.2 and 51.1.

If A mortally wounds him and B afterwards does something which would certainly kill him and does kill him, B has killed him, not A. This is laid down by a wealth of authorities, Celsus, Marcellus, Julian and Ulpian, h.t. 11.3, 15.1. The second man's killing is as if he had died in an earthquake that caused his death, not A. h.t. 15.1.

If A's wound was mortal and B's certainly shortened his life, though it is not certain that it would have killed apart from B's both are liable for the killing. Thus the rule saving A applies only where the wound by B would certainly kill. The mere fact that it shortened his life does not protect A, nor of course the fact that it may have done so. If B had cut the victim's finger, that might have shortened his life, but it is no protection to A any more than a spell of cold weather, which might have the same effect.

The alleged conflict is between h.t. 11.3 and 15.1 on one side and h.t. 51.pr on the other. It is enough to say that this view assumes that the words 'he died *ex alio vulnere*' and '*alius postea exanimaverit*' which are those of h.t. 11.3 and show that the second wound was a mortal one in itself mean the same as 'he died *ab alio ictus*' not '*ictu*' which is the language of h.t. 51.pr. They do not mean the same. The second wording means that he died sooner for the second blow, but there is nothing in it to suggest that this would have killed without the other. There is no break of causation. The text has however a peculiarity which has suggested that it is altered. It says '*lege Aquilia teneri*', but that is not the question. Both are liable in any case under one head or the other. The question is whether A or B or both are liable under cap. 1 *de occiso*.

2. HEYDAYS OF INTERPOLATIONISM

In a way, the interpolationist epoch was but an escalation of the systematic textual criticism which had increasingly flourished throughout the 19th century.[134] The upswing of methodical textual criticism had instilled the awareness that all our texts have come to us as the product of a long

134 The interpolationist movement has now been reviewed by an international group of authors, whose contributions appeared as: *Gradenwitz, Riccobono und die Entwicklung der Interpolationenkritik – Gradenwitz, Riccobono e gli sviluppi della critica interpolazionistica* (M Avenarius et al eds, 2018).

and often unreliable chain of transmissions. The sceptical review of our sources now focussed on Justinian's compilers' intensive reworking of the older material in the early 530s. Lacking a clear methodology, the sceptical approach triggered an avalanche of conjectures, often highly speculative as to where, how and why texts may have been corrupted and what might have been the authentic wording written by the classical jurists.

The first modern scholar to expressly doubt the authenticity of a substantial bit of our texts was Fridolin Eisele (1837–1920), who as a trailblazer ushered in, together with others, the interpolationist era.[135] He approached the texts in the context of the thorny topic of joint liability. His main objective was to find arguments against a theory regarding the Roman law solidarity concept advanced by Alfredo Ascoli (1863–1942). The controversial issue was the consumptive effect of *litis contestatio* for the *actio(nes)* based on the *lex Aquilia*, for which *l.*11.2 was relevant. Eisele is irritated that the words *si plures servum percusserint* do not clarify whether the case is about joint (co-ordinated) or isolated actions. He relates the reference to Julian (in *l.*11.2) to his view as set out in *l.*51.1. Although *l.*51.1 could also be read as referring to a joint action, the context suggests that isolated actions of multiple wrongdoers are at issue. If that is so, Eisele concludes, the lack of a liberating effect of the bringing of an action against one offender, which would relieve all others, is self-evident, and independent of the issue of how multiple actors who join in one delict are met with a multiplicity of claims. However, Eisele declares the passage *et si cum uno – liberantur* in *l.*11.2 as interpolated, because, as a matter of grammar, *liberantur* should rather be an infinitive in order to properly link back to *Iulianus ait*.[136]

On different occasions, Gerhard von Beseler (1879–1947) brought his hypercritical perspective to bear on our texts. His elaborate conjectures are reproduced in full p 149 ff. In his first reconstruction he excises *haec – occisus* from *l.*15.1.[137] He takes the change to the second person (*tu*) in the second sentence as a clue for a post-classical intervention. It is not correct, in Beseler's view, to say that *non est passa ruina apparere an sit occisus*, because it is an 'interruption of the causal connection'. The first sentence must have been much longer, he conjectures, because

135 F Eisele, 'Correalität und Solidarität', (1891) 77 *Archiv für die civilistische Praxis* 374, at 466 f.

136 *Ibid*, 467 n 82.

137 G von Beseler, *Beiträge zur Kritik der römischen Rechtsquellen, Drittes Heft* (1913) 8–9; as to *l.*15.1, Beseler later repeated his criticism, albeit restricted to *haec ita – verum est*: G von Beseler, *Beiträge zur Kritik der römischen Rechtsquellen, Viertes Heft* (1920) 69.

Julian decided to see a killing here; Beseler thus seems to equate the cases of *l*.51 and *l*.15.1. He has doubts, however, whether perhaps the first sentence of *l*.15.1 is 'real', and *l*.51 falsified. In *l*.51.2 he takes *quod si – teneatur* to be an insertion, for which, however, a now lost passage must have been excised. *Subtili ratione – quia* is also not authentic.[138] Philological reasons, which are not set out here, are given for the excisions. Seven years later, Beseler changed his mind and quite radically 'rectified' the text attributed to Julian in a different manner.[139] In the *principium*, Beseler now assumes that a <*de occiso*> had clarified the reference to Chapter I liability. He is unhappy with *igitur*, because the matter of an interrupted causation had not yet surfaced in the text before. For §2, Beseler starts with the somewhat doubtful textual transmission concerning the 365 days, which he assumes must originally have been a reference to the 30-day period of Chapter III. He further infers an original juxtaposition not between the measure of damages owed by two killers, but between a Chapter III and a Chapter I liability. This amounts to the assumption that Julian originally supported the same decision as Celsus (and later Ulpian). *Postea ab alio ictus decessit*: Beseler maintains that all three cases, *l*.11.3, *l*.15.1 and *l*.51, share the same material facts, namely that the second man's blow was deadly 'and the only cause of death'. The sentence *idque – iudicaverunt* is 'untrue', since the case here mentioned is unable to elucidate the issue of interrupted causation, and, moreover, in the case Julian starts with, there is no uncertainty as to the person of the killing, Beseler thinks. He is afraid that *multa – ero* and *quamvis – sustulisse* may also be later additions. Beseler, in his laconic style, does not try to explain why decisions by Celsus/Ulpian and Julian, which had initially been *ad idem*, should have been turned into a controversy by Justinian's compilers. In 1925, Beseler came back to *l*.15.1 with some thoughtful deliberations, for once forsaking textual criticism.[140] These are his musings (freely translated), focussing on the cases of *manumissio* and *alienatio*:

> Action and the action's effect are the elements of liability. When is the act accomplished? When the deed is done, not when the effect ensues. But to trigger liability, an effect befitting the required element must materialise.

Referring to the wording of the statute *si quis hominem alienum iniuria occiderit*, he asks whether the element *alienum*, that is the status of the

[138] *Ibid* Beseler (1913) 27.

[139] Beseler (1920) (n 137) 193 f.

[140] G von Beseler, 'Miszelle', (1925) 45 *ZRG RomAbt* 437.

victim as being someone's property, must be met at the moment when the slave dies or at the moment he/she is wounded. Julian, Beseler argues, opts for the latter concept, as he in general emphasises the first moment in time rather than the second. Julian is thus inclined to attach as many elements of liability to that first moment: 'Going by the standards of statutory interpretation, Julian quite certainly got to the correct understanding of the statute'. Beseler's last contribution concerns *l.*11.3. It is an aesthetically motivated criticism: Beseler assumed that Ulpian had not positively asserted the second assailant's liability under Chapter I, most likely because he thought the text dealt with the first attacker only.[141]

Beseler's radical approaches were topped by Wilhelm Rechnitz (1899–1979), one of the few fully professional classicists to look at *l.*51 in close detail.[142] Inspired by Eduard Norden and Tadeusz Stefan Zieliński, Rechnitz relied on Latin metric, accents and long/short syllables, which they had found were used, even in prose, in typical and recurring patterns (*clausulae*).[143] These patterns could, this was the idea, also be used to detect interpolations. Such are the proposals to which his method takes him for *l.*51:[144] *vulgo quidem* is non-Julianic, as is *sed lege aquilia – caede*. Rechnitz found *sed – igitur* to also be full of objectionable elements; it is probably a later addition as well. He also faults the amateur etymology, which he finds not helpful. *Statuendum – iudicaverunt* is non-Julianic, too. Ultimately, Rechnitz sides with Beseler in turning Julian's result upside down: the Byzantine jurists wanted to set out, first, who is liable, and then

141 G von Beseler 'Romanistische Studien', (1930) 1 *TR* 161, at 182.

142 Rechnitz worked as a librarian in Leipzig, where he also adapted Greek plays for contemporary performances and edited the *Bibliotheca Philologica Classica* (3 vols). In 1934 he immigrated to England, where he became a member and then a teacher of the Church of England. Interned as an enemy alien in 1940, he was deported to Australia. After his release in 1943, he resumed church work and was ordained in 1954. As a priest in the Torres Strait, he pioneered linguistic research for the Papua language. He also addressed issues of mother tongue missionary work: 'Over the course of 24 years, he collated articles, journals, language and music translations, poems and photographic records of the Torres Strait Islanders amongst whom he resided. A prodigious linguist, his scholarship includes musical translation of traditional Torres Strait Islander hymns and languages': State Library of Queensland, http://www.slq.qld.gov.au/straithome/exhibitions/slqgallery/rechnitz, accessed 19 October 2017; cf H A Strauss/W Röder, *International Biographical Dictionary of Central European Emigrés 1933–1945* vol II/2 (1983) 945; U Hohoff, *Wissenschaftliche Bibliothekarinnen und Bibliothekare als Opfer der NS-Diktatur. Eine Übersicht über 250 Lebensläufe seit dem Jahr 1933. Teil 1: Die Entlassungen Universitätsbibliothek Augsburg*, http://dx.doi.org/10.5282/o-bib/2015H2S1-32, accessed 3 March 2018.

143 W Rechnitz, *Studien zu Salvius Julianus* (1925).

144 *Ibid*, 77.

to what degree. The work of Rechnitz has drawn heavy criticism from other classicists, most notably from Ernst Fraenkel.[145]

Ernst Levy (1881–1968) in his *opus magnum* looked into all sorts of situations where multiple actions come into play.[146] Taking up the angle first employed by Eisele, he also reviewed our texts, in respect of which he specifically made the case that they imply a concurrence-of-actions issue:[147] in *l.*11.3 there is a Chapter I action against the later offender, and a Chapter III action against the prior offender, a constellation Levy labels a 'double concurrence', since these actions differ formally (different parties) as well as substantively. Levy 'explains' Ulpian's decision with a 'disruption of the causal flow'.[148] He does not go further into this presumed reason. While Pernice had integrated the concept of an interrupted causal nexus into a requirement of *culpa*, on the strength that such an interruption negated foreseeability, no such construct is provided by Levy. Levy thus has to be credited as the first to use the 'interruption of the causal nexus' as a factor negating an implicit causality requirement for Chapter I liability. From Levy's point of view, Julian's solution can only be understood as being developed from the case of multiple contemporaneous perpetrators, as between whom it is impossible to discern the perpetrator of the actually deadly blow (*l.*51.1): as in that case, Julian is supposed to argue, one can hold liable as killers successively acting perpetrators, between whom it is impossible to discern who dealt the actually deadly blow.[149] Levy then addresses details of the joint liability of these two defendants. Although there are two Chapter I actions, they are based on *eadem causa*, and this makes their relationship an issue. His easy diagnosis is based on *l.*11.2: payment of one perpetrator does not liberate the other. The *dominus* thus cumulates the two 'penalties' which Julian (contrary to Celsus) finds are to be differently reckoned (*l.*51.2). Levy strongly disapproves of Eisele's theory. He has, however, some textual criticism of his own: in *l.*11.3 he dislikes *quia ex alio vulnere periit*, which he declares to be a later addition.[150] As to *l.*15.1, he suspects a falsification of the beginning, invoking Beseler.[151] However, Levy does not doubt that *l.*51 in principle gives us Julian's view, and hence he briefly acknowledges a controversy among the classical lawyers.

145 E Fraenkel, *Kleine Beiträge zur klassischen Philologie* vol 2 (1964) 491.
146 E Levy, *Konkurrenz der Aktionen* vol 1 (1918).
147 *Ibid*, 25.
148 *Ibid*, 25.
149 *Ibid*, 485 f.
150 *Ibid*, 25 n 5.
151 *Ibid*, 25 n 4.

We have to record some offhand references to our texts, which support the interpolationist authenticity doubts. Emil Seckel (1864–1924), in his edition of Heumann's Latin *Handlexikon*, records *l*.51.2 as a reference for '*impunitus*', followed by a cautious '(interp.?)'.[152] Giovanni Rotondi (1885–1918) voices the same opinion.[153] *L*.51.2 is also doubted by Ernst Rabel (1874–1955),[154] Otto Gradenwitz (1860–1935),[155] and Fritz Pringsheim (1882–1967).[156] Heinrich Erman (1857–1940) feels that *l*.51.2, with its triple repetition of *constitui* and the change from *nobis* to *ego*, is 'mightily suspicious'.[157] Franz Haymann (1874–1947) comments upon *l*.51 in passing only:[158] for him, the last sentence of *l*.51.2 is just 'nonsense' and hence everything from *si quis absurde* is non-Julianic. He ventures the guess that the jurists here did not discuss the 'yes' or 'no' of Aquilian liability, but only the measure of damages. Paul Krückmann (1866–1943) launched another attack on *l*.51:[159] the *principium* is of questionable authenticity from *sed lege Aquilia* onwards; perhaps *respondit – praebuit* may also have to be rejected. §1 is sandwiched in; it is doubtful whether Julian is the author. The beginning of the *principium* and §2 can be read together. Krückmann chastises the reasoning as a 'broad swaggering in a schoolmaster's pitch'. In this decade, the willingness to accept *l*.51.2 as authentic Julian hit an all-time low.

Fritz Schulz (1879–1957) used the Ulpian lemma of D.9.2.7.1–8 with D.9.2.11pr–5 as an example of the style of high classical commentaries.[160] These do not

> illustrate abstract principles by means of true or fictitious cases; rather does the work consist of a series of cases in which the legal rule occurs, but it is not abstracted from them in a formula. The authors make no theoretical deduction from the series of cases; they confine themselves to the 'merely paratactic and visual association of the analogy' (Max Weber).[161]

---

152 *Heumanns Handlexikon zu den Quellen des römischen Rechts* (1914) 253.

153 G Rotondi, *Scritti Giuridici* vol 2 (1922) 452 n 2.

154 E Rabel, 'Grundzüge des römischen Privatrechts', *Enzyklopädie der Rechtswissenschaften* (1915) 399, at 457.

155 O Gradenwitz, 'L. 27 §3 de R.V. und der bösliche Ersitzer', *Festgabe für Dr. Karl Güterbock* (1910) 303, at 311.

156 F Pringsheim, *Der Kauf mit fremdem Geld* (1916) 66 n 9.

157 H Erman, 'Entstammt BGB. §266 Tribonian oder Celsus?', (1904) 25 *ZRG RomAbt* 352, at 361.

158 F Haymann, 'Textkritische Studien zum römischen Obligationenrecht', (1919) 40 *ZRG RomAbt* 167, at 219 with n 2.

159 P Krückmann, 'Miszelle', (1940) 60 *ZRG RomAbt* 234.

160 F Schulz, *Principles of Roman Law* (1936).

161 *Ibid*, 51–2.

The rules pertaining to *occidere* and *causam mortis praebere* 'are shown by the cases cited, but are not expressed. […] The ensuing observations relative to the participation of more than one person […] are again strictly on casuistic lines.' Schulz thinks that the whole lemma is 'disfigured by glosses and interpolations'. In *l.*11.2 he considers *nam ex lege – poena* to be non-classical, but apart from this, *l.*11.1–3 'are in order'.[162] Summing up, Schulz finds that Ulpian,

> though attempting a systematic arrangement of his subject, did not succeed entirely in throwing off the haphazard method of stringing his cases loosely together. […] One thing is certain: the casuistic method, which revealed a law dynamic and struggling, gave to classical literature a vivacity and freshness which could never have been attained by a strict theoretical system; to this method Roman juristic writings owe their peculiarly stimulating power, the encouragement to active co-operation which is produced by their concealment of a leading principle – in short just that attribute which has always excited the fascinated admiration of juristic posteriority.[163]

Bernardo Albanese (1921–2004) assumes that Ulpian's text had been subject to very substantial alteration: Celsus, he speculatively suggests, let the first wrongdoer completely off the hook, and the reason he gives is that the amount of deterioration in market value (*deminutio pretii*), that is, the damage caused by the first blow, cannot be assessed in view of the short time remaining.[164] It is this approach, which rejects both Chapter I and Chapter III liabilities, to which Julian refers when he writes of an absurd position (*l.*51.2). Albanese asserts the basic authenticity of *l.*51, although he thinks that a <*de occiso*> or similar had made it clear that Julian really meant Chapter I for the first attacker. The harsh idea of Celsus, not to grant any action at all, was remedied by the compilers, who inserted *sed quasi vulneravit* in *l.*11.3. Albanese thought that in *l.*15.1 (only) the words *vel alio ictu* were non-classical.[165] Of all the contributions of the late interpolationist persuasion, Albanese's work alone has remained a constant point of reference.

---

162 *Ibid*, 63–4.

163 *Ibid*, 64–5.

164 B Albanese, 'Studi sulla legge Aquilia', (1950) 21 *AnnPal* 5: Celsus scribit, si alius mortifero vulnere <servum alienum> percusserit, alius postea exanimaverit, priorem [quidem] non teneri quasi occiderit, [sed quasi vulneravit], quia ex alio vulnere periit, <servus neque quasi vulneravit quia, ex alio vulnere mortuo servo, non apparuit quanto deterior factus sit>, posteriorem teneri, quia occidit. quod et Marcello videtur [et est probabilius], <Julianus autem contra scribit …>.

165 *Ibid*, 167.

Interesting but also vexing comments came from Raphael Powell (1904–1964) in 1951.[166] He ponders whether *alio ictu* in *l*.15.1 could possibly refer to a third person's *coup de grâce*, but even if this were so, no conflict between this fragment and *l*.11.3 can be found. The limitation to a Chapter III liability rests on the inability to prove that the (first) offender had in fact killed the victim, a proof that remains possible after manumission or alienation. Powell also considers the variant, that *alio ictu* merely referred to another wounding: this would make no difference, except that the intervening second offender becomes liable for killing. Coming from the evidentiary aspect, Powell finds that he can easily assimilate the beginning of *l*.51pr: stressing, with Voet, the certainty of the death resulting from the first wound, the second offender's intervention here does not create an evidentiary problem, and hence the first offender can be held liable for killing. The second offender is equally liable for killing as he 'finally dispatched' the victim. Powell now departs from the mainstream in an interesting manner: whereas most authors have understood Julian as resuming the case he set out at the start at the end of the *principium*, Powell toys with the idea that the speedier death referred to a different scenario, namely one without the qualification that death was a certain consequence of the first wound. Unlike anyone else, he is tempted to see two slightly different cases dealt with in the *principium* of *l*.51. The second one seems identical to the one in *l*.15.1, provided one reads *alio ictu* as referring to a human act. For Powell, this would constitute the crux of the matter. Powell discusses three different ways out, all fairly unconventional. First, he considers rejecting his own idea in favour of reading the *principium* in a homogenous way, referring to a certainly lethal wound from beginning to end. Secondly, and more speculatively, he ponders an interpretation according to which the second wound was of such a nature as to make it impossible to establish, in retrospect, whether the first wound was in fact lethal. Thirdly, he considers whether a mechanism of presumption and rebuttal is at play here: the second wound, because it is fatal, gives rise to a presumption that the earlier wound was not fatal, but this presumption could be rebutted. This is, in a way, a reversal of the idea of a break in the chain of causation, according to which the first wound is taken to be lethal unless the second wound is the clear cause of death. Powell ends on a speculative note, wondering whether §1 was sandwiched in by the compilers, due to a misunderstanding of Julian's text. Powell turns to Talmudic law for support

---

166 R Powell, '*Novus actus interveniens* in Roman Law', (1951) 4 *Current Legal Problems* 197.

for the idea that the Romans distinguished between potentially fatal and not potentially fatal wounds, but the difference is only relevant for wounds that did not result in death.[167] Powell also turns to *l*.51.2, which in his view brings *l*.51pr to its proper conclusion (contradicting Lawson): 'There is no question of any interruption in a chain of causation.'

Alan Watson (1933–2018) in 1965 declared *l*.51.1 to be a later insertion.[168] He cites Beseler, adding the deliberation that the case here brought in 'is no authority whatsoever for the proposition it is intended to justify'. He assumes that Justinian's compilers had found the text of §1 elsewhere (leaving undecided whether Julian was the author), since it is unlikely that Justinian made up the reference to the *auctoritas veterum*. Accordingly, §1 may well represent the law (as approved by the *veteres*); it just was not written in the context of what is now *l*.51pr and 2.

David Pugsley's (* 1943) approach to our texts brings a wealth of innovative ideas.[169] Pugsley defends *l*.11.3 and *l*.15 as basically genuine. In the matter of the accrual of the action under Chapter I (*l*.21.1), he sees a doctrinal dispute behind the controversy, with the Sabinian Julian looking at the critical wound as the 'substance' which underlies the whole scenario, while for the Proculian Celsus it is the end-result that counts.[170] However, the differences should not be exaggerated. Moreover,

> [it] does not follow, as Albanese thinks, that because Julian and Celsus differed in h.t.21.1, they must also have differed as to the outcome in h.t.11.3 and 15.1. And Schindler's suggestion of a personal enmity seems wholly unfounded.[171]

Turning to *l*.51, Pugsley supports the view that §1 is a later addition, and he also feels that words *statuendum est utrumque eorum lege Aquilia teneri* make for a weak ending of a thorough analysis and cannot be Julian's. He assumes that in Julian's original the text went on to end with the solution as set out in *l*.15.1. It was the compilers, Pugsley thinks, who desired to see both perpetrators held liable as killers. They were aware that this needed justification, and this is why they shoved in the reference to the *veteres*. §2 gets a better rating. It is high-grade material, and must indeed be the elucidation of a case where two perpetrators are liable for killing; it

---

167 *Ibid*, 204 n 0, citing Sanhedrin 78b, a text Boaz Cohen had already brought to light.

168 A Watson, *The Law of Obligations in the Later Roman Republic* (1965) 245 n 5.

169 D Pugsley, 'Causation and Confessions in the lex Aquilia', (1970) 38 *The Legal History Review* 163.

170 *Ibid*, 165.

171 *Ibid*, 166.

just cannot be the case set out in the *principium*. There must be a special scenario, perhaps referring to two wrongdoers acting in concert. The text, in Pugsley's view tailored to a very specific case (although we do not know which one), offered itself to the compilers to expand and intensify the double liability for killing, which they introduced as a general rule:

> Their reform was then supported by an appeal to the authority of precedent, which was inserted as s.1; and an elaborate argument from principle, which is the second half of s.2, '*quod si quis absurde a nobis haec constitui putaverit*, referring back to the last word of the *principium*'. We have no confidence in the genuineness of any of this passage [...].[172]

In Pugsley's view, the compilers overlooked the two conflicting texts, which retained the original rule (*l.*11.3 and *l.*15.1). Pugsley then adds an interesting observation:[173] Ulp 18 ad ed D.9.2.23.11 in his view deals with the scenario where one person has falsely confessed to having killed, whereas another was the real killer. Pugsley speculates that the slave's owner could sue an attacker under Chapter I, even if the slave was still dying, in order to get the attacker to plead guilty. Pugsley suggests extensive emendations for this text as well, assuming that the compilers wanted to bring this text in line with what they, in his view, had assembled in *l.*51.

In 1971, Ulrich von Lübtow (1900–1995) appeared on our scene as something of an interpolationist latecomer.[174] Like many authors, he takes *l.*11.3 as the reliable starting point, except that he feels that Ulpian wrote *verum* instead of *probabilium*. Von Lübtow believes that Julian and Celsus were *ad idem* with regard to the issue of 'overtaking causation'.[175] The double liability of two killers, von Lübtow finds, is 'simply logically untenable' and hence cannot be attributed to Julian. Von Lübtow discards large chunks of *l.*51 as interpolated.

From the mid-20th century onward, the interpolationist research increasingly turned to the matter of corruptions that texts might have suffered throughout the copying processes over three or four centuries,

172 *Ibid*, 169.
173 *Ibid*, 172 f.
174 U von Lübtow, *Untersuchungen zur lex Aquilia* (1971).
175 To drive this point home, von Lübtow 'reconstructed' the beginning of *l.*15.1 in the following manner: si servus vulneratus mortifere postea ruina vel naufragio [vel alio ictu] maturius perierit, de occiso agi non posse, sed quasi de vulnerato <Iulianus scribit> sed si manumissus vel alienatus ex vulnere periit, quasi de occiso agi posse [Iulianus] <idem> ait.

in between their original 'publication' and their use for Justinian's Digest. Julian's Digesta have been looked at from this angle and the thesis was advanced that at Justinian's time 'the text available was already deeply interpolated'.[176] Hans Julius Wolff (1902–1983) put out a focussed study emphasising this view, which however did not deal with *l.*51 specifically.[177]

Looking at the sum of all specific negations of authenticity, it would be possible, if one cherry-picked doubts from various authors, to discredit *l.*51 in each and every word, eradicating the complete fragment as source material for classical jurisprudence altogether. The scholars of the interpolationist inclination took almost unlimited liberty in creatively rewriting the purportedly original versions as laid down by the classical jurists. Not surprisingly, this led to a terrifying proliferation of a diversity of incompatible ideas.

3. THE PENDULUM SWINGS BACK

By and by, Roman law scholarship turned away from highly speculative reconstructions, reviving a more conservative adherence to the transmitted texts. The change came about in a gradual manner. For decades, authors continued to show a willingness to part with bits and pieces of the texts as non-classical alterations or additions, although the frequency and radicalness of such conjectures continued to decline over time.

An early word of caution had already come from the young Wolfgang Kunkel (1902–1981) in 1929.[178] Rejecting Rechnitz's attack on *l.*51pr, Kunkel stresses the authenticity of *occidisse – praebuisset*, 'the decisive sentence'. He concedes that the bit of etymology *tracta – caede* could be doubted. Kunkel links the discussion to the obvious requirement of 'a certain directness of the infliction of damage'.

In the same year, the Harvard lawyer James Bradley Thayer (1899–1976) advanced a thought-through opinion of his own, based on a critical review of a considerable range of authors,[179] including the textual criticism of Beseler, Levy and others. He rejects their hyper-scepticism: 'If the compilers

---

176 F Schulz, *History of Roman Legal Science* (1946) 230.

177 H J Wolff, 'Concerning the Transmission of Julian's Digesta', (1949) 7 *Seminar (Jurist)* 69.

178 W Kunkel, 'Exegetische Studien zur aquilischen Haftung', (1929) 69 *ZRG RomAbt* 158, at 159.

179 J B Thayer, *Lex Aquilia. Digest IX,2, Ad Legem Aquiliam. On Gifts between Husband and Wife (Digest XXIV, 1, De Donationibus inter Virum et Uxorem)* (1929) 114–5.

had applied themselves to the texts the result should obviously have been the suppression and not an aggravation, of any inconsistency.' Thayer does not accept Grueber's and Vangerow's view, insofar as they suggest that death may not have come with the second wound instantaneously. The solution of the Gloss, that the first wound was not truly lethal, is not satisfying either. In an apologia similar to the one voiced by Ferrini, he suggests that we stick with Julian's own reasons. The case dealt with by Julian is not exceptional, but rather the standard situation of an evidentiary dead end.

F Harry Lawson (1897–1983) addresses the matter of our texts in his *Negligence in Civil Law*.[180] He sets out all three texts and soberly reports the solutions offered by the Gloss, by the Byzantine scholars (of which he was an expert), and by Pernice, Grueber and Monro. He assumes that 'the second blow' (the *alius ictus*) in *l*.15.1 is a later insertion, meant to bring the text closer to *l*.11.3. Even if that were not so, and this variant originated from Julian, it would have to be understood to be 'a blow as catastrophic in its nature and consequences as the fall of a house'. This in turn would qualify as breaking the 'chain of causation'. *L*.51 is about a different case, where both wounds make a contribution, so one is not forced to say that the first wound had not become the cause of death. Turning to *l*.11.3, he sees a possibility – but no more – of understanding *exanimaverit* as 'something of the same kind as Julian seems to have meant in 15.1', citing Grueber's example of cutting the slave's head off. However, Lawson is not sure that this is the way to read the text (which would coincide with Vangerow's understanding). It might well be, Lawson ponders, that Celsus and Marcellus partially disagreed with Julian, somehow keeping to a middle line, going with Julian for the *l*.15.1 case, but not for the one of *l*.51. At this point, Lawson introduces an alternative solution, for which he gives credit to Herbert F Jolowicz (1890–1954), and which, taken up by Dieter Nörr 40 years later, has proved to be the most popular interpretation among the *moderni*:

> Celsus [...] puts the matter merely on the basis of actual result. [...] Julian makes the criterion the originally mortal nature of the blow (and it is only on the assumption that the delict was completed at the moment of striking that the difference in damages in h.t.51.2 and the decision in the second case in h.t.15.1 can be explained). Consequently, if both blows were originally mortal in their nature, both assailants are liable.[181]

180 F H Lawson, *Negligence in Civil Law* (1950) 50–3.
181 *Ibid*, 52.

Julian, in Lawson's view, would have been self-contradictory if he indeed supported the decision in *l.*15.1, as reported by Ulpian. This is the very same idea which had been first brought into play by Noodt. Lawson adds two interesting remarks. Firstly, since the damages for the mortally wounded slave must have amounted to his market value, the only difference at stake here is the year's versus the 30 days' valuation; this proposition is taken from William Buckland (1859–1946) and Arnold McNair (1885–1975).[182] Secondly, Lawson finds that 'the Romans had a firm grasp of the significance of an interruption in the chain of causation',[183] although they grappled to solve the issue. This train of thought is followed into modern law reflections, which need not be set out here. Lawson's book has been reworked, for an updated edition, by Basil Markesinis (* 1944).[184] Regarding our texts, nothing of substance has been added to Lawson's erudite thoughts.

One of the most elaborate exegeses appeared in 1957, Karl-Heinz Schindler's (* 1930) PhD thesis *Ein Streit zwischen Julian und Celsus. Zum Problem der überholenden Kausalität* ('A controversy between Julian and Celsus. Concerning the problem of overtaking causation').[185] First of all, Schindler reasserts the authenticity of *l.*51, in that it is genuinely from Julian. For Schindler, this implies a return to the hypothesis of a juristic disagreement. Schindler identifies two issues over which Julian was at odds with other jurists. One relates to the matter of the calculation of the Chapter I one-year period (*l.*21.1), the other to the matter of the so-called overtaking or, as Schindler prefers, 'aborted' causation. In *l.*51.2, Schindler suspects that *cum – oporteat* is a non-Julianic addition, due to its criminal-policy nature.[186] Apart from this, Schindler tries to fend off over-critical approaches to the texts. Schindler is a specialist on the *Quinquaginta Decisiones*, and it should be noted that he did not connect our problem to any of the presumed constitutions that make up the *Quinquaginta Decisiones.*

---

182 W W Buckland/A D McNair, *Roman Law & Common Law. A Comparison in Outline* 2nd edn (1952) 371 n 1: The authors understand Julian as taking a *per incuriam* decision, 'the wish to date the killing back to the infliction of the mortal wound prevailing over the need for an uninterrupted causation.'

183 Lawson (n 180) 53.

184 F H Lawson/B S Markesinis, *Tortious Liability for Unintentional Harm in the Common Law and the Civil Law* vol 1: *Text* (1982) 30.

185 K-H Schindler, 'Ein Streit zwischen Julian und Celsus. Zum Problem der überholenden Kausalität', (1957) 74 *ZRG RomAbt* 201.

186 *Ibid*, 228: '[E]ine zu betonte Beziehung zu strafrechtlichen Erwägungen'.

Not unlike Schindler's piece, the contribution by Danilo Dalla (* 1943) also marks a retreat from the maelstrom of interpolationist doubts.[187] He finds that Julian identified a legal problem arising out of a longer time period between the wounding and the actual death, to which his solution is presented in D.9.2.21.1. Dalla uses a hypothetical to drive this point home: if the slave's value had dropped in the middle of the year preceding the infliction of the wound, and a considerable time passed before the slave died, it may then have become be impossible for the owner to reach back in time to the peak price. The compensation due under Chapter I would only take into account the already diminished value of the slave. This, in Dalla's view, is the substantive reason for the proposal to let the evaluation period run from the moment of wounding. Since this is a solution to a specific problem of an appropriate determination of the one-year period, it is not dependent on Julian's willingness to accept mortally wounding as *occidere*; hence Ulpian can side with Julian regarding the measure of damages issue. Julian in *l.*51, as in D.9.2.21.1, thinks of a longer period between the first blow and the second blow/death. Here, making the first offender subject to a Chapter III liability is not helpful in view of the problem that troubled Julian, because Chapter III does not allow going back to a past market price. Only a Chapter I liability, triggered by the first attack, allows overcoming a recent price drop that threatens to leave the owner without adequate compensation; securing such compensation is a contribution to the *utilitas communis*. Dalla disputes that there is a discernible self-contradiction between the decisions attributed to Julian. He reads Julian as rejecting the idea of an interruption of the causal flow; rather, Julian is understood as basing the Chapter I liability on the infliction of a lethal wound alone. As to *l.*15.1, Dalla cites other texts where *ictus* refers to accidents. Dalla links Julian's position in *l.*51 directly to the matter of calculating damages under Chapter I.

In his musings about the Roman jurists' methodologies, Manuel J García Garrido (* 1928) used Julian's *l.*51.2 (*multa autem – potest*) as an illustration of the Roman jurists' flexibility and willingness to set legal logic aside for the purposes of utility and justice.[188]

187 D Dalla, 'Guiliano e il *longum intervallum* in tema di applicazione dell'Aquilia', (1974) 187 *ArchGiur* 145.

188 M J García Garrido, *Casuismo y jurisprudencia romana: Pleitos famosos del Digesto* (1973) 76.

Since Sandro Schipani (* 1940), in his important *Responsibilità 'ex lege Aquilia', criteri di imputazione e problema della 'culpa'*,[189] considered the *culpa* element of Aquilian liability specifically, not much attention needed to be given to our texts: after all, according to the majority view, the problem here is not one of *culpa*, occasional dissenters (Pernice) notwithstanding. Schipani refers us back to Schindler.[190]

Ben Beinart (1914–1979) analysed our cases, mobilising his own theory that the *lex Aquilia*, a *plebiscitum*, was originally passed as a political restitution programme for losses suffered during the (third) *seccessio plebis*. This led to a bias, in his view, towards holding as many persons concurrently liable as possible.[191] Among the classical jurists who are our *dramatis personae*, Beinart identifies Julian as the odd one out. Julian, in Beinart's view, was true to the original purpose of the *lex Aquilia*, in that he tried to hold multiple wrongdoers concurrently liable under Chapter I; this is the reason why Julian could invoke the *veteres* in *l*.51.2. The mainstream of Roman lawyers, however, had long departed from this approach, which 'was not an equitable view'. Beinart is thus in line with authors who had tried to show Julian as being inequitably harsh by finding two killers for one slave slain. As to *l*.15.1, Beinart holds that *alius ictus* must be *eiusdem generis* as *naufragium* and *ruina*, and hence cannot include human action. He thus 'rescues' Julian's presumed position from the verdict of being self-contradictory.

Károly Visky (1908–1984) in 1979 reviewed and systematised cases from the field of the *lex Aquilia* that he thought could be understood as dealing with causation.[192] He sets out a fairly conventional concept of causation, including the civilian distinction of two requirements of causation, the second pertaining to the emerging damage. Visky uses selected texts, not really thoroughly dissected, to scan the full range of causation issues. *L*.11.3 in his view addresses a situation where the damaging effect has been triggered not by the tortfeasor's act alone, but also by another, independent factor.[193] While this is taken to be a standard argument, Julian in *l*.51 is seen as dissenting. In the case here addressed, Visky identifies the second blow as the cause of death. He dismisses Julian's position as 'hardly valid', since

---

189 S Schipani, *Responsibilità 'ex lege Aquilia', criteri di imputazione e problema della 'culpa'* (1969).

190 *Ibid*, 22 n 3.

191 B Beinart, 'Once more on the origin of the lex Aquilia', (1956) *Butterworths South African Law Review* 70, at 75.

192 'Die Frage der Kausalität aufgrund des D. 9,2 (ad legem Aquiliam)', (1949) 3 *RIDA* 437.

193 *Ibid*, 486–9.

the inheritance, which Julian includes in the second attacker's liability, is a *lucrum cessans*, and the gain does not seem in reach here, because of the looming death as a consequence of the first wound. However, Julian's opinion is explainable in view of the penal element of Aquilian liability. *L.*15.1 is a case of an interrupted chain of causation. Summing up, Visky confirms that the Roman lawyers did not set out a 'theory of causal nexus', but pragmatically looked for and determined the causal nexus.[194]

The long-time standard work of reference, Max Kaser's (1906–1997) *Römisches Privatrecht*, informs the reader that there has been a controversy regarding the problem of 'so-called "overtaking causation"', and for this *l.*11.3 and *l.*51pr-2 are cited.[195] Kaser later tried to establish the Roman manner to delineate '*ius publicum*' and '*ius privatum*', and in doing so also looked into the emerging uses of phrases like '*publica utilitas*'.[196] He found the term, and what he thought were synonymous terms, employed by late classical authors and in yet later imperial constitutions. From this perspective, Julian appears in a pioneering role, being the first jurist who expressly relied on this topic. Noting the widespread textual criticism, Kaser defensively classifies the idea that the passage should contain a post-classical generalisation as a 'possibility, but not a certainty'. Even if the passage were inauthentic, he thinks, it could still be taken to represent what was a truth for Julian, an oddly forced assertion of a strictly conservative attitude in the matter of textual criticism.

Geoffrey MacCormack (* 1937) has dealt with our problem twice. *Aquilian Studies* is a broadside against the by then prevalent approaches that relied on variants of causation concepts.[197] MacCormack carefully paraphrases *l.*51. As to *l.*15.1, he sides with the assumption that the reference to an *alius ictus* is a later addition.[198] Regarding *l.*11.3, MacCormack finds Celsus at odds with Julian's views in *l.*51. Interestingly, MacCormack manages to rephrase the positions in this controversy without using causation concepts:

> The case in which a slave is mortally wounded by A but dies subsequently from a further wound inflicted by B has commonly been discussed in terms of causation. It is assumed that the wound by A is the start of a chain of causation which is

194 *Ibid*, 501.
195 M Kaser, *Römisches Privatrecht I* 2nd edn (1971) 503 n 2.
196 M Kaser, '"Ius publicum" und "ius privatum"', (1986) 103 *ZRG RomAbt* 1.
197 G MacCormack, 'Aquilian Studies', (1975) 41 *SDHI* 1.
198 *Ibid*, 28.

> either interrupted or terminated by the second wound. Iulian is thought to have held that the second wound does not break the chain of causation between the first wound and the death, whereas Celsus is thought to have held that the second wound breaks the chain of causation and so precludes A's liability under chapter one. This treatment of the problem seems to stem from the pronounced modern concern with questions of causation. There is no evidence in the texts that Iulian or Celsus thought of the relation between the wounds and the death in terms of causation.[199]

We shall return to MacCormack's contributions when the report turns to authors who have looked specifically into the Roman lawyers' methodologies.[200]

The most comprehensive analysis ever put forward came in 1980, from the pen of Hans Ankum (* 1930–2019).[201] Ankum neatly organises the full range of cases and tries to explain the decisions one by one. The following summary cannot do full justice to his systematic disquisition of the whole field. Ankum assumes that Julian indeed disagreed with Celsus with regard to the case set out in *l.*11.3, and that Ulpian's original text informed the reader equally about both jurists' conflicting opinions; the compilers excised the bit relating to Julian, because they gave his view by incorporating *l.*51pr. Ankum takes *l.*51pr as being in direct conflict with Celsus's/Ulpian's approach. He tries to trace back the controversy to the different views held in respect of the relevant moment the slave was to be considered 'killed'. Since Julian – unlike Celsus – was willing to backdate, provided the death had in fact ensued, he could easily also do so in the event that the subsequent death was not a clean-cut consequence of the prior wounding. He finds Julian's solution 'a little problematic, from a strictly logical point of view, as Julian himself felt it'.[202] According to Ankum, Julian gives more weight to the policy consideration dear to him, which in this case trumped strict logic. Marcellus and Ulpian, while in general following Julian in the matter of backdating, were not convinced by Julian's decision (as transmitted in *l.*51pr), due to its logical flaw, and thus stuck with Celsus. Ankum thus thinks he identifies *l.*15.1 as the problematic text, because it could suggest Julian's approval of the mainstream view of

---

199 *Ibid*, 29–30.

200 Below p 80 ff.

201 H Ankum, 'Das Problem der "überholenden Kausalität" bei der Anwendung der lex Aquilia im klassischen römischen Recht', *De Iustitia et iure* (1980) 325.

202 'Vom strikt logischen Standpunkt ist diese Meinung etwas problematisch, wie Julian es auch selbst gefühlt hat', *ibid*, 349.

'overtaking causation'.[203] Ankum, like some of his predecessors – Voorda, Lenel[204] and Beinart come to mind – eliminates the problem by limiting Julian's reported assent to the cases of *manumissio vel alienatio*: a full stop just needs to be inserted between *vulnerato* and *sed*. Unlike the Mommsen edition, earlier editors had punctuated the text in this manner, Ankum informs us. Ankum is not irritated by the consequence that the *non posse* thus can no longer be dependent on the *Iulianus ait*. The emerging standalone sentence *si servus – vulnerato*, which Ankum condones as a possible grammatical construction, in spite of the missing verb, is taken to express Ulpian's own view, and Ulpian's view alone. Ankum also invokes the reading of the vulgate manuscript tradition, which he finds to have *et Iulianus ait*, and he thinks this also supports his view. Last but not least, citing D.9.2.30.4, Ankum concludes that Paulus, unlike Ulpian, most probably adhered to Julian's view.

4. DIVISION OF LABOUR IN ROMAN LAW RESEARCH

While for a long time the fragments as such were the focal point of comments, during the 20th century we saw a massive diversification of Roman law research. Quasi-latitudinal studies emerged, some looking into the legal thinking of specific authors, some devoted to specific substantive topics of Roman legal science, cutting across different authors and their works. This diversification was accompanied by growing specialisation. These are the characteristics of a division of labour. Works of this kind are now reported here, if and insofar as their authors had a closer look at our texts.

a) Ascertaining the Sources

First of all, the textual basis for our Digest texts could now be subjected to an improved review, thanks to Govaert Carolus Joannes Joseph van den Bergh (1926–2005) and Bernard H Stolte (* 1949), who in 1977 edited, as a pilot survey, the Brenkman notes on the Digest title 9.2.[205] They thus also

---

203 In *l*.11.3, Ankum suspects *vel naufragio vel alio ictu* to be a later addition, arguing that *ruina* is the only occurrence the text later comes back to.

204 Otto Lenel (1849–1935), too, had cut the reach of the Julian reference by inserting a colon after *de vulnerato*; *Palingenesia Iuris Civilis* vol 2 (1889) col 525 = Ulp ad ed 651.

205 G C J J van den Bergh/B H Stolte Jnr, 'The unfinished digest editions of Henrik Brenkman (1681–1736)', (1977) 45 *TR* 227.

unlocked the erudite comments by Henrik Brenkman (1681–1736), who followed Noodt's views. A complete set of photographs of the Florentine manuscript had been published in a small print run 1902/10.[206] The mass-market availability of a photographic reproduction, edited by Corbino and Santalucia in 1988,[207] made it possible for everyone to directly check the Florentine reading, without having to rely on one of its printed editions, like the ones by Torelli or Russard. As regards the Florentina, we can see that Mommsen's Digest edition got it right. For the Basilika, which was used, *inter alia*, by Pernice, Ferrini, Lawson, Schipani and Zahn, we now have the new Scheltema edition. Massimo Miglietta (* 1965) has put forward a meticulous comparison of the Digest title 9.2 and its counterpart, Bas.60.3.[208] The micro-structures of the great commentaries that were used for the Digest title 9.2 have been meticulously analysed by Alan Rodger (Lord Rodger of Earlsferry) (1944–2011).[209]

b) *Ideas of Causation in Antiquity*

Boaz Cohen (1899–1968), a leading Talmud scholar of the 20th century, contributed a comparative piece on the principle of causation in the Jewish and the Roman law of damages.[210] He explains the narrow Roman concept of *occidere*, highlighting the effect that indirect causation has to be covered by the *in factum* variant of the Aquilian action. He focusses on Julian's text mostly for the confirmation that *occidere* required the 'direct violence', 'by his hand, as it were'. Sanhedrin 78a deals with a case comparable to the one of *l*.11.3 and proposes holding only the second attacker liable as the killer. Cohen understands *l*.51.2 to be the admission of 'an absence of a logical principle defining what constitutes indirect damage, or causality with relation to damage.'[211]

Robert Röhle (1936–2012) made the attempt to collect, from across a variety of legal fields, instances of what he called 'displacing causation'.[212]

---

206 *Justiniani Augusti Digestorum seu Pandectarum Codex Florentinus, olim Pisanus, phototypice expressus* (1902–10).

207 A Corbino/B Santalucia, *Justiniani Augusti Pandectarum Codex Florentinus* (1988).

208 Miglietta (2014) (n 16); Miglietta (2015) (n 16).

209 A Rodger, 'The Palingenesia of the Commentaries Relating to the Lex Aquilia', (2007) 124 *ZRG RomAbt* 145.

210 B Cohen, 'The principle of causation in the Jewish and the Roman law of damages', *Studi de Francisci* vol 1 (1956) 305, at 318 ff.

211 *Ibid*, 330.

212 R Röhle, 'Zur Frage der sogenannten verdrängenden Verursachung im Römischen Recht', (1965) 31 *SDHI* 305–11.

In a way, his is a companion piece to Schindler's, trying to broaden the basis for a reconstruction of refined causation *topoi*, recurring in different contexts. As to *l.*15.1, Röhle for palingenetical reasons thinks that text was originally about the matter of standing only, and could have run similar to this:

> *Si servus vulneratus mortifere postea manumissus vel alienatus ex vulnere periit, <dominum suum> [quasi] de occiso agi posse Iulianus ait.*

This also results in Ulpian no longer being at odds with Julian. In a surprising statement, Röhle finds that both Julian and Celsus operated with a concept of hypothetical causation.[213]

A number of works have been devoted to Roman lawyers' concepts of causation, or whatever we take as the nearest Roman equivalent. Reinhard Willvonseder (* 1942) was a breath of fresh air, setting himself apart from many, but not from all of the mainstream arguments that had been advanced so far.[214] Willvonseder has some general remarks on the role of causation in the handling of the *occidere* chapter of the *lex Aquilia*.[215] For the Roman jurists, to affirm *occidere* involved the finding of a dead slave, while the causal nexus as such was of no particular concern to them; rather they apply the term *occidere* in an 'undifferentiated' manner.[216] By contrast, the handling of Chapter III focusses more on the effect of a *res corrupta* and its causal production. For both chapters, the decisive question, when looking at the statutory *actio directa*, is finding the phenotypic expression of the required act. Turning to our texts,[217] Willvonseder follows Ankum in limiting the Julian citation in *l.*15.1 to the cases of *manumissio* and *alienatio*; he is also attracted to the idea that *ruina* was the sole case the original text dealt with. He points to modern doctrine, which has tried to limit the concept of overtaking causation to the occurrence of damaging events which are not accompanied by anyone's liability. As to *l.*51, Willvonseder assumes that Julian expects his readers to have the *condicio sine qua non* formula in mind, which might raise doubts in cases of 'alternative' and 'overtaking' causation. Willvonseder therefore approves of the comparison made in §1. The potential outcome, i.e. that none of the attackers could

---

213 *Ibid*, 306.

214 R Willvonseder, *Die Verwendung der Denkfigur der 'condicio sine qua non' bei den römischen Juristen* (1984).

215 *Ibid*, 12 f.

216 *Ibid*, 14.

217 *Ibid*, 145 f.

be liable (§2), needs to be taken seriously, since it could be supported by a stringent application of the *condicio sine qua non* formula. Willvonseder does not see Celsus as the jurist against whom Julian turns in §2, since Celsus advocated liability for both attackers, although differentiating the first from the second as to the relevant Chapter. The comparison with the multi-person theft of a beam (§2), in Willvonseder's view, is also meant to support a turning away from a strict adherence to the *condicio sine qua non* formula, which would require letting all thieves go free. To get to a legally more satisfying result, Julian is willing to base the *actio* on the infliction of a mortal wound alone.

While much of the pertinent discussions tended to gravitate around causation analyses, there was also a countervailing trend of those who argued that the Roman lawyers' thinking here was not centred on matters of causation. This is the place to draw attention to Boudewijn Sirks (* 1947), who gave the problem a new twist, highlighting a potentially influential philosophical background for Julian's reasoning.[218] This is his own abstract:

> D.9.2.51, in which a slave is slain twice and dies, and where Julian considers both assailants equally liable for killing, has been interpreted in the context of *causa superveniens*. In that case Julian's opinion becomes contradictory. It is argued that the text should be read in the context of the Stoic theories on causality as current among the jurists in the first centuries AD. In these theories there existed no *causa superveniens* as of the modern causality theory. As such its application is ill at place here. Instead, in applying these Stoic theories Julian's view can be explained as his attributing a *causa antecedens* to the first assailant, with full imputation of the effect of the subsequent *causa principalis* to him, and attributing a *causa adiuvans* to the second assailant, while valuing at the same time the latter not just as a reinforcing cause but also as a *causa mortis* and a full effective cause. For other jurists the latter evidently went too far.

c) *Enter Nörr*

Dieter Nörr (1931–2017) came to our topic trying to elucidate the use (and possibly the development of the use) of the term *causam mortis praebere*. His complicated exegeses of our texts are meant to support the main premises of his book, and conversely also rely on the panoramic

---

218 B Sirks, 'The slave who was slain twice: causality and the lex Aquilia (Iulian 86 dig D.9.2.51)', (2011) 79 *TR* 313; a shortened version of this paper was published in the Edinburgh Law Review: B Sirks, 'The Parallel Universes of Baker, Joblin and Julian: Causation and Law', (2013) 17 *Edinburgh Law Review* 22.

picture which he unfolds. Nörr played down his very dense contribution by declaring it to be a mere 'sketch'.[219] In fairly mild terms he criticises the introduction of modern causation concepts. Nörr himself, however, brings in a distinction from German tort law, namely that between the causation necessary to trigger liability (the tortfeasor's action must be the cause of the tort) and the causation necessary to link a specific damage to the infringement (the violation must be the cause of the specific damage), arguing that the concepts of 'aborted' or 'interrupted' causation are to be localised as issues of the second causation element which comes into play on the measure of damages level. A similar approach had been taken by Windscheid in his *Pandektenrecht*. However, by the time Nörr wrote his contribution, Dieter Medicus had already rejected Windscheid's notion on the basis of a careful study of Roman measure of damage discussions.[220]

Nörr then starts with the obvious disagreement between Celsus and Julian regarding the reckoning of the one-year period for Chapter I. He shows that these two positions do not logically call for the taking up of specific positions regarding cases of third-party intervention. This, he thinks, can be learned from *l*.11.3: relying on *probabilius*, Nörr takes this fragment to betray a controversy. He further finds that Ulpian's decision regarding the third-party intervention in *l*.11.3 is not in conflict with his siding with Julian regarding the start date for the one-year period. Last but not least, he finds also Ulpian's decision concerning the standing after alienation or manumission (*l*.15.1) in line with Ulpian's other decisions. Nörr then closely reads *l*.51. He sees Julian as struggling with a matter of statutory interpretation (*occidere*), and less so with issues of causation. Nörr holds that the 'effect' has not materialised and hence reads Julian as opening up the *occidere* requirement so as to encompass attempt as well. Nörr does not find this objectionable. Nörr's erudite language is sometimes non-committal, not to say a little opaque, but this is how he has been understood by younger authors. The way Nörr reads Julian, the latter has squeezed the *mortis causam praebere* variant into the concept of *occidere*: *mortis causam praebere* and *occidere* would no longer be counter-posed terms (linked to different procedural venues); *occidere* would rather

---

219 D Nörr, *Causa Moris: Auf den Spuren einer Redewendung* (1986) 160–201; Nörr had sketched central ideas already in his contribution 'Kausalitätsprobleme im klassischen römischen Recht', *Feschrift für Franz Wieacker zum 70. Geburtstag* (1978) 115, which had promptly triggered a sceptical response from MacCormack (cf below, n 288). Nörr later provided an English abstract of the views set out in his book: 'Mortis causam praebere', *The Legal Mind: Essays for Tony Honoré* (1986) 203.

220 Below p 73.

become the generic term, encompassing the *mortis causam praebere* variant as well as the more traditional *occidere* act. Dealing with both the everyday use of *occidere* and the lawyers' use (*l.*51pr) should not be taken as juxtaposition, but as a suggestion to open up the legal concept so as to come (back?) in line with plain and ordinary language. Since such a remodelling of the *occidere* concept, so as to cover attempted murder, does not show up in any of the other jurists' texts, Julian's advance must have remained an unsuccessful attempt to revolutionise the reading of Chapter I.

Nörr senses that the idea of Julian radically departing from established doctrine does not sit well with Julian's own claim that his solution is a consequence of the views of the *veteres*. Nörr sets this potential criticism aside, maintaining that the consequentiality here invoked should not be taken too literally. Nörr further finds that the matter of 'hypothetical causation' is at best mentioned in passing by Julian. Nörr has carefully reviewed Ankum's textual criticism and follows in particular the punctuation suggested for *l.*15.1.[221] He does not agree with Ankum's view of *vel naufragio – ictu* as a post-Ulpian addition, preferring to read *ictus* as stroke of fate.[222] He is also opposed to Ankum's insertion of *et*.[223] As to Julian's unnamed adversary, Nörr sides with those who identify *quis* as Celsus.

While Nörr sets out all this at an unsurpassed level of erudite learning, the centre of what is an almost panoramic picture was not his own original idea (as he himself would have been the first to concede): the recognition would rather have to go to a whole line of earlier authors, including Brinz, Jolowicz, Lawson, Schindler, Rastätter, Röhle and Hausmaninger,[224] to name just a few.

As befits an important monograph, Nörr's book has been reviewed and commented upon many times. This report selects reviews which contain substantial contributions to the understanding of our texts. Neil H Andrews (* 1959) specifically looked for supporting evidence (or lack thereof) for the hypothesis that Nörr had advanced regarding the classical uses and interpretation(s) of the term *occidere*.[225] He gives special attention to Julian's

221 Nörr (1986) (n 219) 182 n 95.
222 A number of literary texts are lined up for support.
223 Above in the text following n 204.
224 On Hausmaninger, see p 91 f.
225 N H Andrews, '"Occidere" and the Lex Aquilia', (1987) 46 *Cambridge Law Journal* 315. The piece is not technically a review.

claim (*l.*51) that precise legal terminology and plain and ordinary language do not coincide here. On the basis of a sober analysis of all relevant texts, refraining from high-flying speculations, Andrews concludes:

> [E]ven in the classical era, it is purely linguistic meaning which is crucial and decisive. Ulpian and Julian both take pains to clarify the essence of the core meaning which *occidere* bears in chapter one. They are expositors of a tradition of interpretation and not originators of this core meaning. [...] [T]his interpretation is not the product of careful reference to issues of causation and responsibility but merely the application of a core meaning which the verb *occidere* possessed at the time of the *lex*'s enactment. Subsequent jurists remained faithful to this pattern of restriction.[226]

It is to be regretted that Andrews did not return with these findings to elucidate the problem of *l.*51 and *l.*11.3 more closely.

Wiesław Litewski (1933–2004) cautioned that the phrase *causam mortis praebere* in *l.*51pr is not of operative importance, since it only serves as a comparison with plain and ordinary language.[227] However, one may deduce that Julian acknowledged *causam mortis praebere* as the generic term, covering both direct and indirect killing. This may or may not imply a criticism of Celsus. In a similar vein, Willvonseder in his review clarified the use of *causam mortis praebere* by Julian.[228] Julian did not juxtapose *occidere* and *causam mortis praebere* as respective requirements of direct action and *actio in factum*, but contrasted legal terminology and everyday language. *Causam mortis praebere* here is to be taken as the 'mere' causing of a death which does not necessarily meet the more restrictive requirements of *occidere*, taken as a technical term. Nothing in this passage, Willvonseder thinks, implies a criticism of Celsus or another jurist in their use of the term *causam mortis praebere*.

Bruce W Frier (* 1943) focussed his attention on the main topic of Nörr's book.[229] He approached the subject from yet another angle, taking note of recent linguistic works. This led him to a criticism not unlike that of Andrews: turning away from causation theories more decisively

226 *Ibid*, 327–8.
227 W Litewski, 'Review of Nörr's Causa Mortis', (1987) 53 *SDHI* 438.
228 R Willvonseder, 'Causam mortis praestare', (1988) 105 *ZRG RomAbt* 737, at 742.
229 B Frier, 'Review of Dieter Nörr "Causa Mortis"', (1988) 109 *American Journal of Philology* 618.

than Nörr, Frier sees the establishment of *causam mortis praestare* as distinct from *occidere* as

> primarily linguistic: for what sorts of circumstances do we use the word 'kill' in ordinary speech? Verbs such as 'kill' often have embedded within them a notion of 'prototypical' causation [reference given]. This linguistic notion corresponds to no developed legal concept of causation [reference given], but rests instead upon the psychological perception of intentional physical manipulation.[230]

Only in passing does Frier touch on our texts. In *l.*51 he sees a 'fierce polemic against Celsus' by Julian, who, Frier finds, rejects the distinction between *occidere* and *mortis causam praestare* 'decisively'.[231]

A paper put out by Peter Birks (1941–2004) in 1994 compared the juxtaposition of *occidere* and *causam mortis praestare* with other similarly structured parallelisms. While his piece is not a review, Birks came back to the very issue so intensely dealt with by Nörr.[232] He found Julian abstaining from an outright assertion that 'occidere means, or once meant, killing-by-striking'. Since the word, as set out by Julian, has no natural restriction to particular kinds of killing, an etymological argument needs to be mustered to come to the restrictive Aquilian understanding of the word. That etymology, Birks surmises, was drawn from Valerius Flaccus via Festus. But 'etymology is a guide to nuance, not to usage':

> There is no indication that the etymology reflected an originally narrow usage, and the quidam who favoured the narrow view of occidere need only be the lawyers driven to it by the fact of its having been employed in the active voice in the lex Aquilia.

Regardless of these somewhat muted reactions, by now, more than three decades on, Nörr's explanation, or at least the simple core of it, has been accepted by quite a number of scholars. It may have become the new orthodoxy.

d) *Modern Causation Theorists Chip In*

As most 20th-century Romanists have employed concepts of contemporary causation doctrine, it is no wonder that in turn our cases have been used

---

230 *Ibid*, 619 f.

231 *Ibid*, 619.

232 P Birks, 'Doing and causing to be done', *The Roman Law Tradition* (1994) 32, at 43–4.

as illustrations for modern-day issues of causation theories, mostly from a tort law perspective.

Carl Haß (1871–1930) made an almost Herculean attempt to rebuild a rational causation system from scratch. In doing so he also looked into our cases.[233] The intervening occurrence of an autonomous fact, including the act of a third party, ends the causal nexus, which thus stretches only from the *percussio* to the wound, but not from the wound to the death. It is necessary for this analysis, however, that the first wound has not in any way increased the risk of the intervening event. Relying on the influential study by von Kries,[234] Haß objects to the use of the term 'interrupted causation'. It would be more appropriate, in his view, to speak of a lack of causation. *L.*51, on the other hand, is justified by the uncertainty over whether the first or the second wound was the cause of the death; the liability of both perpetrators is the law's answer to the evidentiary uncertainty.

Herbert Hart (1907–1992) and Tony Honoré (1921–2019), in their seminal work on *Causation in the Law*,[235] report our cases as dealing with 'additional neutralizing cause', a sub-category of 'Additional Causes'. 'Additional Causes' are found, according to the authors, in cases 'in which there are present on a given occasion two or more factors each sufficient with other normal conditions to bring about certain harm.'[236] Very much like the authors of the *Ius Commune*, they felt the need to refine the definition of 'mortal', which to them can mean either an action/wound (1) 'sufficient to cause the death of a person of average constitution under normal circumstances', or an action/wound for which (2) 'given the circumstances, including the constitution of the victim and likelihood of medical assistance, it is highly probable that it will cause death', or an action/wound that (3) 'in fact [...] causes the victim's death even though it was not mortal in either of the two preceding senses, e.g. a mere scratch

233 C Haß, 'Ueber die Verwerthbarkeit des Gegensatzes von adäquatem und inadäquatem Kausalzusammenhang in der Lehre vom Interesse', (1897) 37 *Jherings Jahrbücher für die Dogmatik des bürgerlichen Rechts* 327, at 402–3. On Carl Haß, later a judge in Munich, see the critical comments by M Hirschberg, *Jude und Demokrat: Erinnerungen eines Münchener Rechtsanwalts 1883 bis 1939* (1998) 121 n 34.

234 *Ibid*, 210.

235 H L A Hart/T Honoré, *Causation in the Law* 2nd edn (1985) 243; for the making of this book cf N Lacey, *A life of H.L.A. Hart. The Nightmare and the Noble Dream* (2004) 209 f. Honoré dealt with the same set of cases also in 'Causation and Remoteness of Damages', *IECL* vol XI (1971) ch 7-130 to 7-138.

236 *Ibid*, 235.

which the victim neglected'.[237] The authors take *l*.15.1 to involve an evidentiary aspect, since the 'additional neutralizing cause' (*ruina* etc.) makes it impossible to establish that the first wound was mortal indeed,[238] but this, they find, runs into difficulties with the statement that the first wound was called 'mortal'. The authors are forced to assume that here the first sense of 'mortal' must have been intended.[239] Interestingly, Hart and Honoré take the matter down the same path which has been travelled by a number of *Ius Commune* writers, shifting the problem into matters of probabilities which need to be gauged by medical experts. Julian's case is reported as well, with the cautious remark that 'Julian appears to take a different view from that attributed to Celsus and Ulpian'.[240]

The fact that one is dealing with a victim who suffers a lethal wound had already attracted, among quite a number of *Ius Commune* authors, an interest in a medically more precise definition of 'lethality'. Danuta Mendelson has dealt with our cases in her contribution 'Aspects of Causation in Hippocratic Medicine and Roman Law of Delict' to the book on *Causation in Law and Medicine*, the latest edition of which appeared in 2016.[241] In the tracks of Hart and Honoré, she deals with our cases as examples of 'Multiple Sufficient Causes: Mortal and Fatal Wounds'.[242] She identifies a common feature in the fact that the first would was sufficient to cause death, 'but medicine could not determine which wound was significant and which was an insubstantial cause of death.' The apportioning of causative factors could not come from the field of medicine; the lawyers had to step in. Ulpian is praised for dissecting the facts and 'draw therefrom strict logical conclusions', namely the attribution of the cause of death to the supervening event, leaving a liability for wounding for the first assailant. Having set out Ulpian's case(s), her view of *l*.51 is an interesting mirror of the Romanist mainstream:

> Julian resolved the issue in policy terms. On the basis of essentially identical facts, he attributed legal liability for the killing to both assailants, though he stated that each of the culprits would have to pay the owner a differentiated

[237] *Ibid*, 241 ff. The reader cannot but remark that this typology mixes different levels of criteria, in that (1) and (2) differ as to whether the prognosis is abstract or concrete, while (3) brings in the difference of an *ex ante* and an *ex post* assessment.
[238] *Ibid*, 243.
[239] *Ibid*, 243 n 81.
[240] *Ibid*, 245.
[241] I Freckelton/D Mendelson eds, *Causation in Law and Medicine* (2016) 58 f.
[242] *Ibid*, 75 f.

> amount in damages.[243] From a causal point of view, Julian seemed to have assumed that the inevitability of the slave's imminent death justified the imposition of liability even if the slave did not in fact die of the first wound. Since the first wrongdoer has not in fact killed the slave, the extension of liability was based on policy grounds. Thus, Julian's conclusion did not stem from an investigation of causative factors; rather, it was based on a broad notion of blameworthiness and the social consideration that 'Misdeeds should not escape unpunished, and it is not easy to decide if one is more blameworthy than the other'.

Mendelson sees Julian as 'not entirely satisfied' with his own analysis, but she finds some comfort in the observation that modern causation lawyers likewise use the appeal to a greater social good to excuse sloppy causation analyses.

The case of *l.*51 has also resurfaced in the *Digest of European Tort Law.*[244] Nils Jansen (* 1967), as rapporteur, used the text to illustrate the type of cases where is damage caused by several successive but independent events outside the victim's sphere.[245] The author reports an ongoing controversy, from Roman antiquity to the present day. Jansen sees a possibility that Julian would have decided the case of an intervening natural cause of death in the same way as Celsus. Also, both jurists have the same starting point, namely the interpretation of *occidere*. It is only when their deliberations go over to the field of causation that the two diverge: from Celsus's standpoint, the intervening event nullifies the hypothetical causal connection; Julian, however, viewed the causation of both contributions as doubtful under the *condicio sine qua non*-formula, since even without the second tortfeasor's intervention the slave would have died.[246] This makes for a similarity with cases of evidentiary uncertainty. Jansen notes that the Roman jurists do not discuss the cases 'in a genuinely causal terminology'. He cautions against looking here for a ready-made solution to the problem of 'successive events breaking a chain of causation', especially since one may see good reasons to treat the cases differently. The penal function of the *lex Aquilia* may also have been in play, Jansen maintains.

---

243 Mendelson found that a similar differentiation was arrived at in *Baker v Willoughby* [1970] AC 467.

244 N Jansen, *Digest of European Tort Law* vol 1: *Essential Cases on Natural Causation* (2007). The same author briefly touched upon *l.*51.2 in his work N Jansen, *Die Struktur des Haftungsrechts* (2003) 241 n 443.

245 'Damage [is] caused by several successive, but independent events outside the victim's sphere ...', *Digest of European Tort Law* vol 1 (2007) 353 f.

246 The reader is not told why the causality of the first wounding is doubtful under the *condicio sine qua non* formula.

While Jansen contributed his analysis to a comparative law report, other authors have looked back at the Roman law to elucidate contemporary tort law doctrine in a domestic arena. It is impossible to give an overview, let alone a complete report, of such works. As a general observation, such uses of the Roman law tend to rely on modern Roman law research, selecting what seems the most recent, most accessible or most reliable publication. There is hardly ever an ambition to contribute to the ongoing dispute among Roman law researchers. From a much wider pool of contributions, just two pieces shall be reported here. Alan Rodger (Lord Rodger of Earlsferry) (1944–2011) cited *l*.51 and *l*.11.2 in *Fairchild v Glenhaven Funeral Services Ltd*, since in his view the texts were about situations 'where it was impossible to ascertain the identity of the actual killer among a number of wrongdoers.' While the text may have been altered by the 6th-century compilers, it was noteworthy, he found, 'that all these centuries ago considerations of policy plainly led to a departure from what the law would usually require by way of proof of causation'.[247] Martin Gebauer (* 1963), in a book about the proper place of hypothetical causation in liability systems, expertly summarises our texts and prominent interpreters. He shows that modern civilian doctrine (Carl Haß could be named here) has – like Julian – seen similarities between the liability of all concurrent tortfeasors in a situation of evidentiary uncertainty on the one hand, and asserting liability on the basis of hypothetical causation only on the other.[248] The idea *cum sit poena* seems to be an apt common denominator. Gebauer points to the double effect of a first attack. It inflicts a lethal wound which will bring about the actual death in the future, but also instantaneously and in reality brings about a substantial degradation of the attacked object;[249] this was an aspect already highlighted by Buckland/McNair and Lawson. Gebauer stresses that while the concept of hypothetical or reserve causation is usually employed to restrict liability, it here legitimises an extension of liability.

Makoto Ishikawa (* 1957) has asked whether our Roman jurists' texts can contribute to the understanding of Japanese law regarding concurrent tortfeasors.[250] He reports the relevant sources with the conflicting views of the Ordinary Gloss and Cujas, as well as those of a number of 20th-century authors, including Martin Gebauer. In his view, the Roman law should be summed up as follows: if the first attacker has wounded the victim in a

247 [2002] UKHL 22; [2003] 1 AC 32, at [160].
248 *Ibid*, 22.
249 *Ibid*, 394.
250 M Ishikawa, 'MINPO §719 und das römische Recht. Eine Anwendungsmöglichkeit auf den Nebentäterfall', *Aus der Werkstatt römischer Juristen* (2016) 173.

non-lethal way, he remains liable for wounding only. If the first wound was lethal, there was a disagreement between Julian and Celsus, the latter being followed by Ulpian and Marcellus. With Ankum, he relies on D.9.2.30.4 to argue that Paulus followed Julian. The fact that Julian needs so many words to support his solution is taken to indicate that this was the minority position.

e) *The Measure of Damages Aspect*

Among the many writers, only a few have tackled the matter from the measure of damages angle. Windscheid and Lawson have already been mentioned.[251] There is a general tendency for those who take the delict of killing as being already accomplished with a lethal wound to see the problems of our texts as issues of a 'second' causation requirement, which ensures that compensation can only be sought for damages caused by the accomplished delictual injury. Nörr's study is a case in point.

Coming from the topic of *id quod interest*, Dieter Medicus (1929–2015) looked at our texts in passing only.[252] He wonders whether the Roman jurists had developed a remoteness test which would have allowed limiting liabilities on the grounds that a chain of causation is so out of the ordinary that the resulting damages should not be compensated. The requirement of 'Adequate Causation' is the catchphrase, causation here referring to the damages evolving along a second causal nexus which starts with the liability-triggering event. Medicus found that our texts suggest that such a causal nexus had not yet been sufficiently isolated from other liability requirements, which would be necessary for a direct comparison with concepts of modern causation theories. He also found that the texts turn on the liability-triggering causation, and not the causation element involved in the measure of damages phase.

An obvious issue pertaining specifically to *l.*51 is the inclusion of the inheritance in the measure of compensation based on the second attacker's liability for killing. The matter is dealt with in a number of other texts, too: Ulp 18 ad ed D.9.2.23pr, Gai Inst 3.212, I.4.3.10, and Paul lex Iul et Pap 2 D.35.2.63pr, quoting Sextus Pedius. Marc 21 dig D.9.2.36.1 can also be taken into account. Several authors have looked into this aspect, among them

---

251 T J Gerke, 'Geschichtliche Entwicklungen der Ansprüche aus der "lex Aquilia"', (1957) 23 *SDHI* 68, is concerned with the measure of damages angle, but mentions our texts only briefly.

252 D Medicus, *Id quod interest* (1962) 325 ff.

Schindler,[253] Below,[254] MacCormack,[255] Ankum,[256] Rodger,[257] Schebitz[258] and Sampson.[259] An issue controversially discussed by these authors is whether one has to assume that in this sort of case the designation of a slave as heir as such is taken to immediately increase his market value, and that this increase is taken into account for the Chapter I liability only if it happened in the critical year before the slaying. That increase in market value may then reflect the likelihood of actually becoming an heir and the expected size of the inheritance. The alternative view (Ankum) holds that the testator must have died and the inheritance fallen due, open to being accepted, before the slave is killed; the owner is then assumed to get a dual compensation, the value of the slave and, on a separate account, the full value of the inheritance which he is now hindered from acquiring. Both scenarios were distinguished and dealt with by the classical jurists.

It is tempting to classify the loss of the inheritance in *l*.51 as a *lucrum cessans*. When Karl-Heinz Below (1906–1984) worked on the possible inclusion of *lucrum cessans* in the measure of damages, he also addressed *l*.51. He could not resist venturing into a full-fledged discussion of Julian's text.[260] Below offers the most extensive review of all previous literature of the interpolationist age. He himself is not averse to making a reasoned selection of what is Julianic and what not. He finds the *principium* heavily corrupted and §2 'almost totally not authentic'.[261] Approving of a fair amount of the textual criticism of the preceding half-century, he sides with those who assume that Justinian's compilers used a text of the *Digesta* already severely corrupted. Ultimately, however, he does not share the assumption of Beseler and Rechnitz that originally Julian too advocated a mixed Chapter III/Chapter I solution for the case set out in the *principium*. He understands Julian as boldly loosening the causation requirement. In order to get there, Julian proceeds in a cautious, almost indecisive and not altogether precise manner. In the eyes of the compilers this was welcome,

253 Schindler (n 185) 229–32.
254 Below (n 260) 24.
255 (1975) 45 *SDHI* 1, at 70–1.
256 Ankum (n 201) 336–7.
257 A Rodger, 'Damages for the loss of an inheritance', *Daube Noster: Essays in Legal History for David Daube* (1974) 289.
258 Below (n 260) 290 f (assumes a controversy among classical jurists).
259 J Sampson, 'Revisiting D.9.2.23.1', *Wrongful Damage to Property in Roman Law. British Perspectives* (2018) 163.
260 K-H Below, *Die Haftung für lucrum cessans im römischen Recht* (1964) 9–17.
261 *Ibid*, 16.

because it allowed the text to be included in the Digest, even though *l.*11.3 brought in a divergent solution. The *statuendum est* may point, again, to a Byzantine scholar using Julian's voice. For the topic of his interest, Below finds a confirmation that the measure of damages which Chapter I allows to recovered includes the lost inheritance. To get there, he must rely on §2, which in turn is defended against textual criticism. Partly, however, §2 has to go overboard, too: the *utilitas communis* argument reflects post-classical, Byzantine ideology, which injects criminal law ideas into the private law arena: the case is about compensation, not about punishment, Below maintains. Like so many interpreters, Below rubbishes *neutrum lege Aquilia teneri aut alterum potius*, since a liability, already engaged, cannot be expunged by someone else's later wrong. The reference to the *subtilis ratio* cannot come from a jurist like Julian; it must be post-classical. Below does not think the reference *quis* points to Celsus.

The measure of damages aspect, for the full range of all three *lex Aquilia* chapters, was the topic of Bernhard Schebitz's (* 1959) doctoral dissertation.[262] Schebitz scrutinises *l.*51, starting with a review of various interpolationist attacks.[263] Regarding the matter of 'overtaking causation', he approvingly reports Ankum's opposition to the radical doubts, which had culminated in assuming that Julian in *l.*51.2 had a mixed Chapter III/ Chapter I liability in mind. Schebitz, not unlike Powell, dissects *l.*51 into disjunct pieces which in his view address different cases. The *principium* concerns the problem of 'overtaking causation', where the second attacker inflicts death on a dying victim. In this scenario, the two attackers' actions are distinguished: the first one is a wounding, the second a straight killing action; no issues relating to measure of damages are involved. §2 cannot be about the same problem: the second attacker, in §2, has to be liable for the loss of the inheritance, regardless of whether the first attacker is liable under Chapter I or under Chapter III. Moreover, the first attacker, if liable under Chapter III, may perhaps be liable for the inheritance too, only if the last will was made within the first 30 days after the wounding: the slave's owner would thus be compensated for the lost inheritance twice. The awkwardly complicated reasoning of §2 fuels the suspicion, Schebitz senses, that §2 originally must have dealt with a veritable problem in its own right, which needs to be uncovered. Shifting around the sequence of events, this is his proposal: §2 deals with the case of sequentially inflicted

262 *Berechnung des Ersatzes nach der lex Aquilia* (1987).
263 *Ibid*, 301–17.

mortal wounds, but the appointment as heir followed the second attack, during a drawn-out interval of dying from both wounds; the ultimate death cannot be attributed to one of the wounds. Both attackers have contributed in equal measure; they are on the same level, just like the many thieves of a beam, in the case referred to at the end of §2. It is the jurist's problem, Schebitz thinks, that in this sequence of events the inclusion of the lost inheritance becomes problematic with regard to both attackers, due to the backwards-reckoning approach for the measure of damages. This is Julian's way out, in Schebitz's view: Julian re-interprets the one-year rule, using *in anno proximo* to alternatively allow a forward reckoning in analogy to the Chapter III provision. For this operation Julian picks the second attacker only, because he is closer to both the appointment as heir and the subsequent death. A double compensation would not be appropriate. Schebitz submits that Julian may also have had healing costs in mind, which accrued over the time the slave took to die. In Julian's time, Schebitz argues, the statutory time provisions for the measure of damages had already been subject to quite liberal handling by the jurists. The following arguments, in Schebitz's view, do not contradict his theory, but they may not be authentic Julian either. The sheer quantity of arguments advanced support the idea, he holds, that Julian must have proposed a ground-breaking innovation, deviating starkly from orthodox doctrine. Allowing the forward reckoning would prove to be decisive in another respect: it was no longer necessary to look for the actual case of inheritance; the appointment as an heir was sufficient. If there were a prize for eccentric ingenuity in speculatively re-reading Julian, Schebitz would be a strong contender.

f) Julian's and Celsus's Legal Methodologies

Since the late 19th century, research has branched out which focusses on individual Roman jurists, their oeuvre and/or their biographies. More specific inquiries are devoted to the question whether specific legal methodologies can be attributed to specific individuals. Julian and Celsus, and the legal methodologies they seem to display, have become research topics in their own right. Since Cujas, the hypothesis has been in play that a specific animosity overshadowed the relation between Celsus and Julian. The idea that our texts reflect conflicting legal opinions was indeed first introduced, by Cujas, interwoven with the assertion of a general feud between the two jurists. This view relies on – and in turn supports – the identification of *quis* (*l.*51.2) as Celsus. The hypothesis of a personal enmity is an extrapolation from a number of disagreements between Celsus and

Julian which are indeed registered in the Digest.[264] The range of relevant texts and their interpretations is not covered by this volume, and the hypothesis as such will not be tested here. Pertinent scholarship will be reported insofar as it has given extra scrutiny to at least one of our texts. There is a slight imbalance in the respective harvests: for Julian, *l*.51 is a kind of signature piece, so Julian studies are a little more likely to include in-depth analyses of this text. The study of *l*.51 has become so popular in this regard that a warning was issued not to see this text as a lockpick to the innermost personality of Julian.[265] Mainly biographical works need not be reported here.

The first highly detailed study devoted to Julian, Heinrich Buhl's (1848–1907) *Salvius Julianus*,[266] only got to volume 1, covering the introduction and the law of persons.[267] Regarding *l*.51.2, Buhl remarked in passing that Julian's careful arguments may have been directed against Celsus, as assumed by Cujas.[268] In a study published two decades later, Louis Boulard (1877–1914) covered the same range of topics as Buhl. There is nothing on our text, but one may note that Boulard claimed to have identified a tendency, observable in Julian's texts, to subtly extend the range of applicability of legal norms.[269] More importantly, Boulard credits Julian with a remarkably progressive attitude.[270] Julian was not a partisan follower of all thoughts Sabinian. A little later, scholars exchanged arguments on the matter of whether both jurists followed a policy of not citing the other by name. Iul 29 Dig D.28.2.13pr seems to disprove this argument, but then interpolationist doubts were voiced whether this text was genuine.[271]

Considerable headway was made in 1952, when Roberto Reggi (1923–1990) scanned the material collected by Buhl anew, now specifically

264 Ulp 29 ad ed D.14.6.7pr; Maec 8 fideic D.35.2.30.7; Ulp 5 ad ed D.2.4.8.2; Paul 17 ad Plaut D.45.1.91.3. Whether this makes both jurists disagree more often than other pairs of classical authors has not been established by means of statistical analysis.

265 A Mantello, 'Rec. di Scarano Ussani, L'utilità e la certezza', (1987) 38 *Iura* 240, at 242, speaking of a '*grimaldello per "rifare dall'interno" la personalità giulianea*'.

266 H Buhl, *Salvius Julianus – Erster Teil: Einleitung, Personenrecht* (1886).

267 An early precursor needs to be mentioned: J G Heineccius's (1681–1741), 'De Salvio Juliano, jurisconsultorum sue aetate coryphaeo', *Opera Omnia* vol 2 (1748) 798.

268 Buhl (1886) (n 266)48.

269 L Boulard, *L. Salvius Julianus – son oeuvre, ses doctrines sur la personnalité juridique* (1902) 183 ff.

270 *Ibid*, 145.

271 B Kübler, 'Hermann Fitting, Alter und Folge der Schriften römischer Juristen' (Review), (1911) 49 *Kritische Vierteljahresschrift für Gesetzgebung und Rechtswissenschaft*, 1, at 7–10; C Appleton, 'La date des Digesta de *Julien*', (1910) 34 *Nouvelle Revue Historique* 731, at 769 n 2.

trying to identify instances where Julian employed instruments of rhetoric.[272] It was a ground-breaking study, now almost forgotten. Reggi started with the field of family law; he does not seem to have made good on his intention to also look into property law, the law of obligations and into inheritance law, all as dealt with by Julian. From the field of obligations, he would surely have come back with valuable insights regarding *l*.51.

Peter Stein (1926–2016) praised Julian's flexible realism.[273] On the one hand, he sees a tendency to 'explore the logical implications of juristic rules', fuelled by the 'desire to make the law more rational'. On the other hand, Julian

> was also a realist who recognized that there were many irrational elements in the law, which had to be accepted for the sake of convenience. One cannot expect every decision to harmonise perfectly with every other decision.

In the civil law 'countless examples of illogicalities' had come to be accepted, Julian is understood as saying.

In a full-fledged monograph, Elmar Bund (1930–2008) tried to reconstruct Julian's legal methodology.[274] He identified specific types of argument. Unfortunately, our texts are not among those he selected for close reading. It may be worthwhile, however, to see how he found Julian's work characterised by earlier authors:[275] Julian delivers operable solutions, results which are never one-sided or over-sharp; his towering creative powers made for riches of new solutions, which have always been admired; his intensive writings were transparent and balanced. Furthermore, Julian took the initiative, at the same time remaining true to classical principles. To this conventional picture, Bund added his own observations: while Julian frequently mobilises similarities, this is never a simple matter of analogy, but rather about the 'development of more complex structures'. Julian was able to interpret the law liberally with the public policy objective in view, without overstepping the boundaries that need to be respected in order to uphold the certainty of the law. His thinking is decidedly 'ontological', less abstract than that of his contemporaries.

Erwin Seidl (1905–1987) reviewed the earlier scholarly approaches to the jurist Julian, and tried to reconstruct Julian's legal methodology.[276]

---

272 R Reggi, 'L'interpretatione analogica in Salvio Giuliano', (1952) 2 *Studi Parmensi* 105.

273 P Stein, *Regulae Iuris* (1966) 95.

274 E Bund, *Untersuchungen zur Methode Julians* (1965). A by-product of this study is E Bund, 'Salvius Iulianus; Leben und Werk', *ANRW* vol 2/15 – Principat (1976) 408.

275 *Ibid*, 181–2.

276 E Seidl, 'Wege zu Julian', *Sein und Werden im Recht* (1970) 215.

Since Bund had not made use of *l*.51, Seidl was the first to try to extract information on Julian's methodology from this text. With regard to *l*.51.2, he asks tentatively whether one should read the text as juxtaposing *ius civile* and *ius honorarium*: in the field of *ius honorarium* we may apply logic, but in the field of *ius civile* the common good must be the controlling idea.[277] Seidl relies on a parallel study where he surmises that Labeo used deductive reasoning, but not in cases controlled by *ius civile*.[278] Seidl lets the question hang in the air.

In his influential PhD thesis, Jürgen Rastätter (* 1953) looked systematically into the surviving notes that Marcellus wrote on Julian's Digest.[279] His central argument, emerging out of a multifaceted inquiry, is the idea that Marcellus, probably in his re-edition of Julian's Digest which he organised, commented upon Julian's text, mostly explaining and illustrating, but occasionally also curtailing Julian's innovations. Rastätter in general defends the authenticity of these notes. He identifies *quod et Marcello videtur* in *l*.11.3 as an indirectly transmitted *nota*; this triggered his interest in the suggested feud between Celsus and Julian.[280] Following an idea of Ferrini and Lenel,[281] he assumes that Ulpian had Julian's Digest, and specifically the part later used by Justinian's compilers for *l*.51, in front of him when he wrote the text of *l*.11.3, and that his copy contained Marcellus's glosses. Rastätter notes a parallelism between *l*.51.1 and *l*.11.2 as well as between *l*.11.3 and *l*.51pr. Turning to the substantive issue, he rejects attempts, all duly noted, to distinguish the cases dealt with, and opts for a juristic controversy. He notes, but disapproves of a strong tendency in recent publications to identify the core dispute in the juxtaposition of a 'stronger accentuation of the damaging act' on Julian's side, whereas Celsus, Marcellus and Ulpian had emphasised the resulting effect. For this view he names Lawson, Schindler, Röhle and Hausmaninger. Scrutinising Julian's reasoning step by step, he dismisses Julian's attempt to argue with the case of multiple offenders, who he assumes have to be taken as acting concertedly. The passage is Julian's indeed, Rastätter affirms; it is just not convincing. *L*.51.2 gets a slightly better review. It is yet another attempt to justify the decision set out in the *principium*. It is incorrect, Rastätter finds, that Julian attributes the idea of letting both offenders off the hook altogether to Celsus, since Celsus

277 *Ibid*, 219.
278 E Seidl, 'Labeos geistiges Profil', *Studi Volterra* vol 1 (1970) 63.
279 J Rastätter, *Marcelli Notae ad Iuliani Digesta* (1981, a dissertation-copy publication).
280 *Ibid*, 116–23.
281 O Lenel, *Palingenesia Iuris Civilis* (1889) vol 1 col 633 n 6, vol 2 col 480 f.

does not relieve the first offender of his Chapter III liability. Rastätter then sides with Dalla, acknowledging that there may have been good reason to upgrade the offenders' liabilities. But Rastätter also believes that Julian has agreed with the cases of *ruina* and *naufragium*, which must be seen as an inconsistency, because here a similar need for an evaluation based on the longer one-year period might be found.[282] Unexpectedly, Julian here sides with Celsus and Ulpian. In view of evidentiary problems which would arise when suing the first offender for killing, Rastätter finds that this is the right thing to do: in cases of overtaking causation, the definitive effect should be decisive, and the preceding mortally wounding be captured by a Chapter III liability only. Rastätter, like many of his predecessors, thinks that Julian, for reasons of equity 'left the firm basis of traditional jurisprudence for a singular opportunistic decision'.[283] The compilers must have found the *nota* of Marcellus, in which he rejects Julian's proposition, integrated in the edition of the *Digesta* that they used, but they cut it out, Rastätter believes, in order to eliminate obvious controversies.[284]

Rastätter's thesis has been reviewed by Ralph Backhaus (* 1950).[285] Backhaus unhesitatingly identifies the problem as one of overtaking causation, as all the reasoning, he finds, turns on causation aspects. In *l.*11.3, the first wound has not been the cause of death. For Julian, however (*l.*51), who is concerned with the interpretation of *occidere*, the liability requirements are already satisfied with the accomplishment of the deadly action. §2 adds a *reductio ad absurdum*, which is not just a recourse to equitable considerations and it is also not 'un-doctrinal'; in this respect Backhaus is at odds with Rastätter. Another review came from Christoph Krampe (* 1943).[286] Krampe labels Julian's decision as a 'minority position', but this alone, in his view, did not justify Rastätter's harsh verdict of Julian as 'inconsistent'. Krampe further disagrees with Rasttätter's reading of *alio ictu* in *l.*15.1 as another *force majeure* event, reporting the interpretations advanced by Schindler and Ankum.

Geoffrey MacCormack, who had forcefully rejected all criticism of Julian based on him allegedly missing the niceties of a theoretical

---

282 Rastätter (n 279) 122 n 77, interprets *vel alio ictu* as referring to *force majeure* events.

283 *Ibid*, 123, speaking of Julian, who 'aus Billigkeitsgründen den festen Boden der traditionellen Jurisprudenz [...] verlässt und eine singuläre Opportunitätsentscheidung trifft'.

284 *Ibid*, 292 n 4.

285 R Backhaus (1984) 101 *ZRG RomAbt* 376.

286 C Krampe (1984) 52 *TR* 58.

causation framework,[287] in 1982 singled out instances where Roman jurists in handling the *lex Aquilia* argued by analogy.[288] He confirms the crucial distinction between statutory actions based on the *lex Aquilia* and the *mortis causam praestare* variant, for which liability is sought by bringing an *actio in factum*. He has interesting remarks regarding the Roman jurists' understanding of *causa* in this context, which in his view reflects 'a fact of general experience as to what is likely to happen', rather than any philosophical view of causation. With regard to Julian's essay, MacCormack ponders, but ultimately rejects, the notion that the musings on the word *occidere* (*l.*51pr) reveal a disagreement between Julian and Celsus as to the basic understanding of *occidere*: in substance, they would both 'have accepted that only certain types of act would have constituted an *occidere*'; there is, at best, 'a verbal difference'.[289] Julian's appeal to *dicitur vulgo* should be treated with caution. Could it be that the language of *mortis causam praestare* was borrowed from the 'uncommon' language of the philosophers, and if so, did this imply that the lawyers imported a whole philosophical theory of causation? Mentioning Nörr, MacCormack finds that this would be too rash a conclusion: 'A doubt must be registered'.[290] MacCormack also scrutinises two comparisons, the first between the case Julian decides and the case of several attackers, with uncertainty as to who was the ultimate slayer (*l.*51.1):[291]

> The difference between the two cases is that in one the wounds are not inflicted at the same time whereas in the other they are. This difference is displaced in Iulian's reasoning by the similarity between the cases, namely that in neither it is absolutely clear from whose blow death has resulted [...] and hence the decision of the veteres can be used as an authoritative precedent in the case under consideration by Iulian.

The other comparison is between the case Julian decides and the theft of a beam by several men, which Julian used to rebut the possible criticism of his decision as absurd (*l.*51.2). MacCormack finds that the decision regarding the stolen beam does provide good support 'for holding

287 MacCormack (n 197).

288 G MacCormack, 'Juristic Interpretation of the Lex Aquilia', *Studi Sanfilippo* vol 1 (1982) 253.

289 *Ibid*, 269; this disquisition is noted by C Aedo Barrena, 'La cuestión causal en la "lex Aquilia" y su solución mediante el mecanismo de la culpa', (2015) 37 *Revista de Estudios Histórico-Jurídicos* 37, at 63 n 62.

290 MacCormack (n 197) 270 with n 12.

291 *Ibid*, 260 f.

that both the person who inflicted the initial, mortal would and the person who subsequently inflicted the wound which killed are liable under chapter one of the lex Aquilia.'

Francesco Casavola (* 1931) used Julian's invocation of the *auctoritas veterum* for a comparison with Celsus.[292] Approving the identification of *quis* as Celsus, he sees Julian in the position of the traditionalist, his traditionalism betrayed by his eager confirmation that he relies on the *veteres* and by the proclaimed need for effective punishment. By comparison, Celsus was committed to a more benign handling of older statute material and advocated a more liberal approach.

In a way, the work by Pietro Cerami (* 1938) is the counterpart to Bund's, in that Cerami looked into Celsus's legal thinking.[293] *L.*11.3 comes into his view, which he links directly to *l.*21.1. Celsus is not solely concerned about (and bound to) literal interpretation, as von Lübtow had asserted, assuming that the availability of an *actio in factum* would allow jurists to retain (or return to) a line of strict interpretation of *occidere*. Cerami finds Celsus arguing in a problem-oriented manner, open to lateral thinking.

Jan van Hoek (* 1942) has dealt with 'glimpses of abstract "legal reality"' in the Digest, indicated by the use of *verum est*.[294] The short essay turns on 'legal reality as an intellectual creation'. *L.*51 is his lead example.[295] Although the exegesis remains a bit sketchy, it offers interesting insights. Van Hoek links the matter to the disagreement on the moment of Aquilian killing. Van Hoek rephrases *l.*11.3 in an interesting manner: according to Celsus's view, the same slave could not be killed more than once, and this was so because the moment of Aquilian killing would be the same for both killers. For Julian, who took the moment the mortal wound is inflicted as the moment of Aquilian killing, it was possible that a slave could be killed twice. Julian is not talking about the procedural differences between the statutory action and an *actio in factum*; hence the term *causam mortis praebere* in Julian's text does not have 'its ordinary importance'. The certainty that the slave would die from the first wound is a material fact, which is not a given simply by the resulting death, due to the speeding up by the second wound: 'So at least a surgeon could tell for sure that the wound was lethal'. This allows *l.*51 and *l.*15.1 to be distinguished: in the

---

292 F Casavola, 'Cultura e scienza giuridica nel secondo secolo d.C.: il senso del passato', *ANRW* vol 2/15 – Principat (1976) 31, at 154 f.

293 P Cerami, 'La concezione celsina del "ius"', (1985) 38 *AnnPal* 140, at 163 ff.

294 J van Hoek, 'Verum est: Glimpses of abstract "legal reality" in the Digest', *Viva Vox Iuris Romani* (2002) 115.

295 *Ibid*, 117.

latter case, only the Gods knew that the wound was lethal, and no surgeon's expertise could find out what was the case. This is where van Hoek arrives at the use of *verum est*: the term points to a reality which exists, whether or not it has been established by the human observer. As to *l*.15.1, van Hoek disagrees with Ankum's attempt to dissociate Julian from Ulpian's text. He speculates that Julian set out his view on the *ruina* case of *l*.15.1 first, and only later realised that a surgeon 'would be able to decide that a wound of a slave was lethal beyond any doubt'; the latter realisation became the basis of *l*.51, so Julian's overall approach 'has become more complete, not contradictory'. Van Hoek registers, without comment, the view that Julian was willing to base his decisions on practicality arguments.

Jan Dirk Harke (* 1969), in his 1999 PhD thesis, had closely looked into the methodology presumably employed by Celsus.[296] For the second edition, he rewrote the book so as to provide a juxtaposition between Celsian methodology on the one hand, and Julian's on the other.[297] *L*.51 is addressed.[298] In Harke's view, Julian here deals with an issue of 'overtaking causation'. Relying on Gerkens, Harke starts from the assumption that Celsus's view (*l*.11.3) and *l*.51 are irreconcilable. It is a problem for Julian to overcome the feature that the first attacker's action has not caused the death; to this effect he has recourse to the idea of an alternative causation which had been recognised by Republican jurists before. Following Nörr and Gerkens, Harke does see a comparability of the cases set out in the *principium* and in §1, since both passages deal with a causal nexus that has been interfered with. Although the reasoning, which Harke classifies as an *argumentum a maiore ad minus* (because of the certainty of the death resulting from the wound), is almost watertight, Julian hesitates to let a merely hypothetical death suffice for the *occidere* requirement. In this situation he brings in the public good, which requires an 'adequate punishment of a misdeed'. Ultimately, it is only the public good here invoked which allows *occidere* to be interpreted in an abnormal manner. Julian himself did deal differently with overtaking causation in *l*.15.1, but this is so because in *l*.51 the deadly effect is not certain. This seems to return to the Ordinary Gloss. Subsequently, Harke changed his view in this regard.[299] He now assumes that Ulpian misreported Julian as agreeing

---

296 J D Harke, *Argumenta Iuventiana* (1999).

297 J D Harke, *Argumenta Iuventiana – Argumenta Salviana, Entscheidungsbegründungen bei Celsus und Julian* (2012).

298 *Ibid*, 240–4.

299 J D Harke, *Die Rechtspositionen am Sklaven 2: Ansprüche aus Delikten am Sklaven = CRRS* III/2 (2013) 67.

with the solution set out in *l*.15.1: Ulpian was simply mistaken as to Julian's real position. It is an 'explanation' which had been advanced by von Lübtow.

A number of authors have pointed to Julian's remarkable interest in issues which today one would classify as 'formal logic'.[300] Markus Winkler (* 1971), a trained mathematician, systematically looked for traces of formal logic in Julian's *Digesta*.[301] *L*.51.1–2 is one of the texts he selected on the strength of *idque* as the first word, an unfortunate choice since this passage is part and parcel of Julian's discussion turning on the case set out in the *principium*. Winkler understands §1 as dealing with an evidentiary problem, whereas both the *principium* and §2 each have a different topic, namely two different violations, which happen at different and discernible times (pr), and the joint liability of (co-ordinated) co-perpetrators (§2). If I understand Winkler correctly, no proper syllogism can be found in §1, rather a cogent 'sign-enthymeme' (*tekmerion*), on the basis of a reference to the *veteres*. The *furtum* case in §2, however, can be rephrased in formal logic. Winkler understands the *ratio* in §2 as 'the strictly logical consequence of a syllogistic argument', namely the one leading to a zero-compensation solution, and this result appears unsuitable for a practical legal issue. Could this be another way of saying that we are dealing with an *argumentum ad absurdum*? Winkler also has some reflections on causation theories in Roman and Greek antiquity.[302]

g) *Punishing* maleficia*: Deterrence as a Public Policy Argument?*

As we have seen, the maxim *ne maleficia maneant impunita*, in all likelihood derived from *l*.51.2, became in the early 13th century a catchphrase for the idea of deterrence as the public policy behind criminal law.[303] A neighbouring bit of text that had been successfully broken out of Julian's essay was the acknowledgement that the common good trumps legal logic. Edward Coke (1551–1633) had adapted this sentence for a use in the context of the English common law: *Multa in iure communi contra rationem disputandi pro communi utilitate introducta sunt*.[304]

---

300 To single out just one important contribution, one could name J Miquel, 'Stoische Logik und römische Jurisprudenz', (1970) 87 *ZRG RomAbt* 85, addressing at 103 f Julian's *liber de ambiguitatibus*.

301 M Winkler, *Mathematik und Logik in Julians Digesten* (2015) 274–9.

302 *Ibid*, 141–4.

303 Above p 15 ff.

304 E Coke, *A Commentary upon Littleton* (1628) 70b.

Modern Roman law scholarship has scanned our sources in order to establish to what extent the ideas of deterrence and general prevention were already present in the Roman lawyers' intellectual world. Two aspects are intertwined. One is the more general matter of the degree to which Roman lawyers used and accepted public policy arguments: what was the role of the *utilitas communis* argument in the inventory of Roman legal reasoning? Pertinent research covers the term *utilitas publica* as well, although it has been a matter of debate how close both concepts really are. More narrowly, Julian's specific use of the term has led to the question whether the *utilitas communis* here invoked has to be understood as 'the fight against crime' (Leptien), the public interest in the prevention of crime (Honsell)? Are we looking at 'general prevention' *avant la lettre* (Giaro)? The intellectual history of deterrence and general prevention is a wide-ranging field of research. Here just those works are singled out which specifically scrutinised the relevant passage of Julian's text, which of course has always been an element relied upon to support the penal nature of the Aquilian liabilities.

Among Roman law researchers, who mostly came and come from the side of private law, there has always been a bias towards maintaining a purist, private-law-oriented approach, and therefore to mistrust instinctively recourses to the public good. A leading study, transcending the narrow private-law focus, came from Artur Steinwenter (1888–1959).[305] Steinwenter mobilised a rich intellectual history background, from the Platonic/Aristotelian tradition to Cicero. *Utilitas publica* in his view began to denote the special interest of the Roman state, and thus came to be juxtaposed with individual positions, which he found not to be the case for *utilitas communis*; this term rather points to the *utilitas omnium*. By contrast, the *utilitas* brought into play by Julian is not the common good, but nothing other than an appeal to *aequitas*, invoked to soften the *ius strictum*. One wonders whether Steinwenter's research interest in the *utilitas publica*, published in 1939, was a concession of sorts to the collectivist (fascist, national-socialist) politics of his time. Jean Gaudemet (1908–2001), in his seminal study devoted to *utilitas publica*, cited Steinwenter and cautiously remarked with regard to *l*.51 that the text, with its rhetorical character, could be suspect.[306] Building on these two studies, Giannetto Longo (1904–1987) tried to systematically reconstruct

---

305 A Steinwenter, 'Utilitas publica – utilitas singulorum', *Festschrift Paul Koschaker* (1939) 84.

306 J Gaudemet, 'Utilitas publica', (1951) 28 *Revue historique de droit français et étranger* 465, at 497 n 1.

the development of the *utilitas publica* concept, from Cicero's time to Justinian's *Novellae*.[307] He supports the idea that a state-oriented concept of *utilitas publica* had not fully emerged before Diocletian. As to *l*.51.2, he is unwilling to believe that *utilitas communis* in Julian's time could be invoked to rectify the *ius civile*, hence the text must be interpolated.[308]

A most fruitful contribution came from Ulrich Leptien (1939–1998).[309] Leptien's systematic review leads him to the question whether we are looking at decisions taken on purely utilitarian grounds. His ground-breaking result was that *utilitas* comes into play only where the issue, from the viewpoint of legal logic, could be decided either way. The *utilitas* then works as a tie-breaker. For this situation to occur, the preferred option as such must be supported, at least to some degree, by legal logic already. The *utilitas* argument does not allow the introduction of a purely utilitarian solution, which runs counter to any legal reason. Leptien identifies *l*.51.2 as such a case.[310] Perhaps contrary to the modern private lawyers' purist instinct, the use of *utilitas publica* did not bring odium on the speaker. There is no reason to purge classical texts by disputing the authenticity of mentions of *utilitas publica*. Thomas Honsell's (* 1947) paper marked a return to a more conventional view.[311] He takes the *utilitas communis* as a gateway to a decision that suspends a rule. In *l*.51.2 he sees the *utilitas communis* as outweighing the *ratio subtilis*, but not as a mere recourse to *aequitas* either. Max Kaser's contribution has already been mentioned.[312]

In his much-read study, Vincenzo Scarano Ussani (* 1951) looked into Julian's reasoning in the context of (mostly) 1st-century developments of Roman society and culture.[313] On Scarano Ussani's analysis, *l*.51 gives us a unique insight into Julian's ideological mindset. Julian was unsettled by the perplexing revival of criss-crossing irrational tendencies in his time. Against those, Julian put a decisive value on rationality, but even more

307 G Longo, 'Utilitas publica', *Atti del Seminario romanistico internazionale* (1972) 155.
308 *Ibid*, 170.
309 U Leptien, 'Utilitatis causa – Zweckmässigkeitsentscheidungen im Römischen Recht', (1969) 35 *SDHI* 51, based on U Leptien, *Utilitatis causa – Zweckmässigkeitsentscheidungen im Römischen Recht* (1967, dissertation-copy publication).
310 *Ibid*, 63.
311 T Honsell, 'Gemeinwohl und öffentliches Interesse im klassischen römischen Recht', (1978) 95 *ZRG RomAbt* 124.
312 Kaser (n 196).
313 V Scarano Ussani, *L'utilità e la certezza. Compiti e modelli del sapere giuridico in Salvio Giuliano* (1987). The book has been reviewed often, *inter alia* by P Cerami, (1989) 35 *Labeo* 120; A Mantello, 'Rec. di Scarano Ussani, L'utilità e la certezza', (1987) 38 *Iura* 240.

so on authority and tradition, the need for punishment, the idea of the common good as an important genetic factor of the *ius civile*, and a distrust of pure reason.[314] *Utilitas communis* appears inextricably linked to the determined suppression of any unrest that could unsettle the Roman order of society. Scarano Ussani highlights the extreme harshness displayed in the suppression of slave rebellion. The SC Silanianum is one example, the senatorial speech by C Cassius Longinus another.[315] It is in contexts like these that one finds the *impunitas* argument employed. In this view, *utilitas communis* looks more like a piece of official phraseology, and the *impunitas* argument seems inextricably linked to a rather crass idea of deterrence. A wide-ranging survey of the *impunitas* argument takes the reader through a great variety of Greek and Roman authors. Coming back to Julian's decision, the determination to react as severely as possible to the misdeeds in the scenario set out in the *principium* becomes the linchpin of Julian's legal analysis. Another characteristic which Scarano Ussani thought he identified in Julian's texts is the wish to expunge ambiguities, so secure legal certainty[316] – another semi-authoritarian character streak? Scarcano Ussani sides with those who identify *quis* as Celsus.[317] This view of Julian as a tough advocate of repressive social policies has convinced Detlef Liebs (* 1936), an outstanding exponent of prosopographical research into classical and post-classical jurists. In his general characterisation of Julian, he finds the jurist averse to a 'scientification' of law, respecting the irrational roots of the historical legal order: 'For example, even in a private law context, he retains the idea of deterrence by punishment; against enlightened recourse to deductive logic, he defends his position with the words: *multa autem iure civili contra rationem disputandi pro utilitate communi recepta esse innumerabilibus rebus probari potest*.'[318] In the same vein, Liebs in his Roman law primer suggests that Julian's text has to be understood as expressing an 'archaic idea of atonement': any innovation in this regard would cut into deeply rooted social conventions, and this Julian was unwilling to propose, even if it meant one had to live with logical inconsistencies.[319]

---

314 Scarano Ussani (n 313) 11.

315 Tacitus Annales 14, 43 f.

316 Scarano Ussani (n 313) 161 f.

317 *Ibid*, 7 ff.

318 D Liebs, 'Jurisprudenz', *HLL* vol IV: *Die Literatur des Umbruchs, Von der römischen zur christlichen Literatur 117–284 n. Chr.* (1997) 105: 'So hält er sogar im Privatrecht am Abschreckungsgedanken durch Strafe fest; gegenüber aufklärerischer Berufung auf deduktive Logik verteidigt er seine Position mit den Worten: *Multa* [...]'.

319 D Liebs, *Römisches Recht. Ein Studienbuch* 6th edn (2004) 57–8.

Over several decades, Marialuisa Navarra (* 1959) has worked on Roman jurists' utilitarianism. In 2002, her research led to a monograph.[320] Here we find *l*.51.2 as the key text for Julian's use of the concept.[321] In §2 she detects a *deductio ad absurdum*, accompanied by a reliance on the *interpretatio prudentium* as well as the *utilitas communis* argument. While the identification of *quis* as Celsus is a moot point, it is not doubtful, she thinks, that we are witness to a school dispute. The ferocity of the argument points to a living controversy ('*una controversia viva*'), which makes Marcellus the slightly more likely adversary than the older Celsus. Navarra carefully weighs the arguments advanced to prove the *utilitas publica* argument as post-classical.[322] She thinks that the arguments found in §2 go together, and Julian takes his deliberations to a solution based on traditional views, yet innovative. Julian's methodology is characterised as topical. However, Navarra does not see Julian as classifying his own solution as an *ius singulare* which would stand antithetically in relation to the *ius strictum*.

While *utilitas communis* can surface in a good number of different contexts, the argument that misdeeds should not go unpunished is of a narrower, more specific nature. The use of this *topos* among classical Roman lawyers has been the guiding question for Michael Börsch (* 1974).[323] Börsch devoted a full chapter to an in-depth exegesis of *l*.51.2, drawing on an impressive range of earlier literature. He generally pushes back against interpolationist doubts, and he tends to praise rather than fault Julian's analysis. Since the presumed Celsus/Julian controversy is not pertinent to the arguments advanced in §2, Börsch does not fully confront this issue, but notes that a school dispute between Proculians and Sabinians will have been in play. Börsch, however, applauds Julian for 'his sure sense of the proper evaluation of events'.[324] Julian's argument in §1 does bring in a case of alternative causation, which, however, is not illogical, since alternative causation and intervening causation pose comparable problems. Turning to the *impunitas* argument, he points to the penal element of Aquilian liability. He rejects Rastätter's characterisation of Julian's solution as 'singular opportunistic decision'.[325] Rather, he finds

---

320 M Navarra, *Ricerche sulla utilitas nel pensiero dei giuristi romani* (2002).
321 *Ibid*, 21–9.
322 *Ibid*, 26–7.
323 M Börsch, *Damit Übeltaten nicht ungestraft bleiben: Impunitas als Argument der klassischen römischen Juristen* (2003).
324 *Ibid*, 35 ('sicheres Gespür für die richtige Wertung der Vorgänge').
325 *Ibid*, 39–40.

Julian engaged in an earnest attempt to convince others of his approach. Like many other readers, Börsch sees Julian admittedly departing from legal logic for the sake of the common good. Interestingly, Börsch regards the *impunitas* argument as relevant only for the first attacker's liability. He considers the *poena*, the necessity of which is invoked, to be serving the function of deterrence: potential wrongdoers must get the signal that the legal system will always react to such an infringement as the one coming from the first attacker. But this argument should not be overvalued: Börsch rejects Scarano Ussani's attempt to colour Julian's essay by placing it in the bloodthirsty context of the SC Silanianum.[326] Pointing out that criminal proceedings (*accusatio criminalis*) were available alongside and on top of the private-law proceedings based on the *lex Aquilia*, Börsch stresses that for Julian this did not turn centrally on suppression of criminal activities, but on private-law liabilities. If it is about deterrence, it is deterrence brought about by private law means. Börsch cautions against giving too much weight to historical context, since the jurists first and foremost wrote for specialists, trying to come up with arguments which could convince the legal expert.

The massive contribution Hans Ankum made back in 1980 has already been reported.[327] At this point, his return, in 2010, to *l*.51, now from the angle of the *utilitas communis* argument in §2, needs to be mentioned.[328] Ankum, who had dealt with the *utilitas communis* before,[329] confirms the views he had set out 30 years earlier. He finds Julian's argument that a lack of all liability should be avoided (§2) 'not accurate', and says 'Julian must have been aware of the opinion of Celsus [...] according to whom [the first attacker] is liable as a *vulnerator* [...] and [the other attacker] on the basis of the first chapter'.[330] Ankum deduces from the fact that Julian does not cite the support of others for his view (described as 'a very severe position') that Julian stood alone, and had to compensate for this lack of collegial support by summoning comparable cases.[331] As a general result, Ankum sees the

326 Börsch (n 323) 46–7.

327 Above sub V.3.

328 H Ankum, 'The functions of expressions with *utilitatis causa* in the works of Classical Roman Lawyers', *Libellus ad Thomasium*, (2010) 16 *Fundamina* 5.

329 H Ankum, '"Utilitatis causa receptum" – On the pragmatical methods of the Roman lawyers', *Symbolae Ivridicae et Historicae Martino David Dedicatae* vol 1 (1968) 1; in French: H Ankum, 'Utilitatis causa receptum. Sur la méthode pragmatique des juristes romains classiques', (1968) 15 *RIDA* 133.

330 *Ibid*, 9.

331 *Ibid*, 8.

utilitas communis as being invoked 'to meet the needs of legal practice' and 'to defend a solution that was contrary to strict dogmatic rules'.[332]

In a monumental project, Roberto Scevola has exhaustively studied the use of *utilitas publica* in Greek and Roman thought in general, and among jurists of the Severian age in particular.[333] In his view, *utilitas communis* has a less pronounced political connotation than *utilitas publica*,[334] which seems to be linked to the notion of public law. *L.*51 is dealt with in passing only.[335] *Utilitas communis* here is invoked to allow the introduction, into the *ius civile*, of a new rule *contra rationem*; he points to a similar use in Pap 2 def D.1.1.7.1, regarding the praetor developing the *ius civile*.

h) Absurdus est

Some authors have specifically pursued a research interest in the use of the absurdity argument among Roman lawyers. *L.*51.2 had to come into their view. A leading study was written by Piera Capone,[336] who mentioned *l.*51.2 in passing only.[337] She referred the reader to Cerami's distinction between two kinds of 'absurdity' arguments, the formal syllogistic one and an intuitive-empirical one, which relies on the practical inconsistency of the result; we are looking at an example of the latter. Tomasz Giaro (* 1951) must be considered a foremost specialist in Roman lawyers' methodologies. In his eyes, Julian's absurdity argument does not just add a second-best reason, but encapsulates a deep-seated doctrinal argument. He too sees Julian as going against Celsus.[338] A precise inquiry into the matter, i.e. which of the attackers has actually caused the victim's death, could lead to a dual acquittal, which would be more absurd than the solution Julian proposes himself. Giaro's view stands out from the mainstream, in that he declines to disparage Julian. On another occasion, Giaro saw Julian attacking Celsus's 'harping on about principles'.[339] Andreas Wacke (* 1936) took a more conventional line. He looked into *l.*51.2 only in passing, noting

332 *Ibid*, 22.

333 R Scevola, *Utilitas publica*, 2 vols: *1 – Emersione nel pensiero greco e romano; 2 – Elaborazione della giurisprudenza severiana* (2012).

334 *Ibid*, vol 2, 5.

335 *Ibid*, vol 2, 5 and 372.

336 P Capone, 'Valore ed uso giuriprudenziale di "absurdus/e"', (1997) 63 *SDHI* 199.

337 *Ibid*, 225 n 108.

338 T Giaro, 'Absurditätsargumente in der römischen Jurisprudenz – Ein Überblick', (2006) 11 *OIR* 31, at 59.

339 T Giaro, *Römische Rechtswahrheiten. Ein Gedankenexperiment* (2007) 452, 613.

that *absurdus* allowed a comparative degree.[340] In Wacke's view, Roman lawyers had realised that unflinching deductive logic does not always serve the law well; the term *utilitas* in general signalled that a point had been reached where all-too-subtle doctrine was in danger of being overrated. In *l*.51 he sees Julian settling scores with the sophisms of some rhetors, and he encourages us to translate *contra rationem disputandi* as 'against logic'.[341] Wacke joins the happy few for whom *quis* is not Celsus.

i) All Text, No Context?

The main texts here dealt with analyse hypotheticals, devised by Roman lawyers to test the limits of Aquilian Chapter I liability. Such abstract hypotheticals in general do not reflect or betray any specific context. Not much can be gained by trying to confront our text with the realities of Roman life. Marco Balzarini (* 1961) in 1982 reviewed Roman law texts which deal with death occurring in a brawl.[342] The victim was considered as having died by accident and the culprit got away with a milder penalty. Balzarini looks at *l*.51.1–2 and *l*.11.2, which show that for the liability under the *lex Aquilia* no such privilege was in play.

j) Lex Aquilia *for Student Readers*

All along, the discussion of our texts has primarily served an educational purpose. However, since the early 20th century, a separate type of publication has branched out, specifically geared to student use. The editions by Monro and Thayer come to mind. Such books are incorporated in this volume insofar as they specifically deal with the law of the *lex Aquilia* and express expert opinions on our issue. These books tend to represent (and in turn reinforce) the mainstream, which is understandable, given their purpose. A pioneering work, particularly tailored to didactical needs, is Herbert Hausmaninger's (* 1936) *Das Schadensersatzrecht der lex Aquilia.*[343] Hausmaninger classifies the discussion as a 'special causation

---

340 A Wacke, 'Ne occasio sit maioris tumultus faciendi', *Een rijk gerecht* (1998) 593, at 593.

341 A Wacke, 'Logische Paradoxien in antiker und moderner Jurisprudenz', *Festschrift der Rechtswissenschaftlichen Fakultät zur 600-Jahr-Feier der Universität zu Köln* (1988) 325, at 363.

342 M Balzarini, 'Appunti sulla "rixa" nel diritto Romano', (1982) 28 *Labeo* 17.

343 H Hausmaninger, *Das Schadensersatzrecht nach der lex Aquilia* 2nd edn (1980) 17–9. The first edition appeared in 1976, the 5th edition in 1996.

problem', and our texts are taken to deal with overtaking causation. The controversy is linked to the dissent regarding the reckoning of the one-year-period: 'For Julian *occidere* is obviously completed already with the act, for Celsus only with the effect'.[344]

In 1989, Bruce W Frier (* 1943) published his *Casebook on the Roman Law of Delict*.[345] He reproduces our texts, followed by questions to be discussed. These questions reveal some of the author's views: *l*.51 'is unusual in that it represents a sustained argument on a single legal point. [...] Although Julian does not name Celsus, he is clearly attacking the earlier jurist's views'.[346]

In his monumental *Law of Obligations*, Reinhard Zimmermann (* 1952), relies on Ulpian and Celsus to identify the problem as one of 'breaking the chain of causation'; hence the first offender's 'conduct can [...] not be labelled *occidere*'.[347] Julian is introduced as disputing this position; once again, he is the odd one out. For him, Zimmermann holds, 'it is the action of inflicting a fatal wound as such that must be termed *occidere*'. This seems to be in line with the core of Nörr's views. A critical contradiction is seen in the relation to *l*.15.1, 'which has given rise to a host of speculations'.

Mario Bretone's (* 1932) *Storia del Diritto Romano* is an inspiring essayistic introduction to Roman Law.[348] In a chapter dealing with the interplay of tradition and innovation, Bretone uses *l*.51 as the example of what he calls 'concrete rationality'.[349] He draws the reader's attention to the use of the 'reputation of the old' by Julian, whose pointed remarks may have been directed against Celsus. In Bretone's view, Julian acknowledged that the *ratio disputandi* – the logic of the dispute – would have led to a result that was unacceptable in view of the idea of law as represented by the *auctoritas veterum*. But, Bretone cautions, *ratio disputandi* and *auctoritas veterum* are not to be taken as mutually exclusive mindsets. If both positions are in play – the rational one as well as the authoritative one – they can reinforce each other or point to opposite results. In the latter case, the choice will be guided by principles of utility and practicability. This is the case here. The bias 'for the old' can only get you so far; while 'the

---

344 *Ibid*, 8.

345 B W Frier, *Casebook on the Roman Law of Delict* (1989).

346 *Ibid*, 85 f.

347 R Zimmermann, *The Law of Obligations* (1990) 992 f.

348 M Bretone, *Storia del diritto romano* 3rd edn (1992) 294–7; Bretone had already addressed the text in *Techniche e ideologie dei giuristi romani* 2nd edn (1982) 310, using *l*.51 to dispute the idea of a petrification of traditional interpretations.

349 *Ibid* Bretone (1992) 294 ('*razionalismo concreto*').

old' is in view, it does not in the end stop Julian from letting the *utilitas* argument control the issue. 'The old' can be presumed to be better, but that presumption can be overcome by critical arguments. Dialectic sophistry, pursued as *l'art pour l'art*, should best be avoided.

Alessandro Corbino's (* 1945) *Il danno qualificato e la lex Aquilia* holds a middle place between a student-oriented introduction and a proper monograph.[350] Corbino does not point the reader to any secondary literature. He brings our cases under the heading of causal nexus problems due to a multiplicity of actions,[351] presenting the pertinent cases in a thought-through order, accompanied by sparse remarks. Taking D.9.2.11.4 and 11.2 as dealing with situations where contributions to the death cannot be individuated, Corbino next tackles *l.*51.2, to set the stage for *l.*51pr–1 and *l.*11.3: here he registers a doctrinal dispute, with Julian's adversaries holding liable only 'the author of the last action, which has brought about death immediately'.[352] Turning to *l.*15.1, he concludes that the texts exclude all approaches limited to 'mechanical considerations'. Corbino adds Paul 10 ad Sab D.9.2.45.3 and Ulp 18 ad ed D.9.2.9pr–1.

VII. MORE CONTEMPORARIES

A more recent standard monograph on the *lex Aquilia*, by Bénédict Winiger (* 1955),[353] deals with our antinomy under the heading 'Formes de causalité'. The author cautions that '*la terminologie moderne de la causalité doit être utilisée avec précaution*'.[354] Both solutions are set out and found, based on some *a priori* reasoning, as having been 'discussable'. Going with Julian meant anticipating a future event, which in fact had not materialised. Going with Celsus means limiting Chapter III liability to actors who inflict '*le coup mortel*'. The second actor's killing act seems weightier, since he directs his attack against a slave already weakened, while on the other hand, the victim would have died soon after anyway. Celsus's solution has the advantages of avoiding speculative considerations and of limiting the issue to be proven to the factual development. Julian, who is praised as '*un des grands spécialistes de la causalité*', is found to have given conflicting

350 A Corbino, *Il danno qualificato e la lex Aquilia – Corso di diritto romano* 2nd edn (2008).
351 *Ibid*, 123 f.
352 *Ibid*, 124.
353 B Winiger, *La responsabilité Aquilienne Romaine. Damnum iniuria datum* (1997).
354 *Ibid*, 58 f.

opinions, in *l*.15.1 and in *l*.51. Following Nörr and others, Winiger sees Julian in the latter text as basing liability '*non pas sur le résultat, mais sur l'acte lui-même qui y a conduit*'. He also chides Julian for not taking into account the possible Chapter III liability of the first offender.

In her wide-ranging monograph on the *lex Aquilia*, Amelia Castresana Herrero (* 1957) puts the issue in the framework of solidarity and the cases of '*causalidad alternativa*'.[355] It is in this field that she sees the difference emerge between strictly result-oriented approaches and approaches that loosen the requirement of an undoubtedly attributable effect. This conflict is reflected, in her eyes, in the Celsus–Julian controversy pertaining to the reckoning of the Chapter I one-year period. Julian tends towards an action-oriented approach, so that *mortifere vulnerare*, Castresana reasons, for Julian already qualifies as *occidere*, although the statutory term was narrower. For Celsus, the ensuing death (causally linked to the action) remains the foundation of Chapter I Aquilian liability. With the same starting point, Ulpian tackles the additional issue of proving that the required result was triggered by the (first) offender's stroke, when a third party interferes. As set out by Ulpian in *l*.11.2, cases of '*causalidad alternativa*' lead to a joint and several liability: the owner freely elects the perpetrator he wants to sue, but he gets his compensation only once. Castresana draws attention to the fact that Julian advocates two Chapter I liabilities that differ as to the precise measure of damages, relying on his concept for determining the start point of the Chapter I one-year period. I am not sure how this relates to the rule of solidarity between multiple wrongdoers. Ulpian takes a split view: regarding the starting point, he follows Julian, but with Celsus is unwilling to relinquish the requirement of the effectively deadly outcome. Following Dalla, Castresana sees Julian as granting the victim better protection, in line with the general idea of solidarity in cases of multiple wrongdoers.

Jean-François Gerkens's (* 1968) contribution stands out in many respects.[356] He is it the only author, it seems, who liberally drew from statements of all epochs of Roman law research. For both fragments, Gerkens first sets out the textual criticism, also diligently reviewing the variants in the Digest manuscripts. This is followed by thorough exegeses. On the broadest possible basis, Gerkens then proceeds to compare both texts. He dismisses the harmonisation advanced by the Ordinary

---

355 A C Herrero, *Nuevas lecturas de la responsabilidad aquiliana* (2001) 53–5.

356 J-F Gerkens, *'Aeque perituris ...' – Une approche de la causalité dépassante en droit romain classique* (1997) 159–206.

Gloss as well as the multifaceted approaches from the interpolationist era. In his own assessment,[357] diagnosing a controversy rests on an '*erreur de perspective*'. The authors confirming the controversy theory, he finds, do not accept that Julian approved of an interruption of the main causal link in the case of *ruina* but not in the case of a blow by a second assailant. They also reject Julian's solution on grounds of logic. Gerkens disagrees on both counts. Relying on Ulp 71 ad ed D.43.24.7.4, a text first brought into play by Faber, Gerkens thinks that it was a real alternative that both perpetrators would go free, rather than a fancy *argumentum ad absurdum*. He thinks that the opposition to letting both perpetrators go unpunished is the main thrust of Julian's essay. In this respect, Celsus and Julian do in fact agree. There is even more common ground in that for both jurists, deadly second events that qualify as *force majeure* do not allow the first wrongdoer to be held liable as a killer. They differ only with regard to the *acte humain*. Even in this respect, Celsus and Julian agree on the solution, insofar as they both advocate the second wrongdoer's liability. Why does Julian prefer Chapter I liability also for the second wrongdoer? Setting the *communis utilitas* argument to one side, Gerkens identifies the inability to give preference to one of the perpetrators as the argument that is crucial for Julian. He also comes close to Nörr's analysis when he writes that for Julian, '*"mortifere vulnerare" équivaut déjà à un "occidere"*'.[358] Celsus, on the other hand, stuck with the effective causation, and this did not allow the death to be attributed to the first perpetrator's attack. This is but another solution, which, in Gerkens's view, has no monopoly on logical soundness. All in all, Celsus and Julian, in the narrow band where they disagree, both present respectable solutions, and the closeness of these solutions allowed the compilers, in Gerkens's view, to present the user with both solutions: '*Les divergences sont cependant minimes*'.[359] It is a secondary question, in Gerkens's view, whether the first perpetrator can be held liable under Chapter I or under Chapter III. He points to the wording of *l*.51, which does not even expressly mention the pertinent chapters of the *lex*. Gerkens also analyses this result in view of the Roman lawyers' doctrine '*sur la causalité dépassante*',[360] which is Gerkens's main topic. As a starting point he finds that disconnecting the wounding from its ultimate effect, allowing for a stretch of time in between, is the precondition for problems of overtaking causation. The *lex Aquilia* makes matters a little more complicated, in

357 *Ibid*, 199 f.
358 *Ibid*, 169.
359 *Ibid*, 202.
360 *Ibid*, 203 f.

that prior to the slave's eventual death a liability for wounding is already engaged. This legal effect is an immediate and, in a way, irreversible one. As to the second event, Gerkens sees a crucial distinction between *cas fortuit* and *acte humaine*. In the first category, the jurists do not depart from the factual causation; the hypothetical potential of the first wound to ultimately kill the slave is not taken into account. In D.43.24.7.4, Gerkens sees the reverse case, the *force majeure* coming first, followed by the human act: again, hypothetical deliberations are not allowed to have an impact on the overall solution. With regard to human intervention, '*un certain désaccord*' becomes apparent. It was the majority view, Gerkens concludes, to refuse hypothetical causation considerations in this case too. Whether one agrees with Gerkens's conclusion or not, as far as today's Roman law scholarship goes, Gerkens's piece must be considered at the top of the heap.

Jeroen Kortmann (* 1974) summarised his paper in the following words:[361]

> The Roman jurists' treatment of the problem of the 'supervening cause' has been the subject of many publications in the second half of this century. In particular, an alleged controversy between Celsus and Julian has been singled out. It is suggested in this essay that the discussions have constantly erred in the translation of D.9.2.51.pr. (Julian). This has often led to a misconception of Julian's opinion on the matter. When closely read, Julian's words, as reproduced in D.9.2.51, leave room for the view that Celsus and Julian either did not disagree at all or in any case did not disagree on the matter of the 'supervening cause'.

Kortmann's own view stresses the evidentiary aspect, taking *l.*51pr as a case where it was impossible to attribute the slave's ultimate death to one of the two attacks: the case set out in the *principium*, according to Kortmann, is about alternative causation, not about supervening causation, hence the topic finds a smooth continuation in §1 and the referencing of the *veteres*. Kortmann draws attention to the difference in wording, in that *l.*15.1 leaves no doubt that the slave died *alio ictu*, whereas in *l.*51pr the slave is *ab alio ictus* and then dies, a wording which supports or creates an ambiguity which in itself may be seen as a material fact.

Paola Ziliotto (* 1967) approaches the Aquilian liability from the angle of 'imputation',[362] seeing both *iniuria* and the *damnum corpori corpore datum*

361 J S Kortmann, 'Ab alio ictu(s): Misconceptions about Julian's View on Causation', (1999) 20 *Journal of Legal History* 95.

362 P Ziliotto, *L'imputazione del danno Aquiliano. Tra iniuria e damnum corpore datum* (2000).

requirement as instruments to allocate liability. She reports both texts, and sides with Ankum in that she sees the dispute about the reckoning of the one-year period as being inextricably linked to the antinomy of *l*.11.3 and *l*.51. One could assume that for Celsus, the autonomously intervening event interrupts the causal chain; the typical endpoint does not materialise. Alternatively, one could assume that the event was 'all right', but that the causal nexus (and thus the *occidere* act) was found to be lacking on the strength of the intervening event. She refers to D.9.2.7.3, where a person's intervention also leads to a negation of *occidere*.

In 2004, Isabella Piro (* 1963) produced a monograph covering important aspects of the *lex Aquilia*,[363] followed by a dense investigation of our texts in a separate publication in 2007.[364] Piro reads *l*.51 closely, and this makes her piece one of the most pertinent contributions to date. Celsus and Julian deal with the same case. They differ as to the '*concezione causale*'. Celsus insisted on the certainty with which the effect could be traced back to its cause. Julian, by contrast, sets out his concept of causation step by step. Julian allows the interpreter of the *lex Aquilia* to gauge the necessary certainty in the light of experience. The visible behaviour of the wrongdoers can be made the basis of evaluation. In a new turn, Piro asks whether a general tendency can be found in Julian's (and others') writings to use the interpretational leeway to protect owners. She points the reader to *l*.11.2 with *l*.51.1, where a similar relaxation of traceable causation allows awarding the owner a multiplicity of claims. Taking on *l*.11.4, the full lemma *l*.11.1–4 comes into view, which she attests has '*assoluta coerenza*'. *L*.51.2 also shows Julian's willingness to expand the compensation granted to the owner. And this, in Piro's view, is brought about by '*una ardita operazione interpretativa, magistralmento costruita*'.[365] Finally, Piro also inspects *l*.15.1. Piro thus turns the tendency which Scarano Ussani thinks is detectable in our texts, namely to supress unrest by tightened legal repression, into a private-law-focussed tendency to intensify the protection of ownership by inflating the grantable compensation. In this line of thought, Julian is not alone. Suddenly Celsus, who stuck with a traditionally narrow concept of causation, may appear to be the odd one out.

---

363 I Piro, *Damnum 'corpore suo' dare – rem 'corpore' possidere. L'oggettiva riferibilità del compartemento lesivo e della possessio nella riflessione e nel linguaggio dei giuristi romani* (2004).

364 I Piro, '*In dubio pro domino*? Brevi riflessioni intorno alla valutazione guilianea dell'*aestimatio perempti* in materia aquiliana', *Fides Humanitas Ius* vol 6 (2007) 4313.

365 Piro (n 363) 187.

Triggered by Lord Rodger's use of D.9.2.51 and D.9.2.11.2 in his opinion in *Fairchild v Glenhaven Funeral Services Ltd*,[366] and the subsequent turn taken in *Barker v Corus (UK) plc*,[367] Bastian A Zahn (* 1986) took a closer look at Julian's concept of killing.[368] He rejects Kortmann's theory, which he finds offers no explanation of Julian's discussion of *occidere*. He comes back to the now-prevailing interpretation, that for 'Julian, the accent lies on the act of killing, whereas Celsus considers the result, i.e. death, to be the decisive element of *occidere*.'[369] As usual, this leaves the problem of *l*.15.1, for which Zahn unfolds a very thorough analysis. Zahn carefully reviews Ankum's proposal, which is ultimately rejected on the basis of a new inspection of the *Littera Florentina* and the MSS of the vulgate tradition. Relying on Bas.60.3.15, Zahn considers a Justinianic intervention unlikely. Zahn draws attention to the fact that the two Ulpian texts can be located as belonging to different lemmata, elucidating *occidere*, *erus*, and *quanti id in eo anno plurimi fuit*. However, the *servus mortifere vulneratus* features in each of these. Zahn comes up with a complicated theory on how Ulpian disclosed his view in a fragmented manner, split up so as to emerge in bits and pieces in different lemmata. Ulpian, he hopes to show, is concerned with the evidentiary aspect, that the resulting death must have become apparent. Turning to *l*.51, Zahn finds the act of *occidere* to be the 'touchstone of Julian's analysis'. He notes that in spite of doubts regarding the causality of the first blow, the ensuing death occurs *maturius*, and deduces:

> There remains a nexus between the first blow and the subsequent death, which, despite not being causal, allows the law to attribute the slave's death to the first assailant and make him liable. That Julian considers both attacks as equivalent instances of *occidere* can also be seen in §2. He speaks of the first assailant as *qui prior vulneravit* and in the same sentence calls the second one *posterior*. By speaking of both as *qui vulneraverunt*, he expresses his view that they are both doing the same, i.e. committing acts capable of causing the death. For these acts to qualify as *occidere* no more is needed than the death actually to occur, and before this happens, both can be called *vulnerare*.[370]

366 *Fairchild v Glenhaven Funeral Services Ltd* [2002] UKHL 22; [2003] 1 AC 32.

367 *Barker v Corus (UK) plc* [2006] UKHL 20; [2006] 2 AC 572.

368 B A Zahn, 'Harmful Conduct as a Touchstone of Causation: An Analytical Comparison of *Barker v Corus* and Julian', (2011) 15 *Edinburgh Law Review* 197.

369 *Ibid*, 206.

370 *Ibid*, 214.

Unfortunately, Zahn does not seem to realise that this description could also open up a possibility for distinguishing the cases of *l.*51pr and of *l.*11.3. Turning to §1, Zahn thinks that in cases both of supervening as well as of alternative causation, the link between the act of killing and the death is loosened. But Julian, he finds, does not distinguish between different types of causation anyway. More importantly, here – and for the *veteres* – it is the act of *occidere* that matters. Likewise, we might classify the stolen beam as a matter of joint liability in a case of cumulative causation: again, Julian 'does not focus on causal theories, but on statutory interpretation.' As to §2, Zahn sides with those who find Julian's pondering of a zero liability 'not entirely true, though, because the first assailant would be liable under the third chapter anyway.'[371] Zahn's following analysis of *Barker* and how it relates to Julian's viewpoint need not be set out here.

Helen Scott (* 1975) confirms Nörr's interpretation in central aspects, especially regarding the feature that Julian is taken to include attempted murder in the Chapter I liability.[372] Doing away with the veil of erudition which prevents blindingly blunt results from emerging from Nörr's book, Scott does not mince her words:

> In Julian's view the cause of action under Chapter 1 accrued as soon as the killing act which constituted *occidere* was committed, regardless of whether it actually caused the slave's death.[373]

As an aside, Scott takes *occidere* to refer specifically to 'typical' killing acts only, an idea earlier mooted by Frier. By contrast, Celsus is taken to understand *occidere* as including the slave's death, which leads Scott to attribute to Celsus the understanding that *occidere* is really 'wrongful causing of death – *mortis causam praebere*'. Scott thus reaffirms the notion of a controversy, on a fairly fundamental level, speculating that Ulpian disapproved of Julian's decision in *l.*51pr.[374] Unlike Nörr, Scott does not hesitate to identify the problem as one of 'over-determined causation'. Last but not least, Scott compares Julian's thinking with a more recent English theory of tort liability. She thus sharpens the analysis of Julian's concept: 'killing' for Julian, she finds, is a dualistic, composite concept, comprising

371 *Ibid*, 215 n 86.
372 Scott (2013) (n 5).
373 *Ibid*, 115.
374 *Ibid*, 118.

on the one hand a particular species of conduct, a typical killing act (this is the concept brought into play by Frier), and on the other hand a particular injury to the victim – a mortal wound. Scott does indeed think that Julian did away with the effectively ensuing death as a precondition for Chapter I liability. Some parallelism with Robert Stevens' concept of tort comes in handy to avoid disparaging Julian: 'Seen in the light of modern tort theory, Julian's analysis of Ch. 1 of the *lex Aquilia* seems, if not prescient, then at least not unsophisticated.'[375]

Lucetta Desanti (* 1959) has written what seems to be a new standard work on the *lex Aquilia*.[376] She carefully analyses *l*.51 as well as *l*.11.3.[377] Relying on Dalla and Gerkens, she sees the topic of the causal nexus as being in play, which has led to dissenting views of Julian and Celsus, as well as other jurists. After rephrasing *l*.11.3, she deals with *l*.51 bit by bit. Regarding the *principium*, Desanti summarises Julian in saying that not only is the second perpetrator, who in her eyes delivered the *coup de grâce*, liable under Chapter I, but also the first perpetrator, who had inflicted a mortal wound. Following Dalla, Desanti stresses that Julian deals with two attacks, launched at different times, which makes the reference to the case of multiple slayers in §1 an analogy argument. *L*.51.2 is but an ancillary argument. Desanti does see, with Ankum, Willvonseder and Gerkens, that for both attackers the argument could be advanced that their respective act, taken in isolation, was not necessary for the realisation of the death. Julian, she thinks, overcame this problem by letting the common good override formal logic. Desanti reports the positions regarding the identification of *quis*. Turning to *l*.15.1, Desanti relies on Dalla. With Dalla, she interprets *alio ictu* as referring to an accident rather than another attack. The solution here seems to be in conflict with the one in *l*.51. Desanti reports the interpolationist doubts which have been triggered by this diagnosis. She takes the line of Gerkens that a distinction has to be drawn between cases of '*forza maggiore*' and human acts. Desanti looks only briefly at Paul 22 ad ed D.9.2.30.4. It is noteworthy that Desanti's review does not utilise the popular idea that Julian equated mortally wounding and killing.

Thomas Finkenauer (* 1968) briefly looked into our problem in 2017.[378] Like Scott, Zimmermann and others, he follows Nörr, whose position in

375 *Ibid*, 122.

376 L Desanti, *La Legge Aquilia. Tra verbal egis e interpretazione giurisprudenziale* (2015).

377 *Ibid*, 47–53.

378 T Finkenauer, 'Pönale Elemente der lex Aquilia', *Ausgleich oder Busse als Grundproblem des Schadensersatzrechts von der lex Aquilia bis zur Gegenwart* (2017) 35, at 63 f.

Finkenauer's paraphrasis comes across perhaps more clear-cut than it appeared in the manner in which it was originally set out by Nörr: 'The controversy between Celsus and Julian is to be explained by the situation, that for the issue of imputation, the former considers the effect as the decisive moment, the latter the action'. Finkenauer then adds a scathing critique of Julian: the case brought in by him as a reference concerns 'alternative causation', and thus is not a real match. The *argumentum ad absurdum* (§2) does not hold, because the first wrongdoer does not go free according to Ulpian; rather he comes under a Chapter III liability. For what in Finkenauer's eyes is nothing but a 'gut decision', rhetoric must take the place of a legal argument. Disregarding the suggestion by Ankum and others, Finkenauer sees Julian as being in agreement with all the decisions set out by Ulpian in *l*.15.1.

Joe Sampson (* 1989) only touches on our problem. Similarily to Piro, he finds Julian willing to interpret the *lex* in a manner favourable to the claimant.[379] Sampson identifies the backwards reckoning from the moment the mortal wound is inflicted, as the key favour to the claimant in play in *l*.51. The *neque impunita* phrase is 'straightforwardly an argument from policy'. Julian 'interprets the scenario' so as to give the claimant 'the best shot at fully realising the value of his claim': 'to take the line later adopted by Ulpian is to allow the nefarious killer to evade liability', the very solution branded absurd by Julian.

David Johnston (* 1961), in a survey of distinctively 'British' contributions to *lex Aquilia* research, briefly reviews the positions of Buckland/McNair, Pugsley and MacCormack.[380] He asks whether a 'theory of causation' really was in play for the Roman lawyers. His answer is negative: he asserts that for the Roman jurists 'the concern seems to be a pragmatic one, of identifying on a particular set of facts whether a particular defendant can be said *occidisse*'.[381] He finds support for this view in Nörr's contributions, which display a similar reluctance to see elements of a theory of causation in the jurists' reasoning. Johnston agrees with Pugsley's sentiment that differences among Roman jurists should not be overemphasised. All in all, Johnston's musings confirm the results arrived at by MacCormack. Trying to identify a specifically 'British' approach, he ponders the alleged affinity between English and Roman lawyers' methodologies, based on a

379 Sampson (n 259) 178–9.
380 D Johnston, 'Causation and Remoteness: British Steps on a Roman Path', *Wrongful Damage to Property in Roman Law. British Perspectives* (2018) 211.
381 *Ibid*, 216.

common 'lack of a conscious analysis', a reluctance to come up with general abstract statements or coherent intellectual systems, and the build-up of a stack of rules in the ordinary course of legal business, going from case to case. He cautiously finds 'some explanatory force' in this view. In line with Johnston, it is indeed arguable that concepts such as overtaking causation or interruption of causation have their origin in the specifically pandectistic-civilian striving for grand theories of causation, from which Johnston sets the British Romanists apart.

Armando Torrent (* 1941) has dealt with the link between the *damnum dare* and the *corpore suo* requirements.[382] He unfolds a narrative which stresses the expansion of Aquilian liability, which over time called for restrictions based on the concept of *culpa*. Decisions turning on causation were not so much philosophically anchored, but motivated by practical deliberations. He is tempted to look at *l*.51 as being relevant to the law of multiple tortfeasors, in view of the special causality problems involved.[383] Based on a detailed report of the case, he sees as Julian holding all attackers liable because the infliction of a mortal wound was equated with delivering death.

382 A Torrent, 'La Causalidad Aquiliana. Conexión corpore suo-damnum dare: Gayo 3,219; Ulp. (18 ad ed.) D. 9,1,1,7; IJ 4,3,16', (2018) *RIDROM (Revista Internacional de Derecho Romano)* 465.

383 *Ibid*, 495–8.

CHAPTER 3
THE SUMMING UP

I. THE CHANGING SOCIOLOGY OF ROMAN LAW SCHOLARSHIP[384]

As a prelude, some quantitative observations may be in order.[385] Throughout this volume, no systematic attempt has been made to allocate space in balanced proportion to the numbers of authors working in a specific century. In the 17th century, for example, more authors voiced an opinion on our matter than the ones here reported. And yet, the accelerated proliferation of Roman law research throughout the 20th and 21st centuries is clearly visible (Fig. 10). The increase in numbers is so massive that it eclipses the effect which the displacement of the Corpus Iuris as a part of the 'black letter law' might have had. As the study of the Digest became detached from the hustle and bustle of contemporary legal practice and Roman law became a matter of pure historical research, the formerly steady demand for 'practical' solutions, extracted from the text of the Digest, should have waned. One might have expected the loss of this demand to manifest itself in a slowdown of scholarly production. No such effect can be detected in the data here collected.

What are the drivers of this surprising growth? Roman law activities have typically been pursued in prospering societies, which depend for their operation on a functioning legal framework of high calibre, and in turn provide resources for the maintenance of university studies. Two thirds of all contributions here recorded, which are indicative of an advanced Roman law discourse, originated from what economic historians have called *la banane bleue*, a geographical corridor credited with a consistent above-average activity of trade and industries, allowing accumulation of

---

[384] The following remarks, some of which may appear quite sweeping, are strictly based on the case study of D.9.2.51 v D.9.2.11.3 only. It may well be that other test-cases would yield different results.

[385] The data is presented p 153 ff.

capital and intensification of cultural activities (Fig. 9).[386] If the *banana bleue* thesis holds true, it might be argued that the increase in our research simply betrays the growing prosperity of the contemporary societal environment over the last 150 years.

Today, there are more scholars at work in the field of Roman law than ever before. Both the number of universities and their respective research forces have been steadily increasing. Roman law scholarship is no exception. Essential working tools for Roman law research, physically held only in some advanced libraries and Roman law institutes, are now to a large degree available online and can be accessed from every desk, anywhere in the world. The availability of specialist literature on an international level has hugely improved, compared with pre-Internet times, allowing more scholars to enter the field with professional equipment. Larger and larger cohorts of law students are provided with Roman law textbooks tailored to didactic needs; our antinomy has always been popular study material and thus features in quite a few of them. The number of people alive today who, as students, have come into a contact with our texts, however fleetingly, is difficult to estimate, but hundreds of thousands may still be a conservative guess. The expansion of academic legal education, on a global scale, is also reflected in the considerable number of works here reported which were written as PhD theses in doctoral programmes. The imperative to publish or perish may play a role, too. Insofar as the quantitative expansion of Roman law research is fuelled, in good measure, by young lawyers' PhD theses (or equivalents), the average age at which contributions are produced may have been driven down: a greening of Roman law scholarship? At the same time, the increase in our lifespan allows individual scholars to produce more papers over their lifetime. Since the last third of the 20th century, contributions have also begun to come from female scholars (Fig. 13).

In our scholarly approaches we observe increasing diversity. Isolated topics and angles, as well as individual Roman jurists and their respective legal methodologies, are being scrutinised from scratch. Issues of philosophical or linguistic subtleties, not all rooted in the intellectual world of Roman antiquity, have liberally been brought to the table. We are increasingly revisiting the works of earlier scholars, unearthing and clarifying what ideas they intended to contribute to the discussion (van den Bergh and Stolte on Brenkman, Cairns on Grueber, or Ibbetson on Buckland). Today, we are witnessing an unprecedented wealth of ideas

386 R Brunet, *Les villes europeénnes* (1989). The study has since been subject to controversy.

in Roman law research, conducted all over the world. The proliferation of viewpoints has been another driver accelerating the overall discourse. Last but not least, there is a trend towards longer contributions. Articles like those from Schindler, Dalla, Ankum, Gerkens or Scott are many times longer than even the longest deliberations of *Ius Commune* times. In today's journals, the erudite commentaries like Ulricus Huber's or Cujas's would fill a few pages at best. If we take both the ever-rising number of contributions and their growing length into account, we are looking at exponential growth (Fig. 11). Had this volume been written only 50 years ago, it would have been half as long.

The exponentially increasing output of Roman law research has an inevitable downside. It has become impossible to consider and weigh all previous contributions. We are operating with a continuously shrinking field of vision. A 17th century scholar who used four or five commentaries could expect to have very much the full range of options and arguments in view. An author who relies on the same number of contributions today sees but the tip of the iceberg, perhaps two to three per cent of all available contributions. That ratio continues to fall. In other fields of research, it has long become a standard approach to ignore altogether publications which are more than 10 or 20 years old. One is bound to presume that everything older, if worth preserving, will somehow be still reflected in the latest publications. Is this the way we, too, will have to go?

II. A SPECTRUM OF SOLUTIONS

For a quarter of a millennium, the reading of the Gloss prevailed. It averted an antinomy by distinguishing two kinds of lethality (of the first wound), the absolutely lethal and the merely contingently lethal. The first noteworthy opposition came from Zasius, who advanced a different way to distinguish both decisions, focussing on the effectiveness of the second blow. From then on, one can identify two pivotal shifts in the evolution of interpretations. The first was the assumption, introduced by Cujas, that the sources betray a doctrinal dissent, with Julian in a minority of one. The second turn was the willingness to analyse our texts as statements pertaining to issues – or theories – of causation. The basis of this turn was the mega-trend, identifiable already in the late Middle Ages, to conceptualise homicide as causing death by a lethal wound. Taken together, the two texts are now mostly understood as positions of a doctrinal dispute of a fairly fundamental nature: Celsus and Julian, this is the idea, are engaged in an intellectual dispute about the theoretical role of causation in the handling of *occidere* and *mortis causam praestare*. If one accepts this narrative, we are looking at a highly charged doctrinal battle of causation theorists. This view, however, has also met – and continues to meet – with sceptical responses, advocating an understanding that refrains from borrowing anachronistic causation theories.

Among those who diagnose a controversy, most authors have found Julian's decision the more difficult to accept, whereas *l.*11.3 has generally been taken for sound doctrine. The scepticism regarding Julian's view predates the diagnosis of a classical controversy. From early on, his decision was classified as an exception to the rule or as the result of a legal fiction (Baldus). The aversion to Julian's view was fuelled whenever learned doctrines of delictual liability were transferred into the field of criminal law: Julian's view would then entail two death sentences. Humanist attempts to contain the death penalty thus were at odds with Julian's view. Celsus was seen as the more benign jurist. However, as long as Justinian's codification was the law of the land, i.e. until the coming of national codifications from the 18th century onwards, it was not possible to disregard *l.*51 altogether. Many of those who were critical of Julian's logic tended grudgingly to fall back on the concept, as seemingly presented in *l.*51.2, that the *utilitas communis* overrides legal logic. Modern Romanists, working after the dethronement of Justinian's codification (or, before that, those working outside its jurisdictional reach), did not need to hold back. In some authors' view, *l.*51 could be called Julian's biggest blunder. Others just eliminated Julian's text – or parts thereof – by assuming interpolations. It is noteworthy, indeed shocking, that long after the irrevocable transition of Roman law activities to an historical-critical approach, and the end of the need to present a definitive reading of Roman law as applicable law for today, authors still have felt and continue to feel the urge to 'take sides', declaring their adherence to either 'Team Ulpian/ Celsus' or, more seldomly, 'Team Julian'. This is none of the historian's business, but old habits die hard.

Whenever one attributed different legal views to Julian and to Ulpian, one was bound to ask what underlying legal concepts might have led the jurists to be wired differently here. For many centuries, the approach which diagnosed a jurists' controversy did not pose this question. Rather, the difference of opinion was taken as a matter of fact. From the late 19th century, however, attempts were made to associate the two jurists' views with divergent concepts of causation. It is remarkable that this had not happened earlier, since elaborate theories of causation had been around since the heydays of scholasticism (*causa remota, causa mediata, causa proxima, causa adjuvans, causa efficiens, causa superveniens* and so forth) and were long known to the learned lawyers, too.[387] But, as the topic of causation is not expressly addressed in our texts at all, the close reading that was required by the Justinianic sources as the law of the land here did not invite venturing into the field of causation theories. One is tempted to speculate that the new fashion for reflections on causation was linked to the scientific and/or technological spirit of the 19th century. Quite a number of authors, Schindler most prominently, have linked the presumed controversy to the unquestionable dispute as to the reckoning for the one-year period, pertaining to the Chapter I measure of damages. In another 20th-century turn, the idea has taken hold that Julian departed from the mainstream of his contemporaries and proposed a radically different understanding of what constitutes *occidere* under Chapter I. Julian, it is argued, accepted that *occidere* signified lethally wounding. This approach typically (but not necessarily) merges two decisions of Julian, one regarding the starting point of the one-year reckoning for Chapter I (*l*.21.1), and the other regarding the case of the slave slain twice.[388]

Of these different approaches to understanding the root of a presumed controversy, none has ultimately prevailed over the others. Ideas have become fashionable or gone out of fashion, and the impression of an unscientific herd instinct cannot be dismissed altogether. Today's mainstream can be summarised like this: Celsus and Julian dealt with essentially the same case and disagreed over the decision. The disagreement concerned a causation issue: Celsus insisted on the actual death as an effect brought about in reality by the attacker; for Julian it was sufficient that the attacker had inflicted an absolutely lethal wound, even if the wound did not causally lead to the slave's death. The eccentricity of Julian's position forced him to heap together arguments of varying – and sometimes questionable – quality, even conceding that his solution compromises legal logic – all to no avail: Roman jurists approved of Celsus's view and left Julian in a minority of one.

---

387 The corresponding modern causation *topoi* are but derivatives of scholastic (and thus ultimately philosophical) originals. All medieval lawyers had a basic understanding of *causa* doctrines, since they were part of the *Trivium*.

388 It is noteworthy that in recent times other authors, who have not sided with the view just set out, have also tried to distance our texts from the obviously a-historical frameworks of causation concepts.

III. 'LAWYERS ARE BAD HISTORIANS' – WAS EDMUND BURKE RIGHT?

Throughout its development, the interpretation of Roman law sources has been incessantly in dialogue with the contemporary intellectual worlds of the respective interpreters. As long as Justinian's codification was the law of the land, the interpretation of the Roman law could not but also try to accommodate contemporary practice. However, in this interplay between contemporary legal thought and historical interpretation no recognisable paradigm shift occurred at the very moments when Roman law lost its position as a primary legal authority. In this respect, there never was a discernible watershed between 'modern' and 'pre-modern' exegeses. While the Roman law no longer is of contemporary application, the interpretation of Roman law sources has remained a matter for lawyers. No attempt was made to positively identify those authors who have enjoyed a formal education other than law, instead or on top of formal legal training. Most medieval and early modern authors, lawyers all of them, will have had a fairly broad classicist education. Scholars of a humanist or neo-humanist persuasion often acquired and employed impressive knowledge of all aspects of Roman antiquity. Among contemporary authors, incidental knowledge allows to identify just a handful with a formal education outside law (Rechnitz, Frier, Winkler, Scott, Johnston). Of these, only Rechnitz and Winkler have based their contributions on methods which are not part of the conventional toolbox of Roman law research. It is not too harsh to find that neither of their contributions has paved the way to new levels of understanding. For all other authors, the approach to the problem seems fairly uniform: it is hardly possible to single out, on the basis of the respective contribution alone, those who can be credited with an added expertise in Roman history or Latin philology. It is fair to assume that the bulk of contributions continue to come from university academics, teaching Roman law – and perhaps contemporary law subjects as well – in a faculty of law. All of these law teachers have of course also acquired some knowledge of Roman history. Indeed, division of labour allows the individual researcher, coming from the field of law, to build up an additional expertise of this or that specific aspect of Roman antiquity, be it an element of the Roman economy or a feature of the intellectual development of Roman society. They may thus, in their specific field of expertise, easily surpass the general eruditeness of pre-modern scholars, not to speak of our access to the wealth of insights which Roman historians and archaeologists continue to accrue.

As long as Roman law research is being conducted mostly by trained lawyers, some intermingling of Roman law scholarship and contemporary legal doctrines remains inevitable. We are still struggling with a cross-pollination that works both ways. The cases dealt with by Celsus, Julian and Ulpian have remained focal points of modern tort discourse. We are not concerned here with the question to what extent contemporary doctrinal discourse can profit from studying texts written by Celsus or Julian. At first sight, there seems no reason to object to the heuristic use of these cases in attempts to systematise and rationalise modern tort theories and their causation concepts. One has to note, however, that such use of Roman legal literature tends to considerably distort the texts to extract contributions that seem fitting for modern debates. The work by Hart and Honoré is but one example: Roman lawyers' dealing with *occidere* did not involve, as these authors put it, the handling of 'two or more factors, present on a given occasion, each sufficient with other normal conditions to bring about certain harm.' The Roman statutory action neither required nor allowed the Roman jurists to analyse 'factors [...] which bring about harm'. From the viewpoint of Roman law scholarship, such misrepresentations could perhaps be deemed harmless if we could be sure they would not, one way or another, find their way back into critical investigations of our historical sources. Alas, we cannot perfectly compartmentalise our minds. Modern doctrinal concepts have always seeped back into the exegeses of Roman law sources to some extent.[389] Relying on their present-day frameworks, a great number of 19th- to 21st-century authors, for whom the Roman law should be a matter of sheer scholarly interest, to be pursued with methods of historical research alone, have unashamedly overloaded their own exegetical efforts with modern doctrinal concepts. The 'overtaking causation' is a case in point. The attempts to analyse the Roman jurists' texts relying on elements of modern tort/causation doctrines have not only failed to let us progress to a more historically accurate understanding of the Roman lawyers' thinking: they mark a retrograde move away from the attainable objectives of our research. Taking together the mostly fruitless excesses of the interpolationist era and the many doctrinally distorted re-narrations, the 20th century has little to show, given the vast intellectual energies that have been spent on the matters of our texts.

389 The contamination of historical scholarship – here as in other fields – by modern-day modes of thought is of course an unavoidable and well-known problem. While there is no want of more recent methodological confessions, the balanced statement of an eminent Roman law scholar is still worth recalling: H R Hoetink, 'Les notions anachroniques dans l'historiographie du droit', (1955) 23 *TR* 1.

There is no need to lose our nerve and forsake the legal approach to the Roman lawyers' texts, which are products of high-grade juristic intellectualism. For such texts, trying to shift to a context-centred approach is not an option: what is the historical context of a hypothetical? Ignoring or sidelining the legal content of our texts would lead to a 'Hamlet without the Prince of Denmark'. This is what we can do: we can fortify our determination to accept – and look for – a different, perhaps fundamentally different, understanding in the Roman era of the pertinent liability concepts and a potentially very different use of technical terms. None of the legal concepts brought into play – causation or *culpa*, to name just two – are really timeless, self-evident or derived from the natural state of affairs. On the contrary, all these concepts are legal-culture-loaded, undergoing considerable and sometimes fundamental change over time. If the Roman jurists are to be properly understood, we must overcome the bias towards doctrinal pattern recognition. All arguments relying on the specifically modern (but in fact often neo-scholastic) use of such terms and concepts need to be discarded if we want to make a serious attempt to understand them in their specific context of Roman antiquity. The affinity – or lack thereof – of a Roman jurist's idea to this or that modern doctrine is not a matter of praise or criticism – it is, for any seriously historical approach, irrelevant. Modern scholars with a legal background, when dealing with Roman law, therefore need to de-familiarise themselves with the specific content of present-day lawyers' doctrinal tool-boxes, without altogether forsaking the legal point of view. As far as possible, cases need to be looked through the Roman jurists' eyes. With this in mind, let us return to Julian.

CHAPTER 4
VERDICT ON JULIAN

I. THE LEGAL BACKGROUND

The cases dealt with concern *occidere*: the Roman jurists here discussed the statutory *actio directa* under Chapter I of the *lex Aquilia*.[390] For them, it made a world of difference whether liability could be asserted by the statutory *actio directa*, based on *occidere*, or the *in factum* variant for *mortis causam praestare*. The former is an application of *ius civile*, while the latter plays out on the basis of *ius honorarium*. Coming from a modern law perspective, it is easy to overlook the fundamental difference the Romans must have seen, under the rules of procedure alone,[391] between *mortis causam praestare* and *occidere*. The jurists here at work did not fail to point out when a liability needed to be realised by an *in factum* proceeding. For them, *occidere* and *mortis causam praestare* were two different and differently structured delicts, the latter supplementing the former. Not even the post-classical transition to the *per cognitionem* procedure did away with this distinction, which – albeit in a somewhat distorted manner – made it prominently into Justinian's codification (I.4.3.16). Dieter Nörr's attempt to show this distinction as in flux, subject to evolutionary re-arrangements, seems untenable, even if such an alleged change would have been just the minority concern of a leading lawyer of the time.[392] It would have been a doctrinal earthquake if notable support had been given to a blurring of the difference between the *actio directa* and

---

390 It is of no import here whether the phrase interpreted is taken from the pertinent edictal *formula* or directly from the text of Chapter I of the Republican statute.

391 For the purpose of this study, it is not necessary to attempt to reconstruct, in close detail, the distinct features of an Aquilian-oriented *in factum* proceeding, modelled after Chapter I of the *lex Aquilia*.

392 This is not to say that there was not an interplay in the developments of the direct action and its *in factum* variant. The shifting relationship between the statutory actions, their accessory *actiones in factum* and the *actiones utiles*, an issue which has rightly attracted much scholarly attention, is of no concern here.

the corresponding *in factum* variant of the same action, which then might even have become superfluous. Repercussions should be traceable in many of our relevant texts, which would inform us about or turn around this procedurally imminently important distinction. Ulpian's statement *nihil interest, occidat quis an causam mortis praebeat* (Ulp 8 ad Leg Iul et Pap D.48.8.15) shows that a merger of both concepts, wherever it occurred, was noteworthy, but could also be expressed in no uncertain terms. Whatever the palingenetical context of this statement may have been, it makes for a stark contrast with Ulpian's and his contemporaries' discussions of Chapter I cases.[393]

Liability under Chapter I was triggered by the completed performance of an intentional act, *occidere*. While *mortis causam praebere* could be seen as a 'crime of result', *occidere* was a 'crime of conduct', with the penalised conduct completed only by the full arc of action, spanning from the killer's strike to the victim's last breath. The conduct encompasses the result: no *occidere* without corpse. When death does not occur instantaneously at the very moment the wound is inflicted, when a temporal hiatus opens up between the infliction of the wound and the death, this can still qualify as *occidere*: *Aquilia lege teneri existimati sunt non solum, qui ita vulnerassent ut confestim vita privarent, sed etiam hi, quorum ex vulnere certum esset aliquem vita excessurum*: Iul 86 dig D.9.2.51pr. Liability in such cases needed not be re-based, due to this hiatus alone, on the *in factum* variant of the Aquilian Chapter I action, which was satisfied by *causam mortis praestare*.[394] For all we know, none of this was controversial, some second-level disputes notwithstanding.

In determining whether *occidere* can be found in a specific chain of events, a kind of graphical (visual) thinking seems to be at work: you watch reality run by, like a movie, and you ask yourself whether what you see can be called *occidere*.[395] As a lawyer, you do not have recourse to a counterfactual, parallel movie, in which the perpetrator's conduct is removed, in order to legally evaluate what you see. All this is far from mysterious. Rather, the legal approach shows a striking immediacy, not letting any doctrine get in between the wording of the statute (or *formula*)

393 When Ulpian quotes Celsus (Ulp 18 ad ed D.9.2.7.6), who had expressed the distinction in a classical manner, he is relying on Celsus's authority; he is not singling out Celsus for an extravagant view, which others had rejected.

394 This is confirmed by the host of problems which arise in such cases; see below p 115 f.

395 Similar views have been expressed by, *inter alia*, Frier (with a linguistic turn), Willvonseder ('phenotypic expression of the required *occidere* act'), and N H Andrews. G MacCormack pointed in the same direction.

and the legal answer to the one and only relevant question: does a lawyer relying on the *lex Aquilia* see *occidere* (the term used in the way the statute is handled) accomplished in what has happened in real life? Quite a few of the authors who have attested to the Roman lawyers' tendency to look for a phenotypical killing act have put their views forward with a linguistic turn, reducing the matter to a question of the recognised use of language alone (Frier, Willvonseder, Scott, Andrews, Zahn and others). The Roman jurists had to approach the *verbum legis* from a linguistic angle, insofar as an issue of statutory interpretation was at stake – how could it be otherwise? – but its handling was interwoven with careful regard for the legal effects any possible answer could have. The linguistic question is asked with its legal relevance in mind: 'do we use the word *occidere* here – in view of the liability/liabilities which a positive answer triggers under the *lex*?' If one wants to find linguistics here, it is legal linguistics.

Today, we analytically split up the performance of the act of killing into, on the one hand, a human action, completed with the infliction of a mortal wound at the latest, and its separate effect, the ensuing death, on the other hand. We do so as if it were the most natural approach. The Roman jurists did not dissect the performance of *occidere* in this manner. The liability under Chapter I was not based on an aggregate of distinct elements, which could be 'ticked off' separately. Liability was triggered, plain and simple, by *occidere* as a holistic action, stretching from the killer's resolution and bodily movement to the wound inflicted and on to the ultimate death. Death is not the effect of a killing action; it is the endpoint and completion of the killing act itself. Looking for isolated 'elements' into which *occidere* could be broken down is of no import for the Roman jurists, since finding isolated elements alone could be of no legal relevance.

Many interpreters almost instinctively tended and tend to analyse our cases as if they were about *causam mortis praebere*. They look separately at both 'action', the administering of the mortal blow *corpore corpori*, and 'effect', the ensuing death, with a link between 'action', and its 'effect', called 'causality'. The presumed causation issue may then be discussed in close detail, bringing in ever more nuanced concepts, for example of an 'interruption of the causal flow' or of the 'overtaking causation' by another, later event. This was not the view of the Roman lawyers. I side with Geoffrey MacCormack, who found that 'questions involving what a modern writer would describe as a causal point arose for a Roman jurist in the context of the operative words of the first and third chapter of the "lex"'.[396]

[396] G MacCormack, 'Aquilian Studies', (1975) 41 *SDHI* 1, at 12.

Insofar as Roman jurists discussed, for specific scenarios, whether the tort defined by the *lex Aquilia* was accomplished, their discussions did not turn around a secondary causality requirement, especially cultivated in German tort doctrine, which is presumed to link a specific loss to the accomplished tort (the primary infringement), thus shifting the issue onto the measure of damages level (Medicus, *contra*: Windscheid, Nörr, Scott).

Looking for the possible completion of an *occidere* act, in a deferred, but still 'matching' death, is not the same as testing a causal link between an event of death and a prior, completed action. Rather, these different perspectives make for markedly different analyses (MacCormack, Johnston). The holistic approach to finding or negating an accomplished *occidere* act in a certain scenario did not allow an issue of causation to be separately addressed. Since the finding or negating of *occidere* in a specific sequence of events did not involve a theoretical causation test, it was not at all a happy turn to read modern concepts like 'overtaking causation' or 'interruption of the causal flow' into our texts. If our texts are read as disquisitions of causation issues, they are not simply rephrased in a universal – and hence harmlessly neutral – terminological framework. Rather, reading the texts as causation essays distorts and obscures their original meaning. Dismissing Julian's deliberations because he did not have a proper grasp of the concept of 'aborted causation' is clear exegetical misconduct, by any standard of historical research. As the Roman jurists did not dissect the act of killing into separate elements, the modern concept of 'imputation', or 'attribution', of an effect or of the completion of the overall statutorily required act, is equally unsuitable to furthering our understanding of the classical lawyers' reasoning: leaving the cases of noxal liability aside, the idea that a killing action could be attributed to someone other than the actor, by virtue of a legal imputation, is absent in our texts, and indeed in all *lex Aquilia* sources of which I am aware.

The attempts made since the 19th century to read fine-spun causation problems into our texts have severely hampered a full understanding of the Roman jurists' decisions. There is no need to scrutinise here the concepts of aborted or interrupted or overtaking causation as such. Whether these concepts are intellectually valuable contributions can only be decided within the framework of a specific tort system, and the precise role this system assigns to a causation requirement. Suffice it to say that Roman lawyers did not rely on such concepts to determine the statutory Chapter I Aquilian liability.

Under the terms of the *lex Aquilia*, mortally wounding did not constitute killing. This should go without saying (Pollock). There is not a single Roman jurist who could be credited with the notion that attempted murder counted as murder, provided that the wound inflicted is truly lethal. For them, attempted murder was not (yet) murder, even if the attacker had managed to mortally wound the victim. It did turn into murder once the lethality of the wound materialised in an actual death. *L.*15.1 shows that mortally wounding does not necessarily lead to a liability for killing: 'there's many a slip 'twixt the cup and the lip'. If it had been possible to bring a statutory Chapter I action on the basis of a lethal wound alone, interesting complications would have arisen, for example if the slave died from another cause during the proceedings, or after judgment had been rendered and damages paid. There is no trace of such complications, and indeed the texts dealing with how a subsequent death impacts a pending law suit for wounding (which has turned out to be actually mortal) are direct contrary evidence.[397]

*L.*21.1 cannot be taken as evidence that Julian (or Ulpian, who approved) supported the view that an action for killing could be brought on the basis of lethal wounding alone. The discussion reported in *l.*21.1 is about the reckoning of the evaluation period, as a measure of damages issue, not about the accrual of the Chapter I action. Accrual of action – the earliest moment an action can be successfully brought in court – and the relevant time period for the evaluation of damages are distinct legal topics. If Julian had been of the opinion that a statutory Chapter I action had already accrued with lethal wounding alone, the general rule for the reckoning of the one-year period would have applied. One could argue therefore that pointing to a special rule regarding the evaluation period for cases with a temporal hiatus between the infliction of a lethal wound and the ensuing death indeed confirms that the action accrued only at the moment when the slave died.

Roman jurists addressed a number of second-order issues which arose out of the occasional hiatus between the affliction of a mortal wound and the death of the slave. (1) As a natural world occurrence, the killing action can be finished after the mortally wounded slave – the initiated killing act still pending completion – has been set free or made over to someone else before he dies: Ulp 18 ad ed D.9.2.15.1. The action under the *lex Aquilia* in such cases accrued for the person who was *dominus* at the time the slave was mortally wounded.[398] A variant of this issue is the case that

[397] Ulp 57 ad Sab D.9.2.46 and Iul 86 dig D.9.2.47.

[398] Faber (n 77) 903; Ankum (n 201) 345; Dalla (n 187) 171 f.

the mortally wounded slave becomes heir to the owner before he dies: Marc 21 dig D.9.2.36.1. (2) It was a matter of doubt, and in fact of controversy, whether for the reckoning of the Chapter I year the completion of the *occidere* action was backdated to the moment of the wounding, provided that the slave later died from this wound. Julian thought so, while Celsus took the death as the controlling moment in time: Ulp 18 ad ed D.9.2.21.1. (3) Ulp 57 ad Sab D.9.2.46 and Iul 86 dig D.9.2.47 address the matter of how the early bringing of an action under Chapter III influences the position under Chapter I, once the slave dies. (4) Most importantly to us, in such cases it was not sufficient to just find that the slave was dead at the end of the day; his death must have come about in such a manner as to complete the first offender's pending *occidere* action. In the absence of a 'matching' death – if a tear in the film prevents the action from being completed – there is no *occidere*. This is what Ulp 18 ad ed D.9.2.15.1 is all about.

II. ULP 18 AD ED D.9.2.15.1 AND ULP 18 AD ED D.9.2.11.1–3

1. ULP 18 AD ED D.9.2.15.1

In Ulp 18 ad ed D.9.2.15.1, the actual death does not qualify as an event which completes the unfinished performance of the act of *occidere*, as begun by the attacker. There is a tear in the film, so to speak. The death which has overtaken the victim does not 'match' the wound inflicted by the attacker. The initially attempted act has proceeded to the mortal wounding of the slave, but no further. The killing action remains forever inchoate. No elaborate theory was required to justify or explain why a mismatch between the actual death and the mortal wound inflicted by the attacker ruled out a direct liability under Chapter I. It is an obvious consequence of the statutory requirement of an *occidere* act: it is simply impossible to find here a graphic arc of action extending without interruption from the attacker's blow to, and only completed by, the victim's death. That, and that alone, constituted 'slaying' – a straightforward, natural understanding of the controlling word used in the *lex*.[399] Since the *occidere* act is not

[399] The natural arc of action which constitutes *occidere* is also incomplete when there is a suitable endpoint, but the action has not started in terms of a killing. A non-mortal wound leads to the slave's death because he has been treated negligently after the attack (Paul 22 ad ed D.9.2.30.4): in the absence of a graphic *occidere* act, there can be no liability on the strength of a Chapter I direct action. Since causation does not seem

accomplished and no liability triggered, there is no need to artificially negate direct Chapter I liability on the strength of deliberations like the 'interruption of the causal nexus' or similar concepts. There is no evidence that such concepts were at all in play in the Roman jurists' handling of *occidere*.

The *occidere* act being aborted, Ulpian supports basing liability on Chapter III, as proposed by Celsus. The attacker is held liable *quasi de vulnerato*. Since *vulnerare* was not a term used in Chapter III, only *frangere* or *rumpere* could be the controlling word here, with *rumpere* already widened to *corrumpere*.[400] *Vulnerare* was used when a slave suffered the *corruptio*. We find the concept of *quasi corrumpere* employed in a number of cases, and the characteristic seems to lie in a difficulty with presenting the object as literally torn asunder: dirtying of clothes (Ulp 18 ad ed D.9.2.27.18), mixing sand into grain (Ulp 18 ad ed D.9.2.27.20), causing a female slave or a mare to miscarriage (Ulp 18 ad ed D.9.2.27.22), sinking a ship by drilling a hole in the hull, thus destroying the cargo (Ulp 18 ad ed D.9.2.27.24). In each of these cases, the perpetrator has undoubtedly illegally meddled with the owner's object and is held liable, based on Chapter III, although the object of his delict cannot be produced in court in a torn-apart state. It may be on a similar rationale that Ulpian proposes holding the first attacker liable under Chapter III *quasi de vulnerato*, since the drowned slave cannot be brought into court to have his/her wound inspected and evaluated. Be that as it may, the *quasi*, here as in the other texts, signals an affirmation of the direct (statutory) action. Using an anachronistic term, one might dub it a case of extensive interpretation. Loosely translated, the *quasi* can be read as 'by way of interpretation'.[401]

Ulpian brings in the case that the mortally wounded slave dies after being set free or conveyed to a new owner. He asks, why the person who was the owner at the moment of wounding is allowed to bring an action

---

doubtful, a causation analysis might trigger a search for elements that allow liability to be negated; the idea of contributory negligence could come into view. Nothing in the text hints at such a turn. In this case, the infliction of a non-mortal wound does not seem to merit a liability for *causam mortis praestare*, at least if one relies on an argument *ex silentio*: the *causa* which the attacker provided could not as such cause death. Liability for wounding is an unproblematic given. Cf Ulp 18 ad ed D.9.2.25pr for a similar mismatch, concerning the Aquilian *actio confessoria*.

400 Cf Gai 3.217.

401 *Quasi* can also be used with respect to the element of the *in factum* variant, i.e. *causam mortis praestare* (D.9.2.11.1): here, you can have borderline cases as well. *Quasi* is not used, however, to indicate the necessity of switching from the direct action to the praetorian *in factum* variant.

under Chapter I, while no such action lies for the owner whose wounded slave dies in the collapse of a building. One can only say that the slave has been killed by you, when you wounded him, *quod mortuo demum apparuit*: 'which only becomes apparent by his death'. The deed may long be done, but whether it can be qualified as killing depends on whether later on death does or does not ensue. The alteration in ownership does not prevent the completion of the killing act *in natura*; it does not constitute a film tear. Rather, the natural dying process continues and leads to a 'matching' death.

Quite a number of interpreters have found that Ulpian's decision is contingent on an evidentiary gap (Pernice, Hart and Honoré, and others). They see the reason for Ulpian's negation of Chapter I liability in the slave owner's loss of the crucial means of evidence: the slave's body, which would have to be used to prove the lethality of the wound, has vanished under the collapsed building or drowned in the high seas. It is not the case that the ensuing death is just a means of proof of the lethality of the wound, which, if proven, would as such already satisfy the statutory Chapter I requirement: the death ensuing from the wound is necessary to qualify the attacker's act as *occidere*. There is no support in the text for the idea that for Ulpian a liability for killing would have been incurred by mortally wounding alone, but here simply could not be made the basis of a successful *lex Aquilia* lawsuit because the plaintiff could not prove the mortality of the wound to a judge. If such an idea were at play, Ulpian's decision would need to be qualified, in that a Chapter I liability could successfully be asserted if only the owner would be able to prove in retrospect the lethality of the wound beyond any doubt prior to the slave being killed by the collapse of a building. Supplementing the text in this manner is an act of creative writing. The text expressly drives home the essential point: you not only need to see the slave dead – his death must have come about in a manner which appears as a completion of the attack, in order to qualify the attacker's action as killing. The decisive 'mismatch' here is obvious and not overshadowed by any uncertainty as to the facts of the case.

There is no basis then, either in the text or in its logic, to limit this decision to cases where there is only a reduced likelihood of ensuing death, in order to ensure 'harmony' with other texts, most notably with *l.*51. Nothing in the text supports interpretations which turn on different degrees of lethality. Even if the slave's death were a prognostic certainty, as a result of the wound already inflicted, the scenario of *l.*15.1 rules out any chance that *occidere* can ever be completed. From the point of view of logic, it is rather the *a fortiori* argument which could be made: whatever the prognostic probability of an ensuing death, the liability can never more be upgraded to Chapter I.

The text, as it has been transmitted, does not address the ensuing measure of damages aspect. Wounding someone mortally, in all likelihood, would allow the market value to be awarded, since the lethal wound immediately brings the slave's value down to zero. It will be necessary to revert to *l*.15.1, and its mention of Julian in particular, in our discussion of *l*.51.[402]

2. ULP 18 AD ED D.9.2.11.1–3

a) Si alius tenuit – cum sit poena *(§§1 and 2)*

Many authors have assumed that the chain of decisions in *l*.11.1–3 is altogether unproblematic, free of surprises, conforming to legal common sense. They may have underrated this passage. *L*.11 needs to be taken as a continuous comment, the *principium* and §§1–4 dealing with the involvement of several suspects in one single incident which ends in a slave's death. Our division into paragraphs is of medieval origin and should not detract from the *Leitmotif* permeating the whole lemma (Schulz, Piro).[403]

L.11.1 deals with two criminals, one holding the slave while the other slays him. They are both liable; however, only the one who slew committed an act of *occidere*, while the other is liable on the strength of an *actio in factum* for *mortis causam praebere*. If one assumes that both wrongdoers acted in concert, one can conclude that no concept of joint tortfeasorship was in play: if a concept of joint tortfeasors had been in the ambit of the *lex Aquilia*, it would not have been necessary, in the case of *l*.11.1, to base the liability of the perpetrator who holds the slave on the *in factum* variant for *mortis causam praestare*.

L.11.2, beginning with *sed si*, is very much an associative continuation: here multiple attackers have beaten a slave to death. As in the preceding case, Ulpian is addressing the events of one single incident; otherwise the distinction taken up from Julian would not work at all. According to Julian, whose view is approved by Ulpian, we need to distinguish whether or not we can identify one attacker who administered the ultimately deadly blow.

---

402 Below p 135 f.

403 Ulpian continues to deal with variations of the same thematic subject matter (one incident/several attackers) in the following §§4–6.

If not, Julian supported holding all attackers liable under Chapter I. We shall return to this proposition once we have looked closer at the variant of the identifiable killer.

If we can identify the one deadly blow, that very actor is statutorily liable for killing. While there is no express explanation as to the other wrongdoers' liabilities, the statement that the attacker who dealt the deadly blow is liable (statutorily) under Chapter I implies that this is not the case for the other attackers. Without theoretical ado, the *occidere* requirement works in a way which gives prevalence to the last killing act. The attacker who can be identified as having finished off the victim with his deadly blow, and he alone, is 'the' killer. He, and he alone, attracts statutory liability under Chapter I, to the exclusion of all other attackers from the same liability. Once the successful killer has landed his deadly blow, others blows my follow, but any further blow can only hit a corpse and hence cannot qualify as killing act.[404] The one accomplished killing act prevents all others from becoming killers on the basis of both earlier and later blows.

Regarding Chapter I of the *lex Aquilia*, if one act of homicide can be found to have been performed by an identified killer, no other act, performed by another during the same incident, can qualify as *occidere*, too. We must not view this exclusionary effect as a fancy doctrinal oddity, a 'theory' superimposed on the terms of the statute: it is rather a plain consequence of a liability based on a conduct, the performance of which ends in, and thus requires, an event which can occur only once. In this respect the *occidere* analysis works in stark contrast to all causation analyses. While the *occidere* analysis is directly geared to – and capable of – determining the one and only killer, causality tests will at the outset throw up a multitude of causative agents. It is a typical task of causality theories then to filter out causers and by this filtration to establish which of the many causes should trigger a liability. No such process is needed if one looks only for the one decisive *occidere* act.

Let us briefly dwell on the question of why no other liability for the rest of the gang is in play. If we look back at the case set out in §1, the attacker who holds the slave is instrumental for the other attacker's ability to administer a deadly blow, and as an aider is held liable using the *in factum* variant for *causam mortis praestare* (Chapter I). In §2, the prior blow(s) cannot have been a contribution to the last blow's deadliness,

---

404 The rest are not killers, *quia non hominem, sed cadaver vulnerarunt*, to use a phrase Carpzov loaned from Patristic Christology (cf c Iul Imp 4.47), B Carpzow, *Practica nova imperialis Saxonica rerum criminalium* (1677) Qu 25 n 32.

because if that had been the case, the first attacker(s) would have been held liable with a (Chapter I) *actio in factum*. We have to assume that the ultimate blow does not, for its deadly effect, depend on the previous blows administered by the others. Rather, amidst a hail of other blows, one blow is placed which is deadly. The remaining issue, whether other attackers could perhaps be held liable under Chapter III, is the very question addressed in the next sentence (§3), where Ulpian goes on to consider and ultimately assert that there is a Chapter III liability, based on an identifiable wound suffered by another attacker, thus supplementing the Chapter I liability of the killer himself. Regarding §2, however, a particular wound inflicted by another attacker is not part of the scenario.

Summing up the situation of the identifiable killer in §2, we have to assume that none of the perpetrators involved – apart from the one identified killer – meets any liability for the attack on the slave. Identifying the actual killer thus exonerates all other attackers involved in the very same incident from any form of Aquilian liability: there is one incident, ending in the slave's death, and his ultimate death is 'used up' to complete the one determinable *occidere* action. Commentators who overlook the fact that, on the strength of the last-act mechanism, all other attackers escape liability could not in the past and cannot now fully understand the ensuing sentence (§3) and the underlying cause for Celsus's concern.

We return to the scenario where it is impossible to single out the one who delivered the decisive blow. Modern lawyers tend to take Julian's decision to hold all attackers liable, if none can be singled out as the effective killer, as unquestionably good law, but we do so because we are accustomed to the concept of joint enterprise liability based on the consent to a joint action plan and some contribution to its implementation. Julian's decision to hold all attackers liable, however, cannot depend on the notion of a joint action plan, agreed by all as the basis for their respective actions. Nothing in the text speaks of or hints at such a requirement. On the contrary, if a joint action plan were in any way the basis of Aquilian liability, the alternative scenario where one ultimate killer can indeed be singled out could not be decided differently from the one where this is not the case.[405] There was no separate 'joint (co-ordinated) action' variant of Aquilian liability.[406]

405 It is not suggested that Ulpian envisaged the case where unconnected attackers just happen to hit on the same victim as several concurrent tortfeasors. The attackers may or may not be taken as having acted in a co-ordinated manner: that element is just not relevant for the determination of the Chapter I liability/liabilities.

406 Ulp 18 ad ed D.9.2.9.3 highlights the absence of the concept of a statutory liability based on joint tortfeasorship: someone who leads a slave into an ambush, where

Moreover, the idea is absent altogether that, by virtue of a joint action plan, someone could be the genuine performer of an *occidere* act even though he did not himself physically bring about the victim's death.[407]

There is no extra variant for aiding and abetting, either: aiders come under the *in factum* variant for *causam mortis praestare* (*l*.11.1). Only one type of wrongdoer qualifies for direct statutory liability under Chapter I, i.e. the person who in reality by his/her own hands performs an accomplished *occidere* act. Julian did not see a need to activate the *in factum* variant. Julian's affirmation of a direct Chapter I liability for all attackers implies that the actual death which the slave meets is legally taken to complete simultaneously all attackers' individual actions, so that the judge can rightly say for each and every one: *(quasi) occidit*. The *quasi*, here as in *l*.15.1, may signal that the case falls just outside the limits of the *occidere* requirement of the *lex*, if strictly construed, but is close enough still to merit a direct Chapter I liability. There is no need, the *quasi* implies, to go over to the *actio in factum*, which would allow and also require sidestepping the concept of *occidere* altogether. All of this is reported by Ulpian without hesitation, suggesting unqualified approval. In *l*.51.1 Julian attributes the same solution, which avoids a zero-compensation result, to the *veteres*. The solution may thus predate the availability of the praetorian *actio in factum* for *mortis causam praestare*.

A last half-sentence addresses the question of solidarity. This brief disquisition is not an abstract statement regarding Aquilian liability in general, which would not be ideally placed here. Since for the given case the liability of all is brought in to avoid a zero-compensation result, one might indeed harbour the idea that – deviating from standard practice – payment on the part of one might here relieve all others. However, Ulpian rejects this idea in view of the penal nature of the action. Due to the cumulative liability of multiple killers, the slave's owner is better off if no specific killer can be identified, in which case all attackers become cumulatively liable.

---

another kills him, can be held liable on the strength of an *actio in factum* (Ofilius), although both perpetrators acted in pursuance of a joint action plan.

407 If one and the same killing act was administered by the joint action of several attackers, they were all held liable (Ulp 18 ad ed D.9.2.11.4): when several attackers dump a heavy beam onto the victim, there is but one indivisible killing act, which is performed by the co-attackers together. This is not a case of joint enterprise liability. All attackers have in fact together performed one and the same indivisible killing act. To use a phrase coined by Labeo in another context, it is an *opus quod a pluribus pro indiviso factum est* (Ulp 71 ad ed D.43.24.15.2). There is no concept in play that every party to a joint action plan, whatever his/her specific factual contribution, is held legally accountable for the acts committed separately and individually by any of the others.

b) Celsus scribit – et est probabilius *(§3)*

*L.*11.3 has to be read as a seamless continuation of the two preceding paragraphs. We are dealing with another case of a brawl, or a scenario similar to one. Ulpian lifts this case and its analysis from Celsus. Celsus envisaged one singular incident, involving (at least) two attackers. One of the attackers (*alius*, not *alter*) is identified as the one who unquestionably delivered a deadly blow (*ex alio vulnere periit*), thus the mortal wound inflicted by an earlier attacker cannot materialise in the victim's death. In order to avoid any misunderstanding: a one-incident scenario is characterised by a unity of place and time; it does not require that everything happens simultaneously: there may still be a 'before' and 'after' (*postea*) in one and the same incident.

Since the actual death is attributed one-to-one to the later blow, at first sight all others appear to be free of liability, as could be seen from §2. One is led to ask: does the identification of the one single deadly blow, by virtue of the prevalence of the last act, exonerate even an earlier co-attacker who had already administered a blow which itself would have led to the victim's death? It must have been Celsus's concern not to let this earlier attacker, who had already mortally wounded the slave, walk away without any liability, enjoying immunity on the strength of the principle that, in relation to Chapter I, if one act of murder was committed by an identified murderer, no one else's action could qualify as *occidere* with regard to the same murder. Celsus pondered two options, taking as the basis of liability either a *quasi occidere* or a *quasi vulnerare*. The *quasi* indicates that neither was seen as a clear-cut case. Neither alternative, however, would imply a move to the *in factum* variant of the respective statutory action. On the contrary, by employing the concept of *quasi*, the discussion is focussed on a liberal applicability of the direct actions. These are the scruples which may have stood in Celsus's way: statutory Chapter I liability is 'monopolised' on the strength of the last and deadly blow, and for the *in factum* variant it is impossible to assert that the first attacker provided a *causa mortis*. As to Chapter III, one may hesitate with regard to the transient nature of the wound inflicted: we are looking at a one-incident scenario, which ends when a blow, attributable one-to-one to a specific attacker, kills the slave.[408]

---

[408] Sequences of wounding and killing are analysed in Gai 7 ad ed prov D.9.2.32.1. While an interval between the two acts gives rise to two actions, one under Chapter III and another under Chapter I, merely transient wounds which result in death do not constitute separate causes of action under Chapter III: the Chapter I liability absorbs

Celsus, however, advocated squeezing in a Chapter III liability, regardless of the limited time-span in which the slave's existence was overshadowed by the mortal wound.[409]

As to the measure of damages, the text is silent. Wounding someone mortally should allow the market value to be awarded, since the lethal wound brings the slave's value down to zero. We have no indication that the sum would have to be discounted in view of the slave's limited life-span after the attack. Although the measure of the Chapter III liability may well have been geared towards the slave's full market value, it remained compensation for wounding, not for killing. Even if the slave's owner was effectively granted fairly similar, or in fact identical, sums in pursuance of both actions, these were not two liabilities for 'killing': the one-year rule applied to the second attacker, but not to the first. It is not helpful to call the difference 'minimal' (*contra*: Gerkens): even minimal differences matter. To round off this case, there is no reason to presume that there is a solidarity joining (and thus cushioning) the two attacker's liabilities; rather, both have to be taken to be concurrently liable. Both perpetrators are guilty of different delicts.

Celsus tried to take the edge off the last-act doctrine, in the case where a would-be killer sees his almost successful attack frustrated by a swifter co-attacker's effective killing blow. By holding the earlier attacker, who had inflicted a deadly wound, liable under Chapter III, Celsus countermands the exonerating effect (regarding Chapter I) of what we would call a last-act doctrine. One might even find that the Chapter III liability is here instrumentalised as a substitute for the wanting liability for attempted murder.

Celsus opted for the less harsh of two possible correctives, holding the earlier attacker liable for *quasi vulnerare*, rather than for *quasi occidere*. Focussing on this preference, Celsus has been understood as taking a restrictive position. In truth, Celsus advocated liability in relation to the frustrated attacker, where, we must assume, there previously was none. In doing so, he chose the slightly less harsh option as the gap-filler. Last but not least, there is no reason to assume that the word *mortifere* in *l.*11.3 is used in any other but its ordinary meaning.

---

the liability for the infliction of the transient wounds from which death ensued (cf Iul 86 dig D.9.2.47). These cases deal with the liability/liabilities of one and the same attacker, whereas in the case of *l.*11.3 wound and death are accomplishments of different attackers, who, however, go after the victim in one and the same incident.

409 As to the use of *quasi vulnerare*, see already above p 117, regarding *l.*15.1.

We shall return to the Marcellus reference, and Ulpian's characterisation of Celsus's decision as *probabilius*, when we later on confront *l*.11.3 with *l*.51.[410] For the time being, it is sufficient to record that Marcellus and Ulpian approved of Celsus's solution and that *l*.11.3 does not mention a contrarian position. At this point, a brief comparison of the cases in *l*.11.3 and *l*.15.1 is in order. *L*.11.3 deals with the death resulting from one singular incident which involves two (or more) attackers who are simultaneously in action, whereas the event which in *l*.15.1 eventually kills the slave appears unrelated to the earlier single-person attack. Most importantly, the Chapter III liability in *l*.15.1 comes in as a substitute for a Chapter I liability, for which the requirement is not met. This ensures that there is at least one person liable, whereas in *l*.11.3 the Chapter III liability of the earlier attacker merely supplements a Chapter I liability of the ultimate killer, which is an unproblematic given. This squeezing in of an additional Chapter III liability, alongside a straightforward Chapter I liability, may have appeared more questionable than the Chapter III liability in the case of *l*.15.1, where it is indispensable to see that the owner gets some compensation in the first place. In the latter case, it may have seemed a tad easier than in the case of *l*.11.3 to hit the attacker with a Chapter III liability, especially because here the slave, mortally wounded, must have lived on for a while. Indeed, the atmospheric elements of caution which accompany Ulpian's report of Celsus's solution (*quasi, probabilius*) have no counterpart in *l*.15.1.

III. IUL 86 DIG D.9.2.51 REVISITED

1. THE PROVENANCE OF THE TEXT

Julian's *Digesta* were written probably over a lengthy stretch of years, to be 'published' in the middle of the second century CE, perhaps a little earlier.[411] Within Julian's *Digesta*, the fragment was part of the comments

---

410 Below p 136 ff.

411 Points of entry for biographical research: (1) T Giaro, s v 'Iulianus [1]: L. Octavius Cornelius P. Salvius I. Aemilianus, Roman jurist, 2nd cent. AD', *Brill's New Pauly*, <http://dx.doi.org/10.1163/1574-9347_bnp_e317640>, accessed online 21 October 2017; (2) D Liebs, *HLL* vol 4 §414; (3) R Baumann, *Lawyers and politics in the early Roman empire* (1989) 237 ff; (4) F Wieacker, *Römische Rechtsgeschichte. Zweiter Abschnitt* (2006) 99 ff, 422 (bibliography); all with ample references. For Julian's Digesta cf E Bund, 'Salvius Iulianus; Leben und Werk', *ANRW* vol 2/15 – Principat (1976) 431.

on the statutory/edictal word *occidere* (Rodger, Zahn). We have no reason to presume that the text of *l.*51 was patched together by the compilers, who would have used material which originally related to different factual scenarios or to different questions of law (as pondered by Powell, Schebitz or Winkler). Rather, we are faced with a continuous text, structured according to the standard literary *responsum* scheme: facts of the case (*ita – decessit*), *quaestio* (*quaero an – possit*), and *responsum* (*respondit – fin*). The case dealt with by Julian did not have to be a real-life case. The element of the intervening inheritance rather smacks of a hypothetical and this points to a teaching environment. There is little in the textual state of *l.*51 that would trigger drastic doubts regarding the text's authenticity. The numerous attacks on the authenticity of *l.*51 have been fuelled mostly by incomprehension of the legal content, not to speak of the climate of distrust which has spread from the interpolationist authors over much of 20th-century scholarship.

2. *ITA VULNERATUS – LEGE AQUILIA TENERI* (*PRINCIPIUM*)

It is the gravest possible misunderstanding of Julian to attribute to him the view that by mortally wounding alone the act of *occidere* was already committed and liability for killing engaged, regardless of whether the wound then actually resulted in the slave's death or not.[412] Julian did not relinquish the requirement of an ensuing 'matching' death as the endpoint of the act. Nothing in the extensive reasoning set out by Julian supports this idea. On the contrary, Julian's whole reasoning seems an attempt to prove that his solution is compliant with the traditional handling of the statutory term *occidere*. In particular, Julian's invocation of the *veteres* is incompatible with the idea that he could have turned radical iconoclast.

If one sets aside the fancy idea of an extravagant break with orthodox *lex Aquilia* doctrine, finding two Chapter I liabilities in Julian's case could only be supported if one and the same death was taken to be the endpoint of two independent killing acts. Two arcs of killing acts meet in the common endpoint of the same actual death. The same real death is thus put to a dual use: it perfects two killing acts; it gives rise to two liabilities

412 Brinz, Jolowicz, Lawson, Schindler, Rastätter, Röhle, Hausmaninger, Willvonseder, Nörr, Winiger, Gerkens, Scott, Mendelson, Zahn, Finkenauer and others; *contra*: Pollock, Desanti and others.

under Chapter I. The last-act doctrine is not an impediment here, since the two actions did not originate in the same incident. In no uncertain terms, we are informed that the two attacks are separated in time: *medio tempore* and *ex intervallo* (Dalla, Desanti).

Both attackers are on an equal footing, as the death must be seen, from Julian's perspective, as completing both their actions in the same manner. The situation cannot be envisaged as allowing an unquestionable one-to-one attribution of the actual death to either of the attacks (Zasius, Luden, Vangerow, Monro, Kortmann). The victim dies 'having been hit by another', not 'by another's blow' (Buckland, Kortmann). In *l*.51.2, Julian expressly argues with the impossibility of singling out one attacker over the other (*nec facile – teneatur*). It is the very element which allows Julian to rely, in *l*.51.1, on the case of multiple attackers wounding the slave, *ut non appareat, cuius ictu perisset* (Donellus, Vangerow). An immitigable uncertainty is part and parcel of the scenario set out by Julian: both attackers' contributions to the actual death cannot be disentangled to allow a one-to-one attribution.

Is it problematic to see the actual death as the endpoint perfecting both attacks? It is a hard case; otherwise Julian would not have provided such an elaborate essay on why the answer should be positive. In Julian's view, the actual death is indeed fit to complete the prior *occidere* action, too, which is only brought forward in time due to the second attack. According to Julian's view, this mere bringing forward in time, as a result of the second offence, does not destroy the adequacy of the actual death as the matching endpoint that completes the first offender's killing act (Grueber). To support this, Julian stresses the requirement that the initial wounding would have resulted in the slave's death 'with certainty'. This is a condition for disregarding the inextricable interplay with the effects of the second wound and thus allowing the actual death to be considered as a completion of the first as of the second wounding. The second attack has not coloured the actual death to an extent which would stand in the way of seeing it as the completion of the first attack. Taking the actual death as the endpoint of the second attacker's action must be regarded as doubtful, too. Otherwise the death could be attributed one-to-one to the second attacker's action. Julian, however, advocates setting aside these doubts.

The reasons Julian gives for his result in the *principium* are straightforward: he stresses the holistic nature of the *occidere* act which triggers Aquilian liability (Chapter I), which does not permit bringing just any causation of a death into the ambit of the statute, even if common-language usage could suggest this. The wrongdoer's bodily force must bring about the deadly state of the victim *quasi manu*. On the other hand, it is not required that the death follows instantaneously. All this is well in line with our general understanding of the Aquilian liability under Chapter I.

The accomplishment of the *occidere* act, for Julian as for all the lawyers of his time, is based on the death the slave in fact meets. This is here true of the first as of the second attacker. The first attacker's liability is not based on an inchoate act. The notion that for the first attacker only an inchoate act can be found has given rise to different theories, which 'explain' how an inchoate act can be sufficient to count as *occidere*. The earliest of these ideas was proposed by Baldus de Ubaldis: the Chapter I liability which Julian finds for the first attacker implied a legal fiction. For those who see the text from a causation-theory angle, Julian acknowledged a hypothetical causation which allowed an inchoate killing act to be completed by an unreal, imagined or fictitious death which has not in reality ensued, but which would have resulted from the wound provided only that the causal nexus had not been 'broken': a constructive death must complete the *occidere* action. Last but not least, there are the many authors who see Julian as an outsider who subscribed to the minority view that for *occidere* an act of mortal wounding was sufficient.[413] This approach simply does away with any causation-theory superstructure. All these ideas have not enhanced our understanding of Julian's actual reasoning. There is no support in the text for the concept that the perpetrator's liabilities are linked to separate endpoints of a markedly different ontological status, the real death for the second attacker, and an unreal death for the first attacker, a purely imagined death which in a hypothetical world would have materialised as an effect of the lethal wound. Perhaps it is correct that Roman legal thought in general was reluctant to pay attention to hypothetical alternative scenarios, brought in specifically as a means to legally dissect the real world and its flow of events (Gerkens). There may have been deep-seated, philosophical reasons why that was so (Sirks), but addressing those is beyond the scope of this humble contribution.

3. *IDQUE – IUDICAVERUNT* (§1)

Why does Julian bring in the case of multiple slayers with uncertain contributions to the death? Many authors have seen Julian's train of thought derailing here, betraying a muddled thinking that does not keep cases of 'interrupted' causation apart from cases of 'alternative' causation. One of

413 See n 412.

the more common interpolationist hypotheses sees §1 as sandwiched in between the *principium* and §2 by Justinian's compilers. Rather than taking exception to the presumed change from one causation topic to another, the flow from the *principium* to §1 suggests that the reasoning is not about causation and its doctrine at all. In the case of multiple slayers one and the same event of death is used as a consummation/completion of several killing acts, thus overcoming the inability to dissect the intermingling attacks into neatly attributable contributions of individual attackers.[414] The case Julian has started with is different first and foremost insofar as there is a noticeable time lag between the two offences (two incidents), whereas the multiple slayers in *l*.11.2 seem to act more or less simultaneously. Since Julian is not approaching the issue from a causation angle, it is absurd to blame him for not realising that he is using a case of 'alternative causation' to support his solution for a case of 'overtaking causation'. Julian's reasoning does not broach the issue of a joint action plan, and it is not helpful to ask for specific objective or subjective requirements for joint tortfeasorship (*contra*: Eisele, Pacchioni, Rastätter). There is no such concept in play.

From a legal point of view, Julian's dual use of one and the same real-life death event as an endpoint of two distinct killing acts is not at all incompatible with his view that for the two killing acts different moments in time mark the starting point for the evaluation period for the damages due.

There is another reason why the comparison has struck many as unconvincing. The liability of all tortfeasors, referred to in *l*.51.1 as well as in *l*.11.2, seems commonsensical today, whereas Julian's solution for sequentially and independently operating attackers is taken to be rather eccentric. One considers these cases to be incommensurable, since a joint action plan, which for some is the assumed basis for each and every attacker's liability in *l*.51.1/*l*.11.2, is missing from Julian's scenario in *l*.51pr. But as we have seen, the jurists have not relied on the idea of a joint action plan as the *ratio decidendi* for the cases addressed in *l*.11.2 and *l*.51.1. If a joint action plan was not the *ratio decidendi* for the decision in the case in *l*.11.2 and *l*.51.1, then the solution set out in *l*.11.2 was just as bold as the one advanced for the case in *l*.51pr. It is remarkable that this decision has been accepted without much ado as a no-nonsense solution, in stark contrast to the one proposed in *l*.51pr. Both solutions use the actual death of the slave to construe several killing actions as accomplished, and they do so in order to avoid the result that in spite of mortal attacks, ending in the victim's death, none of the attackers would be held liable. In this

414 See above p 119 f, with regard to D.9.2.11.2.

respect, both solutions resemble each other. It is perfectly understandable that Julian, in his *l*.51 essay, relies on the decision also reported in *l*.11.2, especially if it had been introduced by the *veteres* already.[415] It is an argument that 'works'.

4. *AESTIMATIO AUTEM – EAM SUSTULISSE* (§2)

The measure of damages aspect for Julian is in play with regard to the consideration of the inheritance in determining the amount owed by the second killer under Chapter I. The wording is plain: here, the higher sum owed by the second killer is expressly based on the increased market value of a slave who has been named heir (*quanti homo plurimi venire poterit*). It is not necessary to assume that the inheritance has fallen due before the second killer's strike (*contra*: Ankum). The text makes no statement as to the relationship between the two liabilities under Chapter I. Both attackers must become liable cumulatively, not because this is the general rule for liability in *eadem causa* (Ernst Levy), but simply because in Julian's view we are dealing with two independent deeds, not one. As each is liable for his own, independent killing act, there cannot be a joint liability, which would override the subtle difference as to the respective measure of damages, highlighted by Julian.

Again and again, Julian has been faulted for the subsequent argument that one should avoid letting both offenders off the hook (*quod si quis absurde – potius*). I side with all authors (Gerkens, Willvonseder, MacCormack and Giaro, for example) who read this as a serious deliberation and not just as a rhetorical and somewhat fishy *argumentum ad absurdum*. Julian's concern is the possible qualification of the actual death as the event, which, as a 'matching' death, could complete either of the two killing actions. If here the uncertainty as to the overlay of effects from both attacks prevents one from seeing the actual death as completing the first attacker's killing act, one would equally have to negate the qualification of the actual death as the matching endpoint of the second offender's killing attack. Therefore, a strict insistence on a specific death that evidently 'matches' and completes the action that had reached the stage of a mortal wounding would indeed point to a solution where none of the attackers were held liable for killing.

There is no way, Julian thinks, that one perpetrator could be preferred over the other. In a case where two subsequent attacks have affected the

415 In *l*.51.1 the liability of the multiple slayers is not based on *quasi occidere*, as in Ulp 18 ad ed D.9.2.11.2.

victim in a manner which does not allow the separation and individual attribution of the effects of respective injuries on the victim's body, legal logic therefore reduces the options to holding either both perpetrators liable for killing, or none of them. Of these two remaining options, one could tend to absolve both attackers of liability as killers, since for both of them it is doubtful whether the statutory requirement is really and unquestionably met. To overcome this stalemate, the public policy argument is brought in. In view of the penal function of Aquilian liability, one is nudged to accept the dual Chapter I liability, even if a legal case for two acquittals could be made.

Anyone who reads *l*.51 and *l*.11.3 as conflicting statements, exchanged in a dialogue of quarrelsome legal writers, must be tempted to see Julian as conceding that strict legal logic points to the very solution he is supposed to reject. Julian is taken to say: 'For the case at hand, my opponent Celsus has the legal logic on his side, in that he limits the first attacker's liability to Chapter III, but I propose to override legal logic for the common good.' Read without bias, the text dismisses the option of holding only one of the two attackers liable for killing without much ado: *nec facile constitui possit, uter potius lege teneatur*. Considerably more momentum is given to the argumentative effort directed against the option of finding neither attacker liable for killing (Gerkens). This includes the *impunitas* argument and the final example of the stolen beam where the *subtilis ratio* could suggest that none of the perpetrators has 'stolen'.

Since Julian is rejecting the result that none of the attackers is held liable for killing, the *impunitas* argument is indeed spot-on. In evaluating the role of the *utilitas communis* argument, not enough attention has been given to the progress made by systematic reviews of this and similar terms, notably the study by Leptien. The *utilitas communis* argument here (as in other situations) works as a tie-breaker between two legally feasible solutions: either both attackers are liable for killing, or none of them. The recourse to the *utilitas communis* in Julian's text does not override legal logic from beginning to end; it does not legitimise a solution which as such would have no support in law (Backhaus). With the public policy angle, Julian does not turn upside down what he would see as the proper legal analysis of the case. There is not a hint of a concession to the effect that the combination of Chapter I/Chapter III liabilities, in Julian's own view, would be the 'correct' solution for the case set out in the *principium*, if only one were to stick to the *subtilis ratio*. No *sacrificium intellectus* is required from the lawyer, as legal logic does not abdicate.

Has Julian been off his guard and overlooked the fact that the unnamed adversary cannot possibly have negated Aquilian liability altogether, since he surely would hold the first offender liable on the basis of Chapter III? Julian does not address Chapter III liabilities at all. The *quaestio* which underlies the text does not encompass Chapter III issues: *quaero an cum utroque de occiso lege Aquilia agi possit.* §2 expressly reminds the reader that the issue being addressed is how to best solve the case of a slave, who, in between two inflictions of mortal wounds, has been named heir. No Chapter III liability could possibly cover this loss of the inheritance: Chapter III liabilities are for wounding, not for killing. Even if it is to be assumed that compensation for lethally wounding led to an award of the full market value, the loss of inheritance is a consequence of death only: a slave, however badly he may be wounded, may still become heir. Since Chapter III liabilities could in no way include the loss of the inheritance, they are rightly not brought into play here.

Given that Chapter III is simply not topical, one cannot rely on a hyper-literal reading of §2 to show that the alternative which Julian fended off was the negation of all liability *lege Aquilia* (which could encompass both relevant chapters). The text, which is dealing exclusively with Chapter I, has to be understood as speaking about 'liability *de occiso*' throughout (Basilika, Below, Schebitz and others). Likewise, the *impunitas* argument has to be taken as referring to impunity for killing. After all, the whole scenario set out in the *principium* is designed as a test for the outer limits of the statutory liability for *occidere*.

If both Chapter I liabilities had been negated, nothing in our sources suggests that Julian, or any other jurist, would have had difficulties in considering the attackers liable under Chapter III here. If one relies on *l.*15.1, perhaps both attackers could have been held liable under Chapter III, which, however, would still leave the owner without compensation for the loss of the inheritance. It is fair, then, to say that Julian advocated a double liability for killing and rejected as insufficient the solution of clearing both attackers of killing, even though holding both liable under Chapter III must have been possible. The element of the loss of an inheritance is an ingenious addition, brought in by Julian to emphasise the difference between his decision and the result at which his opponent (*quis*) could arrive at best if none of the attackers were held liable for killing. It is misleading to dub the difference between Chapter I and Chapter III liabilities in our setting as '*minime*' (*contra*: Gerkens). If the element of an intervening institution as heir is brought in for the purpose of better setting Julian's own solution apart from alternatives, it works only against the solution of refusing all compensation for killing (Schebitz). This confirms that Julian's main line of argument is directed against a negation of all Chapter I liabilities, and not against the solution of holding the first attacker liable under Chapter III, the second under Chapter I, since the latter liability would include the value of the inheritance as well.

The *utilitas communis* argument is used to tip the balance in favour of holding both attackers liable for killing, rather than neither. It is over the top to interpret this as the expression of a criminal policy move to strengthen the effect of deterrence in 2nd-century Roman society at large, as suggested by Scarano Ussani (Börsch). The half-sentence *cum neque – oporteat* is an argument that an actual tort, which leaves a slave dead, should indeed result in appropriate compensation for the loss of the slave's life. *Maleficium* is not the word for a crime which calls for retribution; it is a mildly rhetorically loaded synonym for *delictum* ('wrong' or 'tort'), sometimes with the connotation of a breach of ethical or sacral standards.[416] There is not the slightest hint here at the psychological underpinnings of deterrence that holding someone liable now will impress others so as to deter them in the future from committing the same type of delict.[417] What could the effect of deterrence possibly be if potential attackers learn of Julian's decision and conclude that none of them will get away in a real-life replay of the scenario Julian has envisaged? Even if the *impunitas* argument were seen as implying an idea of deterrence, it is brought up only as a tie-breaker for a problem which is centrally concerned with securing compensation for the slave's owner (Piro, Sampson), as emphasised by the element of the intervening institution of the slave as heir.

IV. ROMAN JURISPRUDENCE: A PRODUCT OF GROUP INTELLIGENCE

1. JURISTS' OPINIONS: COMPLEMENTARITY AND DISAGREEMENT

Driven by an instinct of legal workmanship, Roman jurists of the second century designed hypotheticals to test the limits of the Statute-based liability for damage to personal property. On the basis of the barren wording of the *lex Aquilia*, they weaved an ever-finer net of intriguing

416 T Mommsen, *Römisches Strafrecht* (1899) 11 n 4.

417 The concept was of course well known: cf Seneca's *punitur ne peccetur* and on the legal side C.9.27.1.

casuistry. It is difficult to gauge with some accuracy the measure to which individual Roman jurists of the classical era agreed or disagreed in their legal views, on average. In the large commentaries on the edict, and even more so in Justinian's Digest, a selection of their writings is presented so that their contributions nicely supplement each other, the occasional report of a disagreement notwithstanding. This may or may not be a fair representation of the live discourse in the first and second centuries CE. In this study, with its narrow basis of texts, we can tackle only the limited question whether and to what extent our specific cases betray substantial disagreements regarding a few pertinent legal issues.

2. THE RECKONING OF THE ONE-YEAR PERIOD

There was an attested disagreement between Julian and Celsus pertaining to the reckoning of the one-year period under Chapter I, in cases of a hiatus between the moments of wounding and dying. One does not need to (and should not) blow up this controversy, which has a limited subject matter, into a full-fledged doctrinal dispute between these two jurists, pertaining to the fundamental structure of the delict: there really are two ways which in such cases offer themselves for the reckoning of the critical year, none of which is expressly preferred by the *lex*. This is a typical situation for a – fairly minor – scholarly disagreement. Justinian's Digest obviously here, with Ulpian, adopted Julian's view, preserving, however, Celsus's dissent.[418]

Connecting this dispute to *l*.51, Julian's reasoning here does nicely match his view on the backdating of the critical moment for the start of the one-year period. For him, the starting point for this reckoning is the moment of the mortal wounding, provided that the *occidere* act has come to completion at a later stage. Julian thus distinguishes the two killings in terms of the moment from which one reckons the year backwards; the two killings can therefore differ as to the respective measure of damages. To illustrate the difference, the element of the slave being named heir is brought into play (*l*.51pr and *l*.51.2). As a matter of legal logic, it would not be impossible to follow Celsus's line in cases of a hiatus between mortally wounding and the effective death, while at the same time going with Julian in holding both offenders liable as killers, in a two-incidents

418 This was the view already held by *ius commune* writers; cf. Baldus (n 56) ad *l*.52 (recte 51).

scenario as set out in *l.*51 (Nörr, Pugsley; *contra*: Albanese, Schindler, Ankum, Hausmaninger, Cerami, Castresana Herrero, Ziliotto). In this – hypothetical – merger of the two legal positions, one would only lose the nice illustration of markedly divergent measures of damages for both killings, since the reckoning of the year would start simultaneously for both actions.

3. *L.*51 AND *L.*15.1

Cases where the mortally wounded slave dies in a shipwreck or a collapsing building are easily distinguished from the case Julian decided in *l.*51: when the slave meets another kind of death, the first offender never sees his *occidere* action completed. In these cases, there is a tear in the film. We are looking at two incidents, but the death that comes at the second incident does not 'match' the wound inflicted at the first. There is no evidentiary aspect to Ulpian's deliberations for the case of *l.*15.1, whereas *l.*51 concerns an epistemological uncertainty.

In view of *l.*51, a problem only arises from *l.*15.1 if the *alius ictus* must be understood as a reference to the very scenario underlying *l.*51, namely an additional wounding, brought about by a second attacker, which aggravates and brings forward in time the 'same' death which already awaits the victim with certainty. If this case were addressed here, a difference of opinion between Ulpian and Julian would have existed; a follow-up problem would arise regarding the invocation of Julian as a supporter of the law as set out by Ulpian. This, however, is not how one has to read *l.*15.1. *Vel alio ictu* works as a sweeper clause. One should expect the *alius ictus* to be of the same nature as *ruina* and *naufragium*. Since the incidents specifically named have as a characteristic the 'mismatch' between wound and death, killing the slave regardless of his state as mortally wounded, the continuation 'or by a similar blow', to translate this bit freely, can only cover incidents which appear as a similar 'mismatch'. This is almost *opinio communis*. It may not be strictly necessary that the *ictus* here qualifies as a *casus fortuitus* (Stephanos, Zasius, Pacchioni, Ferrini, Dalla, Rastätter, Nörr, Gerkens, Desanti and many others), although the coupling with *ruina* and *naufragium* supports this notion. There is no stringent reason to restrict *ictus* to non-human blows, although if some other attacker's blow were being referred to, one could perhaps expect that the second attacker's liability and its eventual impact on the first attacker's liability would have been brought into view.[419] The only material fact remains the 'mismatch' of the actual death and the wound previously inflicted. There is no reason to take the casual mention of *alius ictus* as an outlier which would let the text take a completely new turn.

Turning to matters of textual reliability, it is not necessary to go for any one of the explanations that have been advanced in this regard, namely (a) seeing *alio ictu* (or even *vel naufragio – ictu*) as a post-classical gloss, and hence not covered by the original citation of Julian, or (b) restricting Julian's reported approval to the cases of *manumissio* and *alienatio*, for example by appropriate punctuation. As far as *l.*15.1 is concerned, why should Julian not have approved all the decisions here set out, regarding *ruina* and *naufragium* as well as *manumissio* and *alienatio*? There is no reason to doubt the text invoking Julian's approval. From the mention of Julian in *l.*15.1, one does not have to deduce that Julian contradicted himself, and there is no need to attribute to him a change of his views (Noodt, Glück, Pernice), nor is it necessary to assume that Ulpian erroneously mis-cited Julian (Harke). Of course, *vel alio ictu* may well be a non-Ulpianic (perhaps Justinianic) addition, but we can't know for sure and it hardly matters: even without such a sweeper-clause, no educated reader would hesitate to deal with comparable events in the like manner.

4. *L.*11.3 AND *L.*51

*L.*11.3 deals with one incident that leaves the slave dead, whereas *l.*51pr deals with two attacks, separated in time (*medio tempore, ex intervallo*) and, in all likelihood, in space, too. The element of the slave's intervening designation as heir crucially depends on, and in turn highlights, this two-moments-in-time scenario. In *l.*11.3, the later attacker is identified as the one who delivered the very deadly blow (*ex alio vulnere periit*), setting him apart from the earlier attacker who had thus only got to the stage of mortally wounding the victim. There is no evidentiary aspect to Celsus's deliberations for the case of *l.*11.3, creating a similarity to the epistemological uncertainty of *l.*51: the injuries suffered in the two consecutive attacks of *l.*51 contribute to the actual death in a manner

419 Buckland and Kortmann have rightly pointed out that *alius ictus* is not the same as *ab alio ictus*.

which does not allow the death to be attributed one-to-one to either of the attackers. For Celsus, it was the starting point that in a one-incident scenario the attacker identified as the one who administered the one deadly blow attracts and monopolises the Chapter I liability, leaving no room to additionally attach the same Chapter I liability to anyone else. Celsus granted an additional Chapter III action against another almost, but not quite, successful attacker. The situation envisaged by Julian in *l.*51pr is strikingly different: the sequence of events here does not allow the actual death to be attributed one-to-one to either of the attacks. If the victim's owner is not to be left without compensation for the killing of his slave, one and the same death has to be taken as the completion of the two separate attacks. For this solution, the monopolising attraction of Chapter I liability is not a problem, since the two killing acts occur in separate incidents, so neither excludes also attaching the same liability for killing to the other.

No other factual element is needed, or suggests itself, to distinguish the cases of *l.*11.3 and *l.*51. The attempts made in this direction have hardly been convincing: the 'degree of lethality', in play since the time of the glossators, is obviously unacceptable.[420] This leaves the idea that the second blow in *l.*11.3 must be taken as instantaneously effective, whereas in *l.*51 the dying process must have continued for a while, albeit speeded up (Zasius, Donellus, Luden, Vangerow, Grueber). Neither *l.*11.3 nor *l.*51 include clear and express information as to a time-span (or lack thereof) between the second attack and the slave's death.[421] One should not rely on a presumably decisive criterion which does not feature in the text at all. The only express temporal information we are given in *l.*51 is the *medium tempus*, the *intervallum*, separating two attacks. In order to find with Julian, in his two-incidents scenario, that two Chapter I liabilities may co-exist, it is not necessary that the victim's life continued for a while after the second blow. The case addressed in *l.*11.3 is a one-incident scenario as

420 In *l.*51, the certainty of the ensuing death for Julian is a material fact, which allows the actual death to be taken as the completion of the first killing act. In *l.*11.3 (as in *l.*15.1) the lethality of the wound, for the respective jurists, is the basis for awarding a Chapter III liability. There is no reason to assume that in either text the word *mortifere* is used in any other but its ordinary meaning.

421 It has been argued that in the case of *l.*51 death must have come instantaneously with the second attack, since the one-year period for the second attacker is reckoned from his death, whereas any hiatus between wounding and death would require, in line with *l.*21.2, starting from the moment of wounding (Buckland, Windscheid). The argument holds up, but it may be an over-interpretation.

the blows came more or less contemporaneously. If the last blow's deadly effect is immediate, this makes it easier to attribute the death one-to-one to that second blow. However, it would not amount to a material change if death did not follow immediately after the last blow, provided the ensuing death could still be attributed, one-to-one, to that last attack (Buckland).

Both texts, *l.*11.3 and *l.*51, are non-trivial. Celsus as well as Julian made fine-tuned moves towards new levels of sophistication. This required transcending the doctrinal status quo, distancing oneself, to some small degree, from conventional wisdom. The slightly cruder 'old' met the slightly more nuanced 'new'. This could have triggered a controversy if the 'old' had found staunch defenders trying to fend off the 'new'. Our next question will address the matter of the respective perception of each jurist's opinion.

5. CELSUS VERSUS JULIAN?

Cujas made us view Celsus and Julian as locked in an intellectual battle. He thereby troubled our research with a red herring, and a long-lived one for that. It was a mistake to take our two fragments as matching counterpoints, each text marking the position opposed by the other. It may be a case of apophenia, a desire to over-fit, to recognise a pattern. The two decisions are not in conflict at all. Celsus's and Julian's decisions have often been juxtaposed as a more lenient versus a more severe handling of the same case. Nörr for example found Julian advocating 'a more severe penalisation' of the wrongdoers than Celsus.[422] On the strength of *l.*51, Julian has even been portrayed as the advocate of a repressive public policy (Scarano Ussani, Liebs). Celsus, as reported in *l.*11.3, fine-tuned delictual liability under the *lex Aquilia*, and this fine-tuning incrementally extended Aquilian liability. In this respect, nothing set Celsus apart from Julian. Indeed, for Celsus's proposal one could also have advanced the *impunitas* argument, given that it was his concern that the first attacker did not walk away without liability. The liability expansion advocated by Celsus may have been overlooked, because he, for his introduction of a new liability which previously was not recognised, opted for the less harsh of two remedies, holding the first attacker liable for *quasi vulnerare*, rather than for *quasi occidere*. Be that as it may, not too much should be made of the expansive nature of both

[422] Nörr (1986) (n 219) 184.

jurists' interpretations of the *lex*: as a general tendency, fine-tuning tort liabilities over time will rather lead to a piecemeal extension than to a restriction of the range of cases captured for liability.

While the cases dealt with by Celsus (*l*.11.3) and Julian (*l*.51) must be distinguished and thus do not betray a direct confrontation between the two jurists, it would still be possible, as a matter of logic, that each of the decisions was opposed by the other jurist. For the sake of completeness, one might ask whether Julian disapproved of Celsus's decision for the one-incident scenario, and whether Celsus disapproved of the decision Julian proposed for his two-incident scenario in *l*.51pr. These questions, which are independent of each other, need not be approached again as a matter of logical compatibility of two legal decisions – there is no incompatibility here – but with a view to our sources: does our source material comprise information which allows us to positively assert that one jurist disapproved of the other's legal opinion? Given that *l*.11.3 and *l*.51 fall away as bases, the answer is an obvious no. *L*.11.3 does not even state that there was a specific jurist who actually advocated the solution not preferred by Celsus, supporting a *quasi occidere* rather than the Celsian *quasi vulnerare*; it may just have been an alternative pondered by Celsus himself. For reasons of chronology, Celsus here cannot have refuted a view set out in Julian's *Digesta*. *L*.51, on the other hand, makes an innominate reference to someone (*quis*) who was highly sceptical of Julian's approach. We have no source material at all to positively assert that Celsus was this someone. It is but a remote possibility, given that Julian was almost a generation younger than Celsus (Navarra): for Julian to record a specific Celsian opposition in his *Digesta*, it would have been necessary that he had voiced his own view on an earlier occasion, meeting Celsus's opposition, which he then later rebutted in writing. All this becomes unduly speculative. It is by no means certain, moreover, that the *quis* needs to be interpreted as a reference to a specific jurist's 'published' work; it may just as well have been a student or a colleague in a 'classroom' or a counsel in a court setting (Wacke). We must resist the temptation to over-fit. It is not possible to take the *quis* in *l*.51.2 as one of the suggested instances where an innominate reference to an adversary is assumed – rightly or wrongly – to prove a personal enmity. There is no need, in this study, to establish whether a broader set of texts would or would not confirm the hypothesis of a continuous quarrel between the two jurists.

Regarding the issue of whether both jurists employed discernible methodologies, the limited material here used does not allow us to make a proper comparison. While for Celsus's view we only have the barren report by Ulpian, Julian's self-contained essay is an invitation indeed to search for methodological characteristics. Julian's proposed solution, and the different arguments he advances to support it, are in line with the findings of the research that has been devoted to Julian's legal methodology, from Reggi to Battaglia[423] and Babusiaux.[424] *L*.51 first and foremost confirms Julian's legal brinkmanship, his ability to stretch legal concepts to a point where they cannot be stretched any further, if the underlying principles are not to be betrayed. As befits a literary *responsum*, Julian decides a case of a stylised nature which is treated as a given. It is of no concern to him how forensic practice can possibly determine that a wound was definitively lethal. The text betrays no interest in matters of impact assessment, nor does it reveal a specific public policy bias (*contra*: Scarano Ussani, Liebs). The approach here does not betray a lack of a 'conscious analysis' (*contra*: Johnston): on the contrary, the approach is highly analytical – it is just not a causation-focussed analysis. If the word 'pragmatic' implies that logic and accepted premises may light-footedly be set aside in the interest of a working solution, we do not find 'pragmatism' in Julian's reasoning. *L*.51.2 does not show that Julian was a worldly-wise 'realist' who knew when legal logic must make way for the interest of the community (*contra*: Stein, Ankum, Wacke and many others). Julian does, however, seem to pursue an educative ambition, an aspect which needs to be addressed more closely.[425]

In no way do our cases betray a radical dispute between Julian and other lawyers regarding the fundamental structure of the statutory requirements for Aquilian liability, Chapter I. It has been a gross misrepresentation to see both jurists battling it out, like 19th-century academic warriors, between incompatible concepts of causation. Julian did not radically question the handling of the *occidere* requirement, initiating a controversial, all-new understanding of what the *lex Aquilia* required for Chapter I liability (MacCormack). For such drastic reform the classical lawyers 'had neither the inclination nor the energy. [...] The sun of jurisprudence still shone, but with an autumn brilliance.'[426] A full-blown controversy between classical lawyers pertaining to the

423 F Battaglia, *Iuliani de ambiguitatibus liber singularis* (2017).

424 U Babusiaux, 'Celsus und Julian zum Edikt SI CERTUM PETETUR – Bemerkungen zu Prozess und "Aktionendenken"', *Dogmengeschichte und historische Individualität der römischen Juristen* (2012) 367.

425 Below p 141 ff.

426 F Schulz, *History of Roman Legal Science* (1946) 129.

heart of Aquilian Chapter I liability would have in all likelihood called for a Justinianic decision. As far as we can see, none of the constitutions assumed to make up the *Quinquaginta Decisiones* addresses such an issue. This brings us to Justinian's law.

V. JUSTINIAN'S USE OF JULIAN: A MODEL ESSAY OF STATUTORY INTERPRETATION

Those who have found Julian blundering must also attribute a severe lack of judgment to Justinian's compilers:[427] if Julian's reasoning here were as inconsistent as some interpreters take it to be, if he really just rhetorically propped up a 'logically untenable gut decision' (Finkenauer), how crude would it be to select this lengthy bit for reproduction in the Digest? Another blunder, legally far more serious, would lie in the inclusion in the Digest of two radically different understandings of the term *occidere*, which, after all, in Justinian's codification continues to be a statutory term. Alas, the jurists' texts selected for the Digest show a uniform approach to the term, some second-level disagreement in this or that case notwithstanding.

The authors who see an outright disagreement between Julian (*l.*51) and Celsus/Ulpian (*l.*11.3, *l.*15.1) should address the issue of why the compilers should have used the controversy to create a glaring antinomy, rather than expunge it one way or another (Thayer). An unintended antinomy within the same title of the Digest is much more difficult to explain as the result of a mere oversight than in cases where the conflicting passages may have been adopted for the Digest at different times in the editing process, and with different editors in charge, for example D.41.1.36 versus D.12.1.18pr.[428] In all likelihood, to the compilers the

427 Literature on the making of Justinian's Digest abounds. Point of entry: W E Voß, s. v. 'Digesta', *Brill's New Pauly*, https://referenceworks.brillonline.com/entries/brill-s-new-pauly/digesta-e317640?s.num=0&s.f.s2_parent=s.f.book.brill-s-new-pauly&s.q=digesta, retrieved 20 April 2019; cf also T Honoré, *Justinian's Digest: Character and Compilation* (2010).

428 *L.*51 came from the Sabinian mass, whereas *l.*11 came from the edictal mass, so different commissioners will have been in charge for both texts; T Honoré, *Tribonian* (1978) 170.

texts must have seemed to stand in a non-conflicting relationship. In the attested Julian/Celsus controversy concerning the reckoning of the one-year period for Chapter I, the compilers, with Ulpian, followed Julian, not Celsus.

L.51 is one of the longest surviving texts of a Roman jurist dealing with a single isolated point of law (Frier). Many authors who found the text over-long and wordy have thought they had identified passages which to them seemed redundant; this has often come with the suspicion that such parts were later mounted onto a shorter Julian original. Leaving such doubts aside, one may indeed ask why the compilers bothered to give Julian's wide-ranging text in its full length (if we assume that nothing of substance was cut out).

Since the sole legal issue for Julian is the finding or negating of *occidere*, as employed in the wording of the *lex*, in the specific scenario set out in the *principium*, the text is to be read as an exercise in statutory interpretation. Julian starts with the word's literal meaning, highlighting the difference between plain and ordinary language on the one hand, and legal terminology on the other. The understanding of the *occidere* requirement had already been relaxed, so as to encompass cases of non-instant lethality: Julian was no originalist. Bringing in the additional scenario of §1, there is a case-to-case reasoning, *de similibus ad similia*, comparable to an *argumentum per analogiam*.[429] Reference to the *veteres* highlights again the historical dimension. An alternative solution is eliminated, using a teleological argument.[430] One is admonished not to let love of dialectic (*ratio disputandi*) keep one from doing the right thing. Last but not least, there is also a systematic argument of sorts: by referring to a similar case regarding *furtum*, an appeal is made for a homogenous treatment of like problems across different delicts. In a nutshell one finds all the elements which a comprehensive statutory interpretation is expected to factor in: literal meaning, historical perspective, teleological considerations, systematic context, and the analogy to similar cases. While the methodological understanding of interpretation has undergone considerable changes throughout the later history of the civil law, not a

---

429 It is not necessary to revive here the controversy whether this reasoning from case to case, especially as advocated by Julian, can (Seidl) or cannot (Bund) be understood as an 'analogy' in a more modern sense; E Seidl 'Wege zu Julian', *Sein und Werden im Recht* (1970) 215, at 216 f.

430 Bauman rightly remarked that in *l*.51.2 *utilitas* comes into play as 'a special canon of interpretation'; *Lawyers and politics in the early Roman empire* (1989) 101–2 n 143.

single one of the canons which later doctrines of interpretation have found to be relevant is missing in Julian's model exercise:

occidisse dicitur – lege Aquilia teneri	literal meaning: *interpretatio vocis* – legal terminology ≠ plain and ordinary language – etymology – established expansion of literal sense (*rursus – teneri*)
idque est – iudicaverunt	analogy argument: *de similibus ad similia* + historical argument
aestimatio – intellegatur	legal consequences spelled out: *respice finem!*
quod si quis absurde – potius	pondering alternatives, the comparatively best must prevail
cum neque impunita – teneatur	public policy (teleological argument)
multa autem – potest	overcoming schematic reasoning for a useful result makes good law
cum plures – sustulisse	systematic argument from a neighbouring field; avoid sophistry

It is a commonplace of civilian methodologies of statutory interpretation that none of the various canons in play should be given preference as the controlling *topos*. For the civil law, which traditionally tended to acknowledge four elements of interpretation (e.g. grammar, logic, history, system), the following statement tried to authoritatively summarise the approach:

> These are not four different kinds of interpretations, among which one could choose arbitrarily, but the four different activities have to be amalgamated if the interpretation is to work out.[431]

Even though in a specific case one element of interpretation may prove to be more influential than others, the diligent interpreter is expected to routinely review all elements, if only to be on the safe side. It is not necessary for a single isolated element of interpretation to be absolutely compelling, so as to cogently demand, just by itself, one specific interpretative result, eliminating any other once and for all. In a taking of stock, for which all

431 F C von Savigny, *System des heutigen Römischen Rechts* vol 1 (1840) 215 (in the original: 'Es sind also nicht vier Arten der Auslegung, unter denen man nach Geschmack und Belieben wählen könnte, sondern es sind verschiedene Tätigkeiten, die vereinigt werden müssen, wenn die Auslegung gelingen soll').

canons of interpretation are scanned, no strict linearity of argument should be expected. One has to let the different elements play themselves out against each other. The multiple elements of interpretation thus activated need not point to the same result of interpretation, but if they do – as is the case in Julian's presentation – so much the better. The logic of interpretation is non-monotonic. Since Julian's essay is an exemplary study in statutory interpretation, his scanning of the full range of viewpoints, some maybe stronger than others, is not to be scolded for redundancy. Nor does the broad range of aspects reviewed by Julian betray an inherent weakness of his legal position, which would call for extra efforts of defensive reasoning (*contra*: Faber, Ankum, Schebitz, Ishikawa and many others).

Julian's essay is not a doctrinal 'cookbook' on how to proceed with schematically interpreting a statutory term. Nor is it a theory of interpretation. Rather, an exemplary exercise shows the student which perspectives come into play when a statute needs to be interpreted. This befits the process of interpretation, which is not schematic in nature, but rather an art (Bretone, Giaro). Art is best taught by example, and Julian the educator here teaches the art of interpretation.

Let us come back to the question whether *l*.51 reveals a specific Julianic methodology.[432] Lo and behold: on a silver platter we are given Julian's approach to interpretation of the *ius civile*, insofar as it was constituted by statutes. It is all in plain sight. The reader is expressly encouraged not to shrink back from creative interpretation simply because one is operating in the very realm of the traditional *ius civile*. The text does technically refer to this specific layer of law to which the *lex Aquilia* belonged (Seidl): the comparable case of the multi-actor theft pertains to *furtum*, another *ius civile* (XII tables) delict. It is the *ius civile* in particular, Julian argues, which has benefitted from interpretation. This implies that to further develop the law one needs not confine oneself to the evolution of the *ius honorarium* with its in-built plasticity; the older layer of the statutory *ius civile*, too, allows – and indeed continues to benefit from – refinement by way of interpretation.

What Julian practices in *l*.51 matches some abstract statements he has made regarding the methodology of interpretation. Julian avowed the need to specify the laws by way of interpretation: Iul 90 dig D.1.3.11. Moreover, since statutes cannot address all factual variations, it is proper

---

[432] Above p 138 ff.

to proceed *ad similia*, if another case obviously fits the legislative purpose, the *sententia*: Iul 15 dig D.1.3.12.[433] All this may not sound spectacular today, but one must not underrate the long way Roman jurisprudence had come: it had started from an absolute, purely verbal fidelity to the statutes' words, an approach which initially had not even allowed asking for a word's meaning.[434]

Did the approach Julian here displayed differ from that of other classical jurists? No definitive answer can be given on the basis of the select texts here scrutinised. If Julian's view of statutory interpretation had been that of an eccentric outsider, starkly deviating from the work of his contemporaries, the model exercise that could be found here would hardly have commended itself to the compilers; it would have been at odds with the many other instances of statutory interpretation featuring in Justinian's Digest. More likely than not, Julian will have been seen as 'mainstream'.

The compilers included *l*.51 as a model for future statutory interpretation of Justinian's laws, which the Constitutio 'Tanta' welcomed.[435] It is as if the readers were meant to be implicitly instructed: this is how you interpret statutes! From the vast material the compilers had at their disposal they will have picked what they thought was a compelling sample. Julian's essay is a model exercise in statutory interpretation indeed, as '[i]t is the masterpiece that educates, and to the masterpiece everything must be referred' (T R Glover).

433 These texts have of course been subject to intensive studies in their own right, which, however, are not included here.

434 The development of legal methodologies, in its interplay with Roman intellectual history at large, has attracted intense research interest, reporting which, however, would take us far beyond the scope of this contribution. To give at least two references, the reader may want to start with H Hohmann, 'Classical Rhetoric and Roman Law: Reflections on a Debate', (1996) 15 *Rhetorik. Ein internationales Jahrbuch* 15, and A Kacprzak, 'Rhetoric and Roman law', *Oxford Handbook of Roman Law* (2016) 200.

435 New valid rulings may be arrived at by way of conjectures and analogies: Const. Tant. 18 i.f. = Const. Δέδωκεν 18 i.f., pairing Julian and Hadrian for both juristic and imperial authority. If, however, new phenomena emerge from future developments, the emperor has to be asked for an amendment of the law (*augustum remedium*). The exact delineation between the 'creative-interpretative monopoly' of the emperor (Falcone) and analogies permissible as *mera interpretatio* does not concern us here. For the compilers, *l*.51 was a model of the latter.

VI. *OMNIA PRAECLARA TAM DIFFICILIA QUAM RARA*

In the history of interpretations, Iul 86 dig D.9.2.51 has been met with disbelief again and again: one corpse and two killers who are supposed to have killed the same victim at different times! Indeed, it may be the least appreciated of all of Julian's solutions that we know of.[436] Even those who do not see a controversy here (in which case Julian loses almost automatically) have often found *l*.51 unsatisfactory in this or that element. The high frequency of persistent hypotheses of interpolations regarding *l*.51 is an indicator of a widespread discontent.

Regardless of the scepticism with which Julian's decision has been viewed, parts of his repertoire of interpretative *topoi* have been extracted to become signature maxims of the western legal canon: *ne crimina remaneant impunita*[437] and *multa in iure civili/communi contra rationem disputandi pro communi utilitate introducta sunt.*[438] However, the text has not been put to the very use for which it should have been foreordained. In the history of Roman law studies since the Middle Ages, professors have taught the art of interpretation using one Digest text or another. Over time, a stock of Digest fragments coalesced, from which teachers took what they thought was a suitable text. Paul 19 ad ed D.6.2.6, Afr 9 quaest D.12.6.38 and I.4.6pr were among those most frequently picked. *L*.51 was not used for such exercises, perhaps because the result seemed unconvincing. The text has thus never been taken on as the model of the art of interpretation. The overall long-range effect of *l*.51 may be symptomatic of all the appropriations of the cultural remnants of antiquity. There is no way that we could restore them to the vibrant brio they must have exuded in their live setting, and all that seems to be left is the possibility of using them as a quarry of high-grade intellectual material, valuable as building blocks for the construction of new systems of ideas. The historian of classical Roman law will cast a cold eye on all such secondary exploitations of his texts, and then move on.

---

436 There are number of authors who have not joined in in Julian's damnation: Donellus, Pothier, Luden, Franz Victor Ziegler, Vangerow, Buckland, Thayer, MacCormack, Willvonseder, Giaro, Börsch and Piro, to name just a few.

437 See above p 15 ff.

438 See above n 304.

It is not necessary to give an exposition here of the innumerable statements eulogising Julian as an all-time great,[439] a view maintained by Hadrian, Leo/Anthemius[440] and Justinian's compilers,[441] as well as by modern scholars.[442] *L*.51 is a fine and blameless example of the exquisitely balanced legal reasoning that was Julian's trademark. Nothing here is illogical, provided only that the matter is approached with the legal question in mind that emerges from the statute: have acts of *occidere* been committed by the two respective offenders? The question is asked and answered. To support the answer, the reader is guided through a nuanced process of interpretation. In the field of multiple wrongdoers, Julian thus achieved, for a highly specific set of material facts, finesse previously not recognised. His decision is the masterstroke of a legal virtuoso. It has all the traits of a great solution to a serious legal problem: it is compelling, yet parsimonious, elegant yet surprising. Unlike much of its secondary handling throughout the centuries, those in our own century not excluded, the text of *l*.51 is not 'sham and empty cleverness and pseudo-philology', it is not built on 'a science of artificially patching up the contradictions and deficiencies of a codification': the text is but a 'product of juristic reflection on a juristic problem.'[443] In terms of sophisticated legal reasoning, *l*.51 is a *non plus ultra*, which should be treasured like a Mozart sonata or a Cezanne painting.

---

439 'With Iulianus, the Roman jurisprudence reached its apogee': A Berger, s v 'Iulianus', *Encyclopedic Dictionary of Roman Law* (1953) 522.

440 C.6.61.5, CE 473.

441 *Summus auctor iuris prudentiae*: C.3.33.15.2 (CE 530): cf for other texts S Di Maria, *La cancelleria imperiale e i giuristi classici* (2010) 61.

442 H F Jolowicz and B Nicholas, *Historical Introduction to the Study of Roman Law* 3rd edn (1932) 385: 'some modern authorities would regard him as the greatest of all the Roman jurists, not excluding even Papinian'.

443 F Schulz, *History of Roman Legal Science* (1946) 331.

GERHARD VON BESELER'S CONJECTURES

Beiträge zur Kritik der römischen Rechtsquellen, Drittes Heft (1913) 8–9:

L.15.1

si servus vulneratus mortifere postea ruina vel naufragio vel alio ictu maturius perierit, de occiso agi non posse, sed quasi de vulnerato, sed si manumissus vel alienatus ex vulnere periit, quasi de occiso agi posse iulianus ait. [haec ita tam varie, quia verum est eum a te occisum tunc cum vulnerabas, quod mortuo eo demum apparuit: at in superiore non est passa ruina apparere an sit occisus.] sed si vulneratum mortifere liberum et heredem esse iusseris, deinde decesserit, heredem eius agere aquilia non posse.

Ibid, 27:

L.51.2

eiusdem ergo servi occisi nomine alius maiorem, alius minorem aestimationem praestabit, nec mirum, cum uterque eorum ex diversa causa et diversis temporibus occidisse hominem intellegatur. <–,> [quod si quis absurde a nobis haec constitui putaverit, cogitet longe absurdius constitui neutrum lege aquilia teneri aut alterum potius, cum neque impunita maleficia esse oporteat nec facile constitui possit, uter potius lege teneatur.] multa autem iure civili contra rationem disputandi pro utilitate communi recepta esse innumerabilibus rebus probari potest: unum interim posuisse contentus ero. cum plures trabem alienam furandi causa sustulerint, quam singuli ferre non possent, furti actione omnes teneri existimantur, quamvis [subtili ratione dici possit neminem eorum teneri, quia] neminem verum sit eam sustulisse.

Beiträge zur Kritik der römischen Rechtsquellen, Viertes Heft (1920) 193–4:

L.51

ita vulneratus est servus, ut eo ictu certum esset moriturum: medio deinde tempore heres institutus est et postea ab alio ictus decessit: quaero, an cum utroque de occiso lege aquilia agi possit. respondit: occidisse dicitur vulgo quidem, qui mortis causam quolibet modo praebuit: sed lege aquilia is demum teneri visus est, qui adhibita vi et quasi manu causam mortis praebuisset, tracta videlicet interpretatione vocis a caedendo et a caede. rursus <de occiso> [aquilia lege] teneri existimati sunt non solum qui ita vulnerassent, ut confestim vita privarent, sed etiam hi, quorum ex vulnere certum esset aliquem vita excessurum. <sed> [igitur] si quis servo mortiferum vulnus inflixerit eundemque alius ex intervallo ita percusserit, ut maturius interficeretur, quam ex priore vulnere moriturus fuerat, <*in which case the causal connection between the first wounding and the death is interrupted, and only the second man is liable de occiso*> [statuendum est utrumque eorum lege aquilia teneri.

[§1] idque est consequens auctoritati veterum, qui, cum a pluribus idem servus ita vulneratus esset, ut non appareret cuius ictu perisset, omnes lege aquilia teneri iudicaverunt.]

[§2] aestimatio autem perempti non eadem in utriusque persona fiet: nam qui prior vulneravit, tantum praestabit, <quanti in diebus triginta proximis> [quanto in anno proximo] homo [plurimi] fuerit repetitis ex die vulneris <triginta> [trecentum sexaginta quinque] diebus, posterior in id tenebitur, quanti homo plurimi <fuerit> [venire poterit] in anno proximo, <ex> quo vita excessit, in quo pretium quoque hereditatis erit. [eiusdem ergo servi occisi nomine alius maiorem, alius minorem aestimationem praestabit, nec mirum, cum uterque eorum ex diversa causa et diversis temporibus occidisse hominem intellegatur. quod si quis absurde a nobis haec constitui putaverit, cogitet longe absurdius constitui neutrum lege aquilia teneri aut alterum potius, cum neque impunita maleficia esse oporteat nec facile constitui possit, uter potius lege teneatur.] <si plures servum percusserint, si quidem apparet, cuius ictu perierit, ille qui coccidit tenetur: quod si non apparet, omnes quasi occiderint teneri receptum est.> multa autem iure civili contra rationem disputandi pro utilitate communi recepta esse innumerabilibus rebus probari potest: unum interim posuisse contentus ero. cum plures trabem alienam furandi causa sustulerint, quam singuli ferre non possent, furti actione omnes teneri existimantur, quamvis [subtili ratione dici possit neminem eorum teneri, quia] neminem verum sit eam sustulisse.

'Romanistische Studien', (1930) 1 *TR* 161, at 182:

L.11.3

Celsus scribit, si alius mortifero vulnere <servum> percusserit, alius postea exanimaverit, <illum> [priorem quidem] non teneri quasi occiderit, sed quasi vulneraverit, quia ex alio vulnere periit, [posteriorem teneri, quia occidit.] quod et Marcello videtur et est probabilius.

CHARTS

The following graphs and maps record only the authors here reported. As to the range of authors captured, see p 3 f.

The authors are apportioned to centuries. For this purpose, the date of birth is taken as the criterion, not the date when the contribution to the theme of D.9.2.11.3 versus D.9.2.51 was published.

The number of authors born in the 20th century in all likelihood is still rising.

For the main university affiliation, authors who have been members of two or more universities are allocated to one university on the basis of length of membership; in the absence of a marked difference, the last university post was chosen. The main university affiliation does not necessarily represent the place where the contribution to the theme of D.9.2.11.3 versus D.9.2.51 was written.

Where one and the same author has written more than one contribution to the theme of D.9.2.11.3 versus D.9.2.51, the number of contributions credited to her/his university is also increased.

Number of contributions

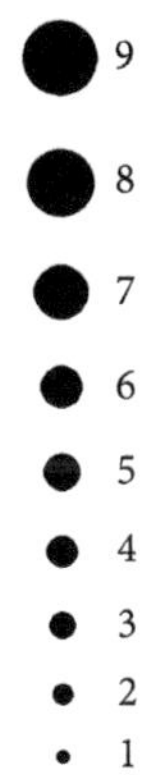

Fig. 1. Authors reported, d.o.b. before 1300, main university affiliation

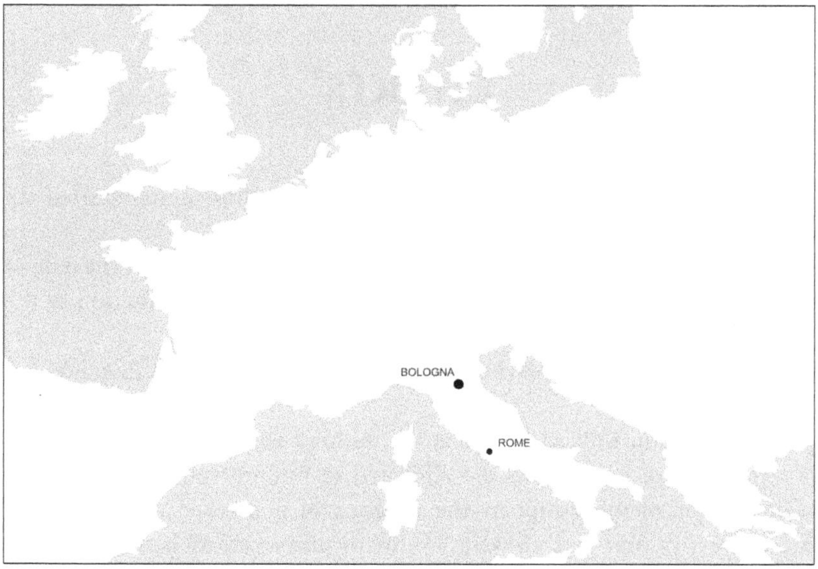

Fig. 2. Authors reported, d.o.b. 1300–1400, main university affiliation

Fig. 3. Authors reported, d.o.b. 1400–1500, main university affiliation

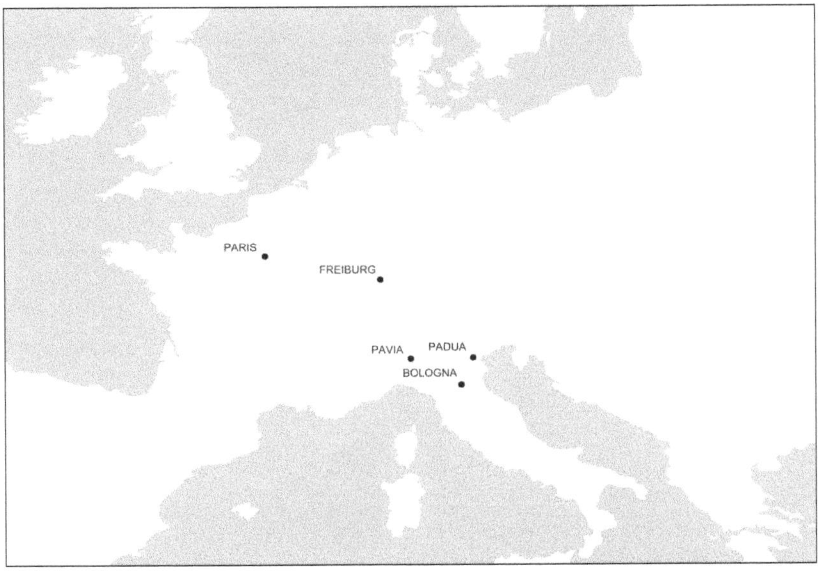

Fig. 4. Authors reported, d.o.b. 1500–1600, main university affiliation

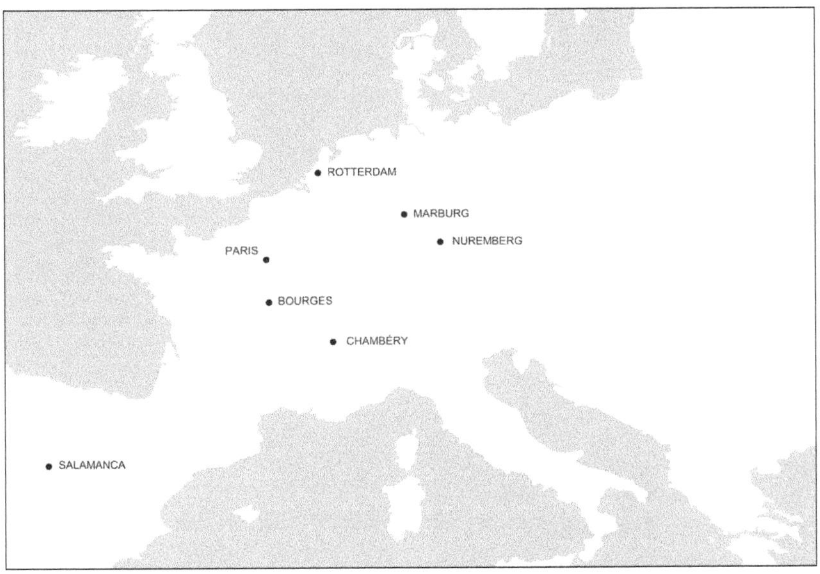

Fig. 5. Authors reported, d.o.b. 1600–1700, main university affiliation

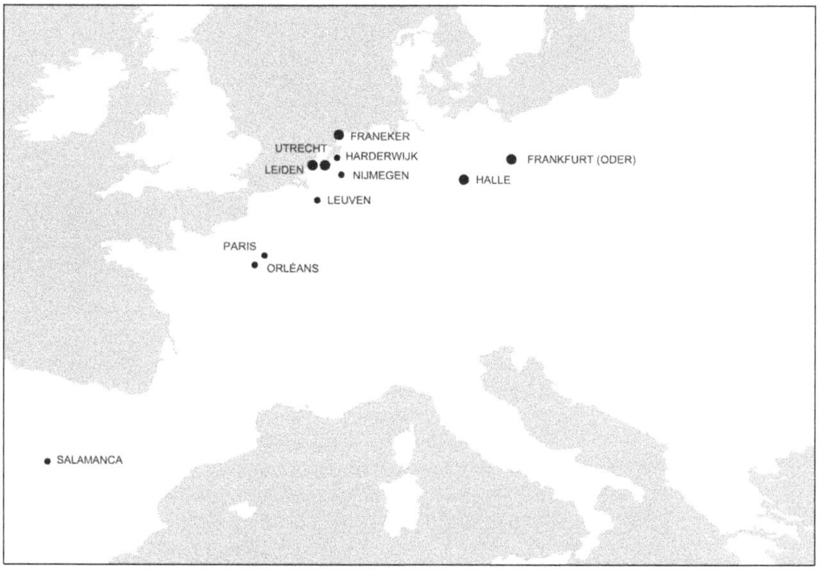

Fig. 6. Authors reported, d.o.b. 1700–1800, main university affiliation

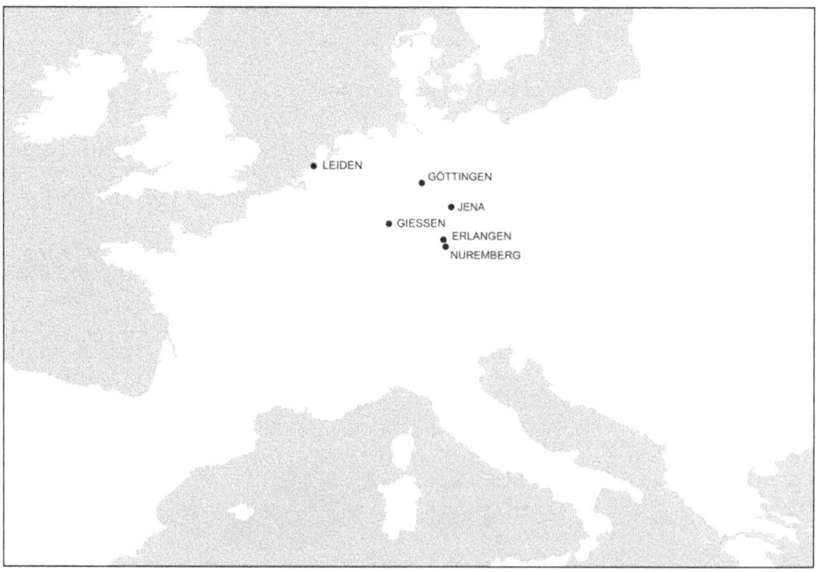

Fig. 7. Authors reported, d.o.b. 1800–1900, main university affiliation

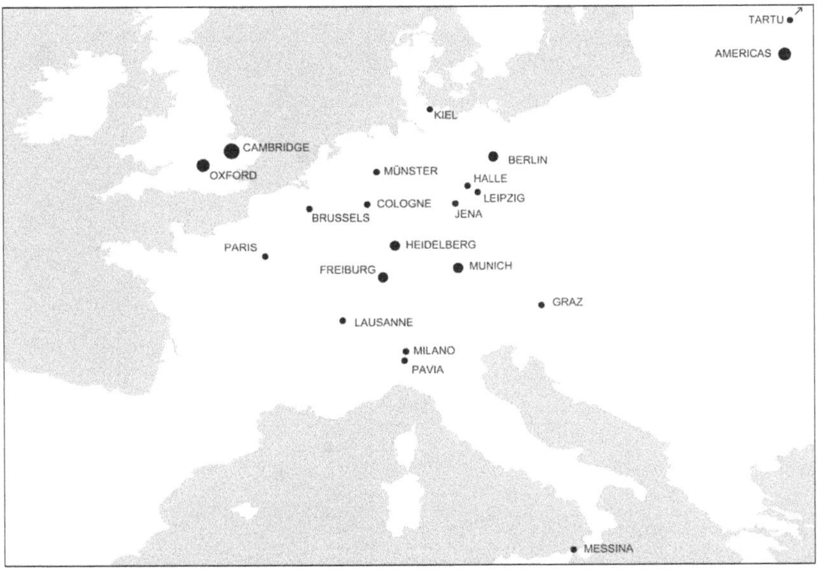

Fig. 8. Authors reported, d.o.b. 1900–2000, main university affiliation

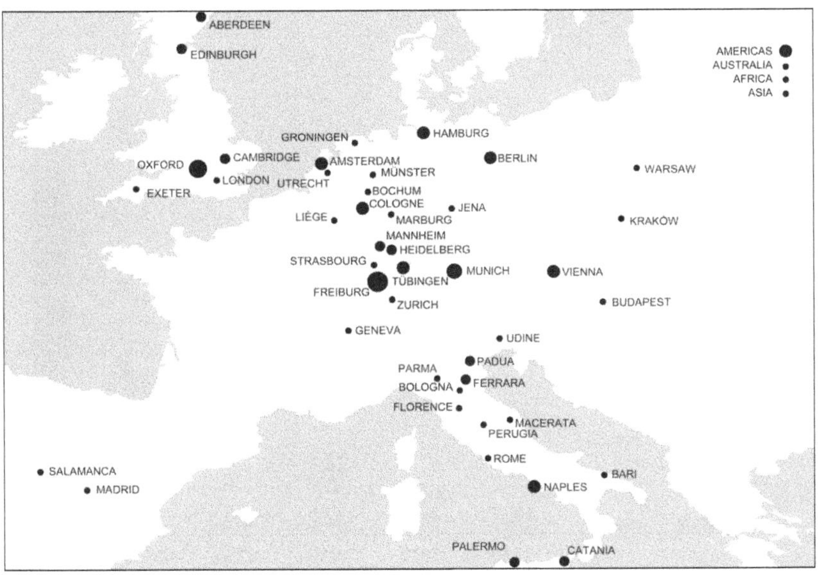

Fig. 9. All authors reported, main university Affiliation ('La banane bleue')

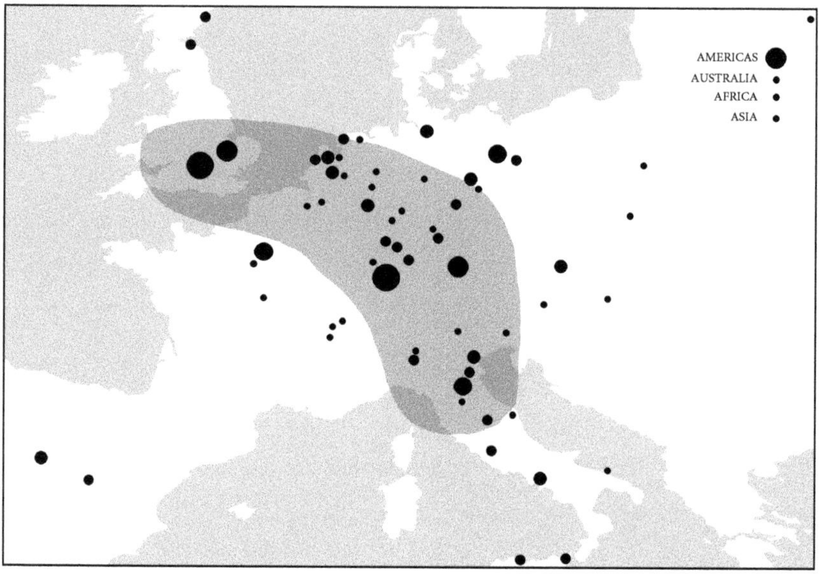

Fig. 10. Number of authors reported/century (sorted by d.o.b.)

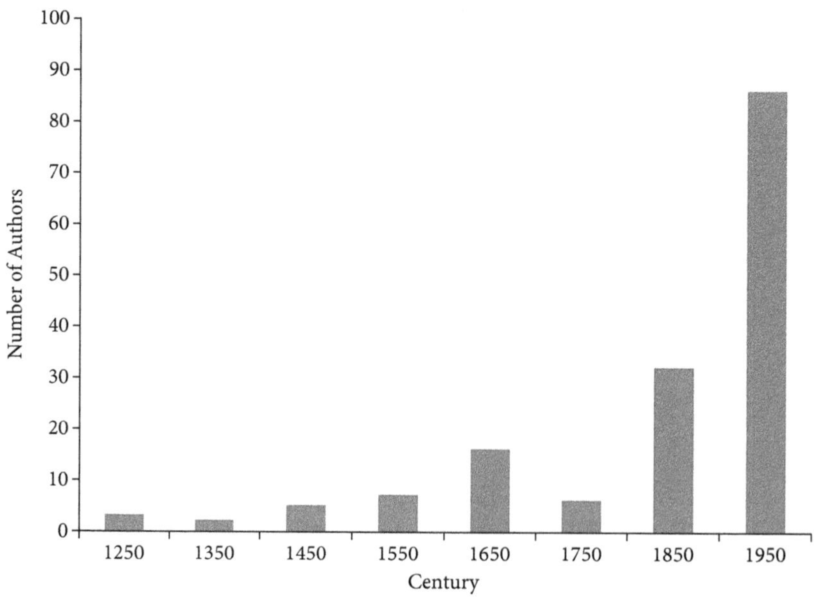

Fig. 11. Sum of pages published by authors reported/century (based on an estimated increase from 0.1 to 5 as average publication length)

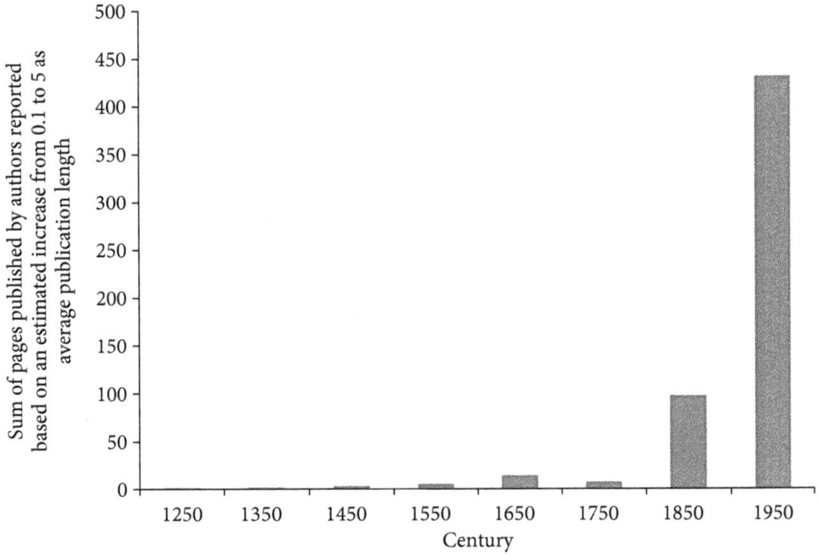

Fig. 12. Languages of contributions/century

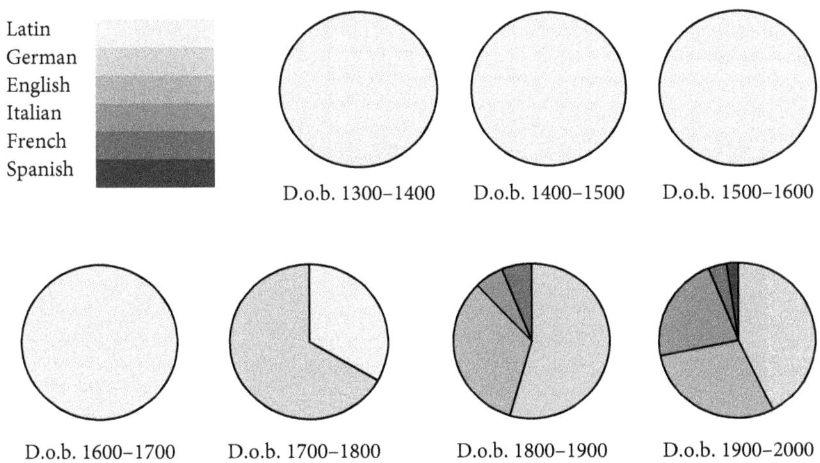

Fig. 13. Gender distribution/century

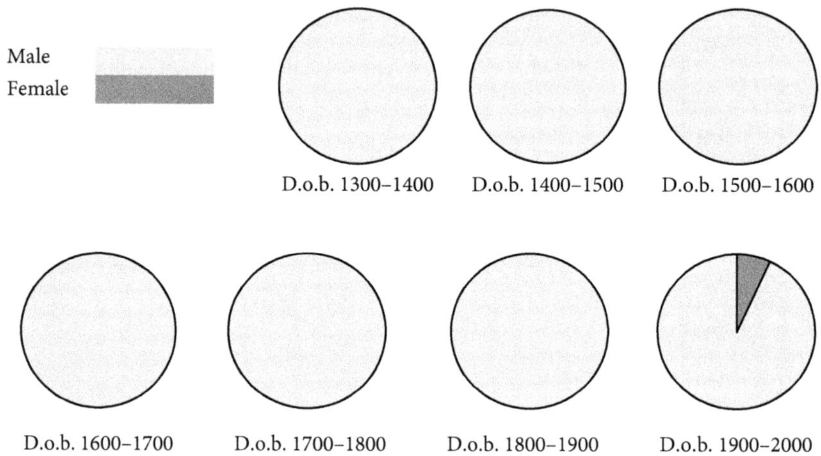

BIBLIOGRAPHY*

Angelus Aretinus, Tractatus super maleficiis, Lyon, 1555.

Ulrike Babusiaux, 'Celsus und Julian zum Edikt SI CERTUM PETETUR – Bemerkungen zu Prozess und "Aktionendenken"', Dogmengeschichte und historische Individualität der römischen Juristen. Atti del Seminario internazionale Montepulciano 14–17 Giugno 2011 =Quaderni del Dipartimento di Scienze Giuridiche, 107 (C Baldus, M Miglietta, G Santucci, E Stolfi eds, Trento: Università degli Studi di Trento, 2012) 367.

Cristián Aedo Barrena, 'La cuestión causal en la "lex Aquilia" y su solución mediante el mecanismo de la culpa', (2015) 37 Revista de Estudios Histórico-Jurídicos 37.

Federico Battaglia, Iuliani de ambiguitatibus liber singularis. Una monografia romana di lingua del diritto tra esegesi e storiografia, Pavia: TCP Edizioni, 2017.

Roger Brunet, Les villes europeénnes: Rapport pour la DATAR, Montpellier: RECLUS, 1989.

Bernardo Albanese, 'Studi sulla legge Aquilia', (1950) 21 AnnPal 5.

Neil H Andrews, '"Occidere" and the Lex Aquilia', (1987) 46 Cambridge Law Journal 315.

Hans Ankum, '"Utilitatis causa receptum" – On the pragmatical methods of the Roman lawyers', Symbolae Ivridicae et Historicae Martino David Dedicatae, vol 1 (H Ankum et al eds, Leiden: Brill, 1968) 1.

——, 'Das Problem der "überholenden Kausalität" bei der Anwendung der lex Aquilia im klassischen römischen Recht', De iustitia et iure – Festgabe für Ulrich von Lübtow zum 80. Geburtstag (M Harder, G Thielmann eds, Berlin: Duncker&Humblot, 1980) 325.

——, 'The functions of expressions with utilitatis causa in the works of Classical Roman Lawyers', Libellus ad Thomasium, (2010) 16 Fundamina 5.

Charles Appleton, 'La date des Digesta de Julien', (1910) 34 Nouvelle Revue Historique 731.

Athenaeus of Naucratis, The Deipnosophists, vol 2, Yonge tr, London: Henry G Bohn, 1854.

Martin Avenarius/Christian Baldus/Francesca Lamberti/Mario Varvaro eds, Gradenwitz, Riccobono und die Entwicklung der Interpolationenkritik – Gradenwitz, Riccobono e gli sviluppi della critica interpolazionistica. Methodentransfer unter europäischen Juristen im späten 19. Jahrhundert Circolazione di modelli e metodi fra giuristi europei nel tardo Ottocento, Tübingen: Mohr Siebeck, 2018.

* No publisher given for works earlier than 1800.

Jacobus Ayrer, Tractatus Methodicus & accuratissimus de Triplici Genere Homicidiorum, Frankfurt, 1647.
Reinhard Bachovius von Echt, Notae et animadversiones ad disputationes Treutleri, vol 1, Cologne, 1688.
Ralph Backhaus, Review 'J Rastätter, Marcelli Notae ad Iuliani Digesta', (1984) 101 ZRG RomAbt 376.
Marco Balzarini, 'Appunti sulla "rixa" nel diritto Romano', (1982) 28 Labeo 17.
Richard A Bauman, Lawyers and politics in the early Roman Empire: a study of relations between the Roman jurists and the emperors from Augustus to Hadrian, Munich: Beck, 1989.
Ben Beinart, 'Once more on the origin of the lex Aquilia', (1956) Butterworths South African Law Review 70.
Karl-Heinz Below, Die Haftung für lucrum cessans im römischen Recht, Munich: Beck, 1964.
Adolf Berger, Encyclopedic Dictionary of Roman Law, Philadelphia: The American Philosophical Society, 1953.
Gerhard von Beseler, Beiträge zur Kritik der römischen Rechtsquellen, Drittes Heft, Tübingen: Mohr, 1913.
——, Beiträge zur Kritik der römischen Rechtsquellen, Viertes Heft, Tübingen: Mohr, 1920.
——, 'Miszelle', (1925) 45 ZRG RomAbt 437.
——, 'Romanistische Studien', (1930) 10 TR 161.
Johann Samuel Friedrich von Boehmer, Meditationes in Constitutionem Criminalen Carolinam, Halle 1770.
Justus Hennig Boehmer, Ius Ecclesiasticum Protestantium, vol 5, Halle, 1736.
Michael Börsch, Damit Übeltaten nicht ungestraft bleiben: Impunitas als Argument der klassischen römischen Juristen, Frankfurt/Main: Peter Lang, 2003.
Johannes Alphonsus Henricus (Hans) Bots, 'Harderwijkse professoren (1648–1812) en net benoemingsbeleid van de Gelderse curatoren', Het Gelders Athene: bijdragen tot de geschiedenis van de Gelderse universiteit in Harderwijk (1648–1811) (J A H Bots, Meindert Evers, Willem T M Frijhoff et al eds, Hilversum: Verloren, 2000) 51 ff.
Louis Boulard, L. Salvius Julianus, son oeuvre, ses doctrines sur la personnalité juridique, Paris: Rousseau, 1902.
Frits Brandsma, Dorotheus and his Digest translation, Groningen: Forsten, 1996.
Mario Bretone, Techniche e ideologie dei giuristi romani, 2nd edn, Naples: Edizioni Scientifiche Italiane, 1982.
——, Storia del diritto romano, 3rd edn, Rome: Laterza, 1992.
Aloys Brinz, Pandecten, 2nd edn, vol 2, Erlangen: Deichert, 1879.
Johannes Brunnemann, Commentarius in Pandectas, vol 1, Geneva, 1752.
William Warwick Buckland, The Roman Law of Slavery: The Condition of the Slave in Private Law from Augustus to Justinian, Cambridge: University Press, 1908.

William Warwick Buckland/Arnold Duncan McNair, Roman Law & Common Law. A Comparison in Outline, 2nd edn, F H Lawson rev, Cambridge: University Press, 1952.
Elmar Bund, Untersuchungen zur Methode Julians, Köln/Graz: Böhlau, 1965.
——, 'Salvius Iulianus; Leben und Werk', ANRW vol 15/2 – Principat (Berlin: De Gruyter, 1976) 408.
Bartholomaeus Caepolla, Cautele varii tractatus legum, Lyon, 1535.
John Cairns, 'English Torts and Roman Delicts: The Correspondence of James Muirhead and Frederick Pollock', (2013) 87 Tulane Law Review 867.
——, 'The Early Historiography of the Lex Aquilia in Britain: Introducing Students to the Digest', Wrongful Damage to Property in Roman Law. British Perspectives (P Du Plessis ed, Edinburgh: University Press, 2018) 3.
The Cambridge Companion to Roman Law, D Johnston ed, Cambridge: University Press, 2015.
Piera Capone, 'Valore ed uso giuriprudenziale di "absurdus/e"', (1997) 63 SDHI 199.
Benedict Carpzow, Practica nova imperialis Saxonica rerum criminalium, Wittenberg, 1677.
Francesco Casavola, 'Cultura e scienza giuridica nel secondo secolo d.C.: il senso del passato', ANRW vol 15/2 – Principat (Berlin: De Gruyter, 1976) 31.
Amelia Mercedes Castresana Herrero, Nuevas lecturas de la responsabilidad aquiliana, Salamanca: Ediciones Universidad de Salamanca, 2001.
Osvaldo Cavallar, 'Agli albori della medicina legale: I trattati "De percussionibus" e "De vulneribus"', Ius Commune 26 (1999) 27.
Pietro Cerami, 'La concezione celsina del "Ius"', (1985) 38 AnnPal 5.
Samuel de Cocceji, Ius Controversum Civile, vol 1, Frankfurt/Leipzig, 1713.
Boaz Cohen, 'The principle of causation in the Jewish and the Roman law of damages', Studi de Francisci, vol 1 (Milan: Giuffrè, 1956) 305.
Edward Coke, The First Part of the Institutes of the Lawes of England, or, A Commentary upon Littleton, not the Name of the Author Only, but of the Law It Selfe, London, 1628.
Alessandro Corbino/Bernardo Santalucia, Justiniani Augusti Pandectarum Codex Florentinus, Florence: Olschki, 1988.
Michael Crawford, Roman Statutes, Bulletin of the Institute of Classical Studies Supplement 64, London: Institute of Classical Studies, 1996.
Iacobus Cuiacius, Opera, quae de iure fecit, et edi voluit, vol 4, Frankfurt, 1595.
——, Opera Postuma, vol 2, Paris, 1637.
John Cunningham ed, The Shock of War – Tunbridge Wells in the First World War, Tunbridge Wells: n p, 2014.
Danilo Dalla, 'Guiliano e il longum intervallum in tema di applicazione dell'Aquilia', (1974) 187 ArchGiur 145.
Philippus Decius, Consilia sive responsa, Frankfurt/Maine, 1588.
Lucetta Desanti, La Legge Aquilia. Tra verba legis e interpretazione giurisprudenziale, Turin: Giappichelli, 2015.

Ettore Dezza, Lezioni di storia del processo penale, Pavia: University Press, 2013.
Digest of European Tort Law, vol 1: Essential Cases on Natural Causation, Bénedict Winiger, Helmut Koziol, Bernhard A Koch, Reinhard Zimmermann eds, Vienna/New York: De Gruyter, 2007.
Jean Domat, Lex Lois Civiles, Paris, 1767.
Christian Heinrich Eckhard, Hermeneutica Juris, Karl Friedrich Walch ed, Lipsia, 1779.
Fridolin Eisele, 'Correalität und Solidarität', (1891) 77 Archiv für die civilistische Praxis 374.
(Karl) Heinrich Erman, 'Entstammt BGB. §266 Tribonian oder Celsus?', (1904) 25 ZRG RomAbt 352.
Anton Faber, Rationalia in secundam partem pandectarum, Geneva, 1616.
Contardo Ferrini, Opere, vol 2, V Arangio Ruiz ed, Milan: Hoepli, 1929.
Thomas Finkenauer, 'Pönale Elemente der lex Aquilia', Ausgleich oder Busse als Grundproblem des Schadensersatzrechts von der lex Aquilia bis zur Gegenwart – Symposium zum 80. Geburtstag von Herbert Hausmaninger (R Gamauf ed, Vienna: Manz, 2017) 35.
Florianus de Sancto Petro, In primam & secundam Digesti veteris partem commentaria, Bologna, 1576.
Ernst Fraenkel, Kleine Beiträge zur klassischen Philologie, vol 2: Zur Römischen Literatur – Zu juristischen Texten – Verschiedenes, Rome: Edizioni di Storia e Letteratura, 1964.
Richard M Fraher, 'Preventing Crime in the High Middle Ages: The Medieval Lawyers' Search for Deterrence', Pope, Teachers, and Canon Law in the Middle Ages (J Ross Sweeney, S Chodorow eds, Ithaca, NY: Cornell University Press, 1989) 212.
Richard M Fraher, 'Tancred's Summula de criminibus: A New Text and a Key to the Ordo iudiciarius', (1979) 9 Bulletin of Medieval Canon Law 23.
——, 'The Theoretical Justification for the New Criminal Law of the High Middle Ages: "Rei Publicae Interest, Ne Crimina Remaneant Impunita"', (1984) 3 University of Illinois Law Review 577.
Ian Freckelton/Danuta Mendelson eds, Causation in Law and Medicine, London/New York: Routledge, 2016.
Bruce W Frier, Review 'Dieter Nörr, "Causa Mortis"', (1988) 109 American Journal of Philology 618.
——, Casebook on the Roman Law of Delict, Atlanta, GA: Scholars' Press, 1989.
Manuel J García Garrido, Casuismo y jurisprudencia romana: Pleitos famosos del Digesto, Madrid: Artigrafia, 1973.
Jean Gaudemet, 'Utilitas publica', (1951) 28 Revue historique de droit français et étranger 465.
Martin Gebauer, Hypothetische Kausalität und Haftungsgrund, Tübingen: Mohr Siebeck, 2007.

Theodor Joseph Gerke, 'Geschichtliche Entwicklungen der Ansprüche aus der "lex Aquilia"', (1957) 23 SDHI 68.

Jean-François Gerkens, "Aeque perituris ..." - Une approche de la causalité dépassante en droit romain classique, Liège: Ed. Collection Scientifique de la Faculté de Droit, 1997.

Tomasz Giaro, 'Die Illusion der Wissenschaftlichkeit', (1994) 22 INDEX 107.

——, 'Absurditätsargumente in der römischen Jurisprudenz - Ein Überblick', (2006) 11 OIR - Journal of Ancient Law Studies 31.

——, Römische Rechtswahrheiten. Ein Gedankenexperiment, Frankfurt: Klostermann, 2007.

Christian Friedrich von Glück, Ausführliche Erläuterung der Pandecten nach Hellfeld, 10. Theil, 1. Abt., Erlangen: Palm'sche Buchhandlung, 1808.

Otto Gradenwitz, 'L. 27 §3 de R.V. und der bösliche Ersitzer', Festgabe für Dr. Karl Güterbock: Zur achtzigsten Wiederkehr seines Geburtstages (Munich: Vahlen, 1910) 303.

Gregorius Papa IX, Decretales cum glossis restitutae, Venice, 1615.

Petrus de Greve, Exercitationes ad pandectarum loca difficiliora, Nijmegen, 1660.

Hugo Grotius, Florum sparsio ad ius Iustinianeum, Paris, 1642.

Erwin Grueber, The Roman Law of Damage to Property, Oxford: Clarendon Press, 1886.

Handbuch der lateinischen Literatur der Antike (HLL), vol IV: Die Literatur des Umbruchs, Von der römischen zur christlichen Literatur 117 - 284 n. Chr. (Klaus Sallmann ed, Munich: Beck, 1997) 105.

Jan Dirk Harke, Argumenta Iuventiana, Berlin: Duncker&Humblot, 1999.

——, Argumenta Iuventiana - Argumenta Salviana, Entscheidungsbegründungen bei Celsus und Julian, Berlin: Duncker&Humblot, 2012.

——, 'Die Rechtspositionen am Sklaven. 2: Ansprüche aus Delikten am Sklaven', Corpus der römischen Rechtsquellen zur antiken Sklaverei III/2: (T J Chiusi, J Filip-Fröschl, J M Rainer eds, Mainz: Akademie der Wissenschaften und der Literatur, 2013) 67.

Herbert Hart/Tony Honoré, Causation in the Law, 2nd edn, Oxford: University Press, 1985.

Carl Haß, 'Ueber die Verwerthbarkeit des Gegensatzes von adäquatem und inadäquatem Kausalzusammenhang in der Lehre vom Interesse. Zugleich ein Beitrag zur Lösung des Kausalitätsproblems in der Rechtswissenschaft', (1897) 37 Jherings Jahrbücher für die Dogmatik des bürgerlichen Rechts 327.

Herbert Hausmaninger, Das Schadensersatzrecht der lex Aquilia, 2nd edn, Vienna: Manz, 1980.

Franz Haymann, 'Textkritische Studien zum römischen Obligationenrecht', (1919) 40 ZRG RomAbt 167.

Johann Gottlieb Heineccius, Opera Omnia, vol 2, Geneva, 1748.

Heumanns Handlexikon zu den Quellen des römischen Rechts, Emil Seckel ed, Jena: Fischer, 1914.

Christoph Haubold, De jure et justitia commutativa, tom I, Ingolstadt, 1671.
Margaret Hewett, 'Voorda resurgens: An introduction to Jacobus Voorda and his unique lectures on the Ius Hodiernum at the University of Utrecht', (2003) 9 Fundamina 103.
Max Hirschberg, Jude und Demokrat: Erinnerungen eines Münchener Rechtsanwalts 1883 bis 1939, Munich: Oldenbourg, 1998.
Hendrik Richard Hoetink, 'Les notions anachroniques dans l'historiographie du droit', (1955) 23 TR 1.
Hanns Hohmann, 'Classical Rhetoric and Roman Law: Reflections on a Debate', (1996) 15 Rhetorik. Ein internationales Jahrbuch 15.
Ulrich Hohoff, Wissenschaftliche Bibliothekarinnen und Bibliothekare als Opfer der NS-Diktatur. Eine Übersicht über 250 Lebensläufe seit dem Jahr 1933. Teil 1: Die Entlassungen Universitätsbibliothek Augsburg: http://dx.doi.org/10.5282/o-bib/2015H2S1-32, accessed 3 March 2018.
Freiherr Rudolph Christoph Karl Sigmund von Holzschuher zu Harrlach und Thalheim-Aschbach, Theorie und Casuistik des gemeinen Civilrechts, vol 3: Obligationenrecht, 3rd edn, Leipzig: Baumgärtner, 1864.
Tony Honoré, 'Causation and Remoteness of Damages', IECL vol XI (Tübingen: Mohr, 1971) ch 7.
——, Tribonian, Ithaca, NY: Cornell University Press, 1978.
——, Justinian's Digest: Character and Compilation, Oxford: University Press, 2010.
Thomas Honsell, 'Gemeinwohl und öffentliches Interesse im klassischen römischen Recht', (1978) 95 ZRG RomAbt 124.
Ulricus Huber, Praelectiones iuris civilis, vol 3, Lueder Mencken ed, Leipzig, 1735.
Zacharias Huber, Dissertationes Juridicae et Philologicae, vol 2, Franeker, 1702.
David Ibbetson, 'William Warwick Buckland on the lex Auqilia', Wrongful Damage to Property in Roman Law. British Perspectives (Paul Du Plessis ed, Edinburgh: University Press, 2018) 46.
Alexander de Imola (Tartagni), In primam partem infortiati commentaria, Venice, 1562.
Innocentius IV, In v. libros decretalium comentaria, Venice, 1570.
International Biographical Dictionary of Central European Emigrés 1933–1945, vol II: The Arts, Sciences, and Literature, Part II: L–Z, H A Strauss, W Röder, general eds, Munich/New York: De Gruyter/Saur, 1983.
Makoto Ishikawa, 'MINPO §719 und das römische Recht. Eine Anwendungsmöglichkeit auf den Nebentäterfall', Aus der Werkstatt römischer Juristen. Vorträge der Europäisch-Ostasiatischen Tagung 2013 in Fukuoka (U Manthe, S Nishimura, M Igimi eds, Berlin: Duncker&Humblot, 2016) 173.
Nils Jansen, Die Struktur des Haftungsrechts: Geschichte, Theorie und Dogmatik, Tübingen: Mohr Siebeck, 2003.
Günter Jerouschek, '"Ne crimina remaneant impunita." Auf dass Verbrechen nicht ungestraft bleiben: Überlegungen zur Begründung öffentlicher Strafverfolgungen im Mittelalter', (2007) 89 ZRG KanAbt 323.

David Johnston, 'Causation and remoteness: British Steps on a Roman Path', Wrongful Damage to Property in Roman Law. British Perspectives (P Du Plessis ed, Edinburgh: University Press, 2018) 211.
Herbert F Jolowicz and Barry Nicholas, Historical Introduction to the Study of Roman Law, 3rd edn, Cambridge: University Press, 1932.
Justiniani Augusti Digestorum seu Pandectarum Codex Florentinus, olim Pisanus, phototypice expressus, a cura della Commissione ministeriale per la riproduzione delle pandette, Rome, 1902–10.
Hermann Kantorowicz, Albertus Gandinus und das Strafrecht der Scholastik, Zweiter (Letzter) Band: Die Theorie. Kritische Ausgabe des Tractatus des Maleficiis nebst textkritischer Einleitung, Berlin/Leipzig, 1926.
Max Kaser, Römisches Privatrecht I, 2nd edn, Munich: Beck, 1971.
——, '"Ius publicum" und "ius privatum"', (1986) 103 ZRG RomAbt 1.
Lotte Kéry, 'Ein neues Kapitel in der Geschichte des kirchlichen Strafrechts: Die Systematisierungsbemühungen des Bernhard von Pavia (†1213)', Medieval Church Law and the Origins of the Western Legal Tradition: A Tribute to Kenneth Pennington (W P Müller, M E Sommar eds, Washington DC: The Catholic University of America Press, 2012) 229.
Jeroen S Kortmann, 'Ab alio ictu(s): Misconceptions about Julian's View on Causation', (1999) 20 Journal of Legal History 95.
Christoph Krampe, Review 'J Rastätter, Marcelli Notae ad Iuliani Digesta', (1984) 52 TR 58.
Paul Krückmann, 'Miszelle', (1940) 60 ZRG RomAbt 234.
Constantin Kruse, Alternative Kausalität im Deliktsrecht: Eine historische und vergleichende Untersuchung, Berlin: LitVerlag, 2006.
Bernhard Kübler, Review 'Hermann Fitting, Alter und Folge der Schriften römischer Juristen', (1911) 49 Kritische Vierteljahresschrift für Gesetzgebung und Rechtswissenschaft 1.
Wolfgang Kunkel, 'Exegetische Studien zur aquilischen Haftung', (1929) 69 ZRG RomAbt 158.
Nicola Lacey, A Life of H.L.A. Hart. The Nightmare and the Noble Dream, Oxford: University Press, 2004.
John H Langbein, Prosecuting Crime in the Renaissance: England, Germany, France, Cambridge, Mass.: Harvard University Press, 1974.
Marie-Clotilde Lault, 'La prise en compte médiévale de la victime dans quelques traités criminels et statuts urbains', (2015) 25 Histoire de la justice, 107.
Frederick H Lawson, Negligence in the Civil Law. Introduction and select texts, Oxford: Clarendon Press, 1950.
Frederick H Lawson/Basil S Markesinis, Tortious Liability for Unintentional Harm in the Common Law and the Civil Law, vol 1: Text, Cambridge: University Press, 1982.
Otto Lenel, Palingenesia Iuris Civilis, vol 1, Leipzig: Tauchnitz, 1889.

Ulrich Leptien, Utilitatis causa – Zweckmässigkeitsentscheidungen im Römischen Recht, Thesis Freiburg/Br, 1967.
——, 'Utilitatis causa – Zweckmässigkeitsentscheidungen im Römischen Recht', (1969) 35 SDHI 51.
Ernst Levy, Konkurrenz der Aktionen, vol 1, Berlin: Vahlen, 1918.
Detlef Liebs, Römisches Recht. Ein Studienbuch, 6th edn, Göttingen: Vandenhoek & Ruprecht, 2004.
——, Lateinische Rechtsregeln und Rechtssprichwörter, 7th edn, Munich: Beck, 2007.
Wiesław Litewski, 'Review of Nörr's Causa Mortis', (1987) 53 SDHI 438.
Egidius von Löhr, Die Theorie der Culpa, Gießen: Heyer, 1806.
Giannetto Longo, 'Utilitas publica', Atti del Seminario romanistico internazionale (Perugia: Liberia editrice universitaria, 1972) 155.
Heinrich Luden, Abhandlungen aus dem Gemeinen Teutschen Straftrechte, vol 2: Über den Thatbestand des Verbrechens nach gemeinem teutschen Recht, Göttingen: Vandenhoeck&Ruprecht, 1840.
Ulrich von Lübtow, Untersuchungen zur lex Aquilia de damno iniuris dato, Berlin: Duncker&Humblot, 1971.
Geoffrey MacCormack, 'Aquilian Studies', (1975) 41 SDHI 1.
——, 'Juristic Interpretation of the Lex Aquilia', Studi in Onore di Cesare Sanfilippo, vol 1 (Milan: Giuffrè, 1982) 253.
Ian Maclean, 'Evidence, Logic, the Rule and the Exception in Renaissance Law and Medicine', (2000) 5 Early Science and Medicine 227.
Antonio Mantello, 'Rec. di Scarano Ussani, L'utilità e la certezza', (1987) 38 Iura 240.
Sabrina Di Maria, La cancelleria imperiale e i giuristi classici: 'reverentia antiquitatis' e nuove prospettive nella legislazione giustinianea del codice, Bologna: Bononia University Press, 2010.
Sabine Mattasch, Der Tatbestand des Verbrechens bei Heinrich Luden, Jena: Boorberg, 2005.
Jason di Mayno, In primam Infortiati partem Commentaria, Venice, 1573.
Hieronymus Christoph Meckbach, Anmerkungen über Kayser Carl des V Peinliche Halsgerichts-Ordnung: Nebst einer Beschreibung und Erklärung der sogenannten Bambergischen Tortur, Jena, 1756.
——, Commentar über den Sachsen-Spiegel, 2nd edn, Weimar, 1789.
Dieter Medicus, Id quod interest, Munich: Beck, 1962.
Gerardus Meerman, Novus thesaurus juris civilis et canonici, vol 2, The Hague, 1751.
Massimo Miglietta, 'Towards a palingenetic study of Bas. 60,3: the contribution of the Byzantine ἴνδικες: part I', (2014) IX Subseciva Groningana 59.
——, 'Towards a Palingenetic Study of Bas. 60.3: The Contribution of the Byzantine "ΙΝΔΙΚΕΣ. Part II', Il diritto romano e le culture straniere. Influenze e dipendenze interculturali nell'antichità (F Lamberti, P Groeschler, F Milazzo eds, Lecce: Grifo, 2015) 283.
Juan Miquel, 'Stoische Logik und römische Jurisprudenz', (1970) 87 ZRG RomAbt 85.
Theodor Mommsen, Römisches Strafrecht, Leipzig: Duncker&Humblot, 1899.

Charles Henry Monro, Digest IX.2, Lex Aquilia, Cambridge: University Press, 1898.
James Muirhead, 'Grueber on the Lex Aquilia', (1886) 2 Law Quarterly Review 379.
Nikolaus München, Das kanonische Gerichtsverfahren und Strafrecht, vol 2, Cologne/Neuss: Schwann, 1866.
Jan Wendelius Napjus/Gerrit Arie Lindeboom, De hoogleraren in de geneeskunde aan de Hogeschool en het Athenaeum te Franeker, Amsterdem: Rodopi, 1985.
Marialuisa Navarra, Ricerche sulla utilitas nel pensiero dei giuristi romani, Turin: Giappichelli, 2002.
Gerhard Noodt, Opera Omnia, vol 1, Leiden, 1724.
Dieter Nörr, 'Kausalitätsprobleme im klassischen römischen Recht', Feschrift für Franz Wieacker zum 70. Geburtstag (O Behrends et al eds, Göttingen: Vandenhoeck&Ruprecht, 1978) 115.
——, Causa Mortis: Auf den Spuren einer Redewendung, Munich: Beck, 1986.
——, 'Causam mortis praebere', The Legal Mind: Essays for Tony Honoré (N MacCormick, P Berks eds, Oxford: Clarendon Press, 1986) 203.
Clifford Ando/Paul Du Plessis/Kaius Tuori eds, Oxford Handbook of Roman Law, Oxford: University Press, 2016.
Tim Whitmarsh (ed in chief), Oxford Classical Dictionary, Oxford: University Press, since 2015.
Giovanni Pacchioni, 'A Disputed Point in the Lex Aquilia', (1888) 4 Law Quarterly Review 178.
Alessandro Pastore, 'Médecine et droit, compétition ou collaboration?', Histoire, médecine et santé (2017) 11 Revue d'histoire sociale et culturelle de médecine, de la santé et du corps 19.
Kenneth Pennington, 'Innocent III and the Ius Commune', Grundlagen des Rechts: Festschrift für Peter Landau zum 65. Geburtstag (R Helmholz et al eds, Paderborn: Schöningh, 2000) 349.
Alfred Pernice, Zur Lehre von den Sachbeschädigungen nach römischem Rechte, Weimar: Böhlau, 1867.
Isabella Piro, Damnum 'corpore suo' dare – rem 'corpore' possidere. L'oggettiva riferibilità del compartemento lesivo e della possessio nella riflessione e nel linguaggio dei giuristi romani, Naples: Edizioni Scientifiche Italiane, 2004.
——, 'In dubio pro domino? Brevi riflessioni intorno alla valutazione guilianea dell'aestimatio perempti in materia aquiliana', Fides Humanitas Ius. Studi in onore di Luigi Labruna, vol 6 (C Cascione, C Masi Doria eds, Naples: Editoriale Scientifica 2007) 4313.
Robert Jean Pothier, Pandectae Justinianeae in novum ordinem digestae, tom 1, Lyon 1782.
Raphael Powell, 'Novus actus interveniens in Roman Law', (1951) 4 Current Legal Problems 197.
Xavier Prévost, 'Reassessing the Influence of Medieval Jurisprudence on Jacques Cujas' (1522–1590) Method, Legal Humanism and its Claims. Petere Fontes? (P J Du Plessis, J W Cairns eds, Edinburgh: University Press, 2016) 88.

——, Jacques Cujas (1522–1590), Jurisconsulte humaniste. Travaux d'Humanisme et Renaissance, no DXLI, Geneva: Droz, 2015.

Fritz Pringsheim, Der Kauf mit fremdem Geld, Leipzig: Veit, 1916.

David Pugsley, 'Causation and Confessions in the lex Aquilia', (1970) 38 The Legal History Review 163.

Ernst Rabel, 'Grundzüge des römischen Privatrechts', Enzyklopädie der Rechtswissenschaften (F Holtzendorff, J Kohler eds, Berlin: Duncker&Humblot, 1915) 399.

Jürgen Rastätter, Marcelli Notae ad Iuliani Digesta, unpublished thesis (dissertation copy), Freiburg, 1980.

Wilhelm Rechnitz, Studien zu Salvius Julianus, Weimar: Böhlau, 1925.

Roberto Reggi, 'L'interpretatione analogica in Salvio Giuliano', (1952) 2 Studi Parmensi 105.

Alan Rodger, 'Damages for the loss of an inheritance', Daube Noster: Essays in Legal History for David Daube (Alan Watson ed, Edinburgh: Scottish Academic Press, 1974) 289.

——, 'The Palingenesia of the Commentaries Relating to the Lex Aquilia', (2007) 124 ZRG RomAbt 145.

Robert Röhle, 'Zur Frage der sogenannten verdrängenden Verursachung im Römischen Recht', (1965) 31 SDHI 30.

Giovanni Rossi, Incunaboli della modernitá. Scienza guiridica e cultura umanistica in André Tiraqueau (1488–1558), Turin: Giappichelli, 2007.

Guido Rossi (a cura di), Bartolomeo Cipolla: un giurista veronese del Quattrocento tra cattedra, foro e luoghi del potere, Padua: CEDAM, 2009.

Giovanni Rotondi, Scritti Giuridici, vol 2, a cura di V Arangio-Ruiz et al, Milan: Hoepli, 1922.

Onofrio Ruffino, 'Cipolla, Bartolomeo', Dizionario biografico degli italiani, vol 25, Rome: Istituto della Enciclopedia Italiana, 1981.

Joe Sampson, The Historical Foundations of Grotius' Analysis of Delict, Leiden, 2017.

——, 'Revisiting D.9.2.23.1', Wrongful Damage to Property in Roman Law. British Perspectives (P Du Plessis ed, Edinburgh: University Press, 2018) 163.

Justo García Sánchez/Beatriz García Fueyo/Diego de Covarrubias y Leyva. Summa de delictis et eorum poenis. Año 1540 (Primer tratado de derecho penal, parte especial, de Europa), Oviedo: Servicio de publicaciones de la Universidad de Oviedo, 2018.

Vincenzo Scarano Ussani, L'utilità e la certezza. Compiti e modelli del sapere giuridico in Salvio Giuliano, Milan: Guiffrè, 1987.

Bernhard Schebitz, Berechnung des Ersatzes nach der lex Aquilia, Diss Iur, Berlin (dissertation copy), 1987.

Karl-Heinz Schindler, 'Ein Streit zwischen Julian und Celsus. Zum Problem der überholenden Kausalität', (1957) 74 ZRG RomAbt 201.

Sandro Schipani, Responsabilita ex lege aquilia criteri di imputazione e problema della culpa, Turin: Giappichelli, 1969.

Johann Friedrich von Schulte, Geschichte der Quellen und Literatur des canonischen Rechts von Gratian bis auf die Gegenwart, vol 2, Stuttgart: Enke, 1877.

Fritz Schulz, Principles of Roman Law, Oxford: Clarendon Press, 1936.

——, History of Roman Legal Science, Oxford: Clarendon Press, 1946.

Eva Schumann, 'Von "Teuflischen Anwälten" und "Taschenrichtern" – Das Bild des Juristen im Zeitalter der Professionalisierung', Ulrich Tenglers Laienspiegel, Ein Rechtsbuch zwischen Humanismus und Hexenwahn (Andreas Deutsch ed, Heidelberg: Universitätsverlag Winter, 2011) 431.

Albrecht Schweppe, Das Römische Privatrecht in seiner heutigen Anwendung, 4th edn, W Meier ed, Göttingen: Vandenhoeck&Ruprecht, 1831.

Helen Scott, 'Killing and Causing Death in Roman Law', (2013) 129 Law Quarterly Review 101.

Erwin Seidl, 'Wege zu Julian', Sein und Werden im Recht. Festgabe für Ulrich von Lübtow zum 70. Geburtstag (W G Becker, L S von Carolsfeld eds, Berlin: Duncker&Humblot, 1970) 215.

——, 'Labeos geistiges Profil', Studi in onore di Edoardo Volterra, vol 1 (Milan: Giuffrè) 63.

Boudewijn Sirks, 'The Parallel Universes of Baker, Joblin and Julian: Causation and Law', (2013) 17 Edinburgh Law Review 22.

——, 'The slave who was slain twice: causality and the lex Aquilia (Iulian 86 dig D.9.2.51)', (2011) 79 TR 313.

Peter Stein, Regulae Iuris. From juristic rules to legal maxims, Edinburgh: University Press, 1966.

Artur Steinwenter, 'Utilitas publica – utilitas singulorum', Festschrift Paul Koschaker (Weimar: Böhlau, 1939) 84.

James Bradley Thayer, Lex Aquilia. Digest IX, 2: Ad Legem Aquiliam. Text translation, and Commentary. On Gifts between Husband and Wife (Digest XXIV, 1: De Donationibus inter Virum et Uxorem) Text and Commentary, Cambridge, Mass.: Harvard University Press, 1929.

Andreas Tiraquellus, Tractatus Varii, Lyon, 1587.

Armando Torrent, 'La Causalidad Aquiliana. Conexión *corpore suo-damnum dare*: Gayo 3,219; Ulp. (18 ad ed.) D. 9,1,1,7; IJ 4,3,16', (2018) Revista Internacional de Derecho Romano 465.

Baldus de Ubaldis, In primam Digesti veteris partem commentaria, Venice, 1599.

Govaert Carolus Joannes Joseph van den Bergh/Bernard H Stolte Jnr, 'The unfinished digest editions of Henrik Brenkman (1681–1736)', (1977) 45 TR 227.

Jan van Hoek, 'Verum est: Glimpses of abstract "legal reality" in the Digest', Viva Vox Iuris Romani. Essays in honour of Johannes Emil Spruit (L de Ligt et al eds, Amsterdam: Gieben, 2002) 115.

Karl Adolph von Vangerow, Lehrbuch der Pandekten, vol 3, 7th edn, Marburg/Leipzig: Elwert'sche Buchhandlung, 1876.

Gonzalo de Villadiego, Tractatus de irregularitate, suspensione et interdicto ecclesiastico, Salamanca, 1589.

Károly Visky, 'Die Frage der Kausalität aufgrund des D. 9,2 (ad legem Aquiliam)', (1949) 3 Revue internationale des droits de l'Antiquité 437.

Johannis Voet, Commentarius ad pandectas, vol 1, Geneva, 1778.

Bavius Voorda, De crimineele ordonnantien van Koning Philips van Spanje, Leyden, 1792.

Andreas Wacke, 'Logische Paradoxien in antiker und moderner Jurisprudenz', Festschrift der Rechtswissenschaftlichen Fakultät zur 600-Jahr-Feier der Universität zu Köln (Cologne: Carl Heymanns, 1988) 325.

——, 'Ne occasio sit maioris tumultus faciendi', Een rijk gerecht: opstellen aangeboden aan prof. mr. P.L. Nève (B C M Jacobs et al eds, Nijmegen: Gerard Noodt Instituut, 1998) 585.

Alan Watson, The Law of Obligations in the Later Roman Republic, Oxford: Clarendon Press, 1965.

Ortwin Westenberg, Opera Omnia Juridica, vol 2, Hanover & Luneburg, 1747.

Joseph Willems, La Loi Aquilienne: théorie du dommage aux choses en droit romain, Louvain: Charles Peeters, 1896.

Reinhard Willvonseder, Die Verwendung der Denkfigur der 'condicio sine qua non' bei den römischen Juristen, Vienna/Cologne/Graz: Böhlau, 1984.

——, 'Causam mortis praestare', (1988) 105 ZRG RomAbt 737.

Bernhard Windscheid, Lehrbuch der Pandekten, vol 2, 8th edn, Kipp ed, Frankfurt: Rütten&Loening, 1900/1901.

Bénédict Winiger, La responsabilité Aquilienne Romaine: damnum iniuria datum, Basel: Helbing&Lichtenhahn, 1997.

——, Responsibility, Restoration and Fault, Cambridge: Intersentia, 2018.

Markus Winkler, Mathematik und Logik in Julians Digesten, Berlin: Duncker&Humblot, 2015.

Hans Julius Wolff, 'Concerning the Transmission of Julian's Digesta', (1949) 7 Seminar (Jurist) 69.

Bastian A Zahn, 'Harmful Conduct as a Touchstone of Causation: an Analytical Comparison of Barker v Chorus and Julian', (2011) 15 Edinburgh Law Review 197.

Udalricus Zasius, Opera Omnia, vol 5, Lyon, 1550.

Franz Victor Ziegler, Die Theilnahme an einem Verbrechen nach P.G.O. Art. 148. Eine criminalistische Abhandlung, Marburg: Elwert, 1845.

Paola Ziliotto, L'Imputazione del danno Aquiliano. Tra iniuria e damnum corpore datum, Padua: CEDAM, 2000.

Reinhard Zimmermann, The Law of Obligations, Cape Town: Juta, 1990.

Henricus Zoesius, Commentarius ad Digestorum libros L, Louvain, 1718.

INDEX OF SOURCES

The entries for D.9.2.11.3, D.9.2.15.1, and D.9.2.51 register only the author's own exegeses (**bold**).

INDEX OF PERSONS*

* Authors of works of reference etc., which are not directly related to the topic of this book, are not listed.

ABOUT THE AUTHOR

Wolfgang Ernst is Regius Professor of Civil Law in the University of Oxford and Fellow of All Souls College. Before joining the Oxford Law Faculty in 2015, he taught Roman law and private law at the universities of Tübingen, Bonn and Zurich, and also as visiting professor in Cambridge and Jerusalem. He is interested in Roman law and the Roman law-based doctrinal history of civilian legal systems. His recent research focusses on the history of monetary law and the legal history of 'social choice' procedures.

www.ingramcontent.com/pod-product-compliance
Ingram Content Group UK Ltd.
Pitfield, Milton Keynes, MK11 3LW, UK
UKHW021825120926
8556IPUK00043B/1034

9 781780 688329